"Katherine is truly gifted! Her magical techniques and seminars are life-changing . . . especially if your heart is blocked to receiving love. Her insight and wisdom can assist anyone wanting to find 'The One.' Her processes worked for me . . . I am now in an amazing committed relationship with my life mate!"

RENEE PIANE, author of *Love Mechanics: Power Tools to Build Successful Relationships with Women* and cofounder of RapidDatingUSA.com

"You can't get what you want until you know what you want. Katherine Woodward Thomas helped me to define what I was looking for and helped me to create a path to call in the love of my life. Now, just about a year later, I'm shopping for engagement rings. It works."

DEBRA TENNEN, M.D., ophthalmologist

"Working with Katherine Woodward Thomas opened my heart and mind to embracing and healing all aspects of 'The One' in me. Yes, I have called in the love of my life, a lover beyond my wildest dreams! Most important, I've called in—and live in—LOVE."

KAREN RUSSO, corporate trainer

"Katherine is brilliant at helping to create an inviting space for your divine-right partner to show up. Within six months of working with her, Paul showed up and we are building a vision of a shared life together. I am grateful to her for her support, clarity, and inspiration."

WANICE LAMOYNE, founder and CEO of Principles at Work

"This course became my lifeline, best friend, and guardian. It gave me what I craved most: the compassionate understanding, loving support, and practical tools to guide me in releasing old blocks and patterns that were inhibiting love from entering my life. The work required some time and dedication, but as I'd made the commitment to do it diligently and honestly, I was amazed to find it comforting and pleasurable. Just two weeks after finishing the course, my life has more meaning, I'm happier, and I actually love 'me.' The most challenging predicament I face is how to schedule time for each of the five great guys who are calling me right now!"

DEBRA KAUFMAN, television writer and producer

"'The One' I had to call in first and foremost was myself; and this course gave me the tools to do that. I am now standing in the vision of the great love I always wanted in my life, but never before truly believed I could have. I am now creating it. A beautiful, healing journey into the heart, expanding it to let more love out, and welcome more love in. Definitely a life-changing experience on many levels."

MAGDA MOLINA, actress

CALLING IN "THE ONE"

7 Weeks to Attract the
Love of Your Life

KATHERINE WOODWARD THOMAS

THREE RIVERS PRESS • NEW YORK

Grateful acknowledgment is made to the following for permission to reprint previously published material: **Broadway Books:** Excerpts from *The Illustrated Rumi* by Coleman Barks and Michael Green. Copyright © 1997 by Coleman Barks and Michael Green. Reprinted by permission of Broadway Books, a division of Random House, Inc. **Harmony Books:** Excerpts from "The Agony and Ecstasy of Divine Discontent," "The Awakening," "Do You Love Me?" "I Am and I Am Not," "Looking for Love," "Looking for Your Face," and "Lost in the Wilderness" from *Love Poems of Rumi* by Deepak Chopra, M.D. Copyright © 1998 by Deepak Chopra, M.D. Reprinted by permission of Harmony Books, a division of Random House, Inc. **HarperCollins Publishers Inc.:** Exercise from "Fourth Chakra Exercises: Exercise to Open Your Heart" from *The Eight Human Talents* by Gurmukh Kaur Khalsa and with Cathryn Michon. Copyright © 2000 by Narayan, LLC. Reprinted by permission of HarperCollins Publishers Inc. **Penguin Group (USA) Inc.:** Excerpts from *Living with Feeling* by Lucia Capacchione. Reprinted by permission of Penguin Group (USA) Inc. **Riverhead Books:** Excerpt from *Ethics for the New Millennium* by the Dalai Lama and Alexander Norman. Copyright © 1999 by His Holiness the Dalai Lama. Reprinted by permission of Riverhead Books, an imprint of Penguin Group (USA) Inc.

Copyright © 2004 by Katherine Woodward Thomas

Published by Three Rivers Press, New York, New York.
Member of the Crown Publishing Group, a division of Random House, Inc.
www.crownpublishing.com
THREE RIVERS PRESS is a registered trademark and the Three Rivers Press colophon is a trademark of Random House, Inc.

Printed in the United States of America

Design by Karen Minster

Library of Congress Cataloging-in-Publication Data
Thomas, Katherine Woodward.
Calling in "the one" : 7 weeks to attract the love of your life /
Katherine Woodward Thomas.— 1st ed.
Includes bibliographical references.
1. Single women—Religious life. 2. Mate selection—Religious aspects.
I. Title.
BL625.7 .T47 2004   646.7'7—dc22   2003017868

ISBN 1-4000-4929-6

20 19

First Edition

To my beloved husband, Mark,

and our beautiful daughter, Alexandria—

the fruits of my labor

Special Thanks

If I have seen further it is by
standing on the shoulders of giants.

—Isaac Newton

All accomplishments in life, both great and small, can be traced to the influences and efforts of many. This book is no exception. It has taken the love and support of many wise and caring people over the years to help me arrive at a place in my life where I have something valuable to say. The collective kindness and generosity that I have received in my life is a debt that I can never repay directly, and can only hope to pay forward for the rest of my life.

I do, however, wish to thank certain people for helping me, not only to write this book, but to become the person who was capable of writing this book. To my "vision keepers," Naomi Benghiat and Jennifer Holt, thank you for steadfastly holding the vision of what love could, and would, look like in my life, when I was too weary to care; and for the depth of your devotion to the fulfillment of my dreams. To Lora Cain, for providing many, many hours of encouragement, editorial advice, and edification. To Tamira Hughes, for being the incredible gift that you are, sweetly arriving in my life just in the nick of time. To Natalie Lehman, for your kind and loving support. To Benjamin Dover, for pointing out potential pitfalls and thus guarding my every step like a pit bull. To my agent, Angela Rinaldi, who, with great kindness and care, skillfully managed to shepherd this work into the world. To my editor, Jennifer Kasius, for blessing this project with the magnitude of your talents and creative abilities. To Nancy Hardin, for your generosity, commitment, and common sense. To Carrie Thornton, for so graciously and adeptly stepping up to the plate as we came into the final stretch. To Karen Minster, for enhancing my words with your beautiful design. To Teresa Alas, for keeping my daughter safe and loved on those long afternoons of writing and rewriting. To Philippa Burgess, for your sound advice and ever-optimistic encouragement.

To Douglas Evans, for being one of those rare and special people who actively seeks to bless and prosper those around you. And to Maureen O'Crean, for insisting that I write all this down in the first place.

I also want to thank my clients and students for trusting me with your hearts, and for teaching and inspiring me constantly. To every psychotherapist, spiritual teacher, and healer I've ever had, including Dr. Anne Brooks, Reverend Chris Faulconer, and Debu Ghosh, for your amazing generosity, wisdom, and counsel as well as your willingness to travel into the depths to help me find my way home. To Marianne Williamson, whom I knew when, and who has consistently modeled for me what it is to be a woman on fire, burning brightly for the forces of love. To the Agape International Spiritual Center and Landmark Education, for helping us all to expand our capacity to love and be loved.

Thank you also to my brothers, Todd Grupe and Scott Grupe, for being a source of love and light in my life. To my mother, Sandra Pullman, for your support and generosity over the years as well as the magnitude of your much-treasured love; and to my father, Robert Kersch, who, after all is said and done, has loved me well. To all of my past loves and ill-fated romantic liaisons, from whom I've learned everything— thank you from the bottom of my heart and please forgive me my flaws.

Most of all, I thank my husband, Mark Austin Thomas, for the steadfast constancy of your love, the countless hours of your wise and encouraging counsel, and for your unrelenting belief in me. To our daughter, Alexandria, thank you, sweetheart, for being born. You've opened my heart wider than I knew possible.

Contents

Preface: My Story   xiii

CONTENTS

Preface: My Story

Be realistic.

Plan for a miracle.

—Bhagwan Shree Rajineesh

This is what being single was like for me. I am an attractive, charismatic woman—petite, with a curvy figure, olive complexion, and unruly dark hair. I love people fervently and I have a profound need to be deeply connected to them. I hated, hated, hated being alone in life. Yet, by the time I reached my fortieth birthday, I was a true-blue, card-carrying member of the fastest-growing group in America, the "never-marrieds."

I had no problem meeting men. As a matter of fact, my favorite advice to my gal pals was that old saying "Men are like buses. If you miss one, another will be along in ten minutes." In other words, don't spend too much time grieving when they disappoint you. And believe you me—I spoke from experience.

When I was nineteen, I had a boyfriend who, responding to my nurturing and caring nature, told me that it would be a tragedy if I never had children. His words haunted me as the (tick, tick, tick) years passed.

When in my late thirties, having just finished graduate school en route to becoming a psychotherapist, I sat reading Gail Sheehy's book *New Passages,* which had just come out. In it, she devotes a whole section to women who, like me, had postponed childbearing. She quotes a gynecologist as calling this phenomenon "a mini-epidemic of . . . deluded, about-to-be desperately disappointed women in their mid-forties." My heart sank. I knew then that it just wasn't ever going to happen for me and that I'd just been fooling myself.

At least once a week, as though he or she had the right to humiliate me, someone would say something like "You've never been married? Why? What's wrong?" For years, I told them that it was because I hadn't met the right person. Eventually, though, I began to secretly wonder if it was because I'd never *been* the right person.

All of our suffering
in life is from
saying we want
one thing and
doing another.
—Debbie Ford

I kept trying to figure out what was *wrong* with me. Here I was, counseling others on how to have great and loving relationships while coming home to an empty apartment night after night. Why wasn't anyone proposing to me? Why wasn't anyone asking me to be the mother of his children? God, it would have been better if I were at least divorced. Then I could say that *someone* had wanted me, only it didn't work out.

This was my pattern. I went for unavailable men: any type, shape, size, color, professional affiliations, or lack thereof. As long as it was an impossible love, I was in. I was a magnet for married men, engaged men, workaholic men, alcoholic men, commitment-phobic men, and gay men who were interested in exploring. And because I worked with ex-cons as an art therapist for several years, I also seemed to possess an unfortunate allure for straight men who were on their way in or out of prison. All of these men found me fascinating and compelling and would go to remarkable lengths to seduce me. I'd like to be able to tell you that available men found me uninteresting or unattractive or . . . something. But, truthfully, so few available men came into my life that I have no idea how they might have responded to me. Consequently, I was alone quite a bit.

Sometimes, I'd give in and become entangled in some drama that wasn't ever going to go anywhere and I'd feel terrible about myself. I'd berate myself for spending time with losers, yet it seemed the only alternative was to be alone. And, as I told you before, I hated being alone. All too often, I found myself getting attached to a man whom I didn't respect, seduced by his desire for me. The occasional man I'd meet whom I did respect and who actually was available seemed to run like water through my fingers. He was always on his way elsewhere.

Finally, right around my forty-first birthday, I met a gracious and classy older man named Daniel. He was a widower whose wife of twenty-something years had passed away a few months before we met. He was good-looking, kind, successful, spiritual, fun to be with, and very, very considerate of me. He told me over and over how beautiful and smart he thought I was and went out of his way to try to please me.

I thought I'd gotten it right this time, completely ignoring the signs that I was simply his transitional relationship in the aftermath of a long and happy marriage. Even though I had stopped dating anyone but him, the truth was, he had several girlfriends whom he was seeing. I was just waiting for him to come to his senses! Perhaps, in my heart of hearts, I didn't believe that I'd ever have what I really wanted. So, I just pretended that even though he wasn't committing to me, the crumbs were good enough. After all, it was a huge step up from some of the guys I'd dated. This included the one who thought being good to me was "letting" me feed his cats while he was away. When he asked another woman out on New Year's Eve, I finally got the hint. Daniel was the last unavailable man I ever dated.

MEETING "THE ONE"

Now, I have to back up several years to 1992. I was dating William, whom I'd met through the personals. He seemed to be the nice guy I thought I was looking for—bright, creative, sweet, and employed. He actually paid for dinner at the nice restaurants he invited me to. I was in heaven. I did not yet know that William was a rage-aholic. That part came later.

When I was invited by a friend to a gathering sponsored by a local spiritual group, I asked William to come along. Now, William had about as much interest in spiritual matters as I have in the mating patterns of armadillos. However, when a man is trying to get a woman into bed, he racks up lots of points by going with her to the kinds of events she's interested in and this fact was not lost on William.

We made our way to the address I was given and rang the bell. A man who introduced himself as Mark answered the door. Welcoming and polite, he invited William and me to join the group that had gathered in his living room. Although Mark gave no overt indication of being attracted to me, I've always had a fairly acute radar about these things. I could tell by the way his glance lingered just a moment too long that he was interested. I was flattered and somewhat intrigued. When he called two days later, I was not completely surprised.

On my first night out with Mark, we attended the backyard wedding of a friend of his. We were so absorbed in our conversation that we barely paid attention to the bride and groom. Afterwards we went dancing. I assured Mark that my relationship with William was not exclusive. I convinced him that it would be perfectly fine for me to date both of them. I

> If you want the whole thing, the gods will give it to you. But you must be ready for it.
> —Joseph Campbell

Don't look for
new ways to
flee across the
chessboard.
Listen to hear
checkmate
spoken directly
to you.
—Rumi

did this for two months, after which time I chose William over Mark. Upon reflection, I see that I let Mark go because he didn't fit the picture in my head of what "The One" would look like. I can also see that it was not the right time for Mark and me to be together. This was for a variety of reasons, not the least of which is that being with Mark would have required a certain level of maturity that I did not yet possess.

A year later, out of the blue, I received a call from Mark. I hadn't heard from him since our sad "I can't see you anymore" talk. After I'd broken up with William, another "bus" had already come along and I was seeing someone else. Once again, though, things had not yet progressed to exclusivity and I agreed to spend time with Mark. But after only two weeks, I had to admit to myself once more that I was really not available, and I had to let Mark know.

For the next six years, I thought about Mark off and on. I would wonder how he was and if he was even single anymore. And I wondered if he ever thought about me. Each time I was between boyfriends, I'd toy with the idea of calling him. Somehow, I always decided against it.

SIX YEARS LATER

December of 1998. In response to my little epiphany about my widower semi-boyfriend, Daniel (i.e., after six months of dating and no New Year's Eve date, get a clue, girlfriend!), I did what most of us do. I called one of my best friends to complain. Now, what I *wanted* her to do was to be in cahoots with me by making Daniel and, for that matter, all men in general, wrong. Instead, she asked me what I was avoiding by choosing to be alone in life. The question startled me. I had so longed for a healthy, committed partnership with a man whom I could love and respect that I hadn't even considered that I might actually be invested in being alone. Yet, as much as the question irritated me, I had to confess that the idea resonated as true. The more I sat with it, the more I realized that I loved my freedom, in spite of my complaints to the contrary. I loved not being accountable to anyone. I loved keeping my options open. In fact, I had to admit that I was terrified of being emotionally dependent on anyone, and vulnerable to the possibility of being left.

Now, I became a psychotherapist from the inside out. Helping others to heal was a natural outgrowth of how I'd been healing myself for close to fifteen years by this time. Believe me, at this point I knew my issues backwards and forwards, and had most of the answers to my own perplexing questions and broken-hearted dilemmas. However, I hadn't yet made the leap of using the insights I had to catapult myself into playing full out in life. I had not yet been willing to surrender hook, line, and sinker to the risk of love. I was still trying to protect myself from being disappointed in ways similar to how I'd been disappointed in childhood. All this time I'd been pining for love and complaining about the lack thereof, and yet I'd been too scared to open up my heart again and get back on the horse.

> The important thing is to be able at any moment to sacrifice what we are for what we could become.
> —Charles Dubois

BECOMING AVAILABLE

You can work on yourself for years and then someone says one little thing and the whole universe opens up. My friend's simple question initiated a profound period of inquiry for me. I simply couldn't go on blaming others—my parents, men, the culture—for my circumstances. For years, I had made my desire to meet "The One" the central drama of my life. Now, I finally understood the difference between wanting something and being ready to have it. As I began to take responsibility at a whole new level for my covert attitudes and hidden agendas, I found myself releasing the resistance I had to being open to love. For the first time in my adult life, I became truly available to create a loving, committed, romantic union.

At the time, I'd been getting positive results in my professional life by setting clear and attainable intentions. I decided to set an intention around finding "The One." To make it official, I called a girlfriend. "Naomi," I said, "I'm going to be engaged by my birthday." "Great!" she replied without skipping a beat. Immediately, she began relating to me as though this intention were true. Looking back, I see that her confidence in my ability to transform my life was vitally important to the process I was in. Our friends are our training ground for loving relationships. They encourage and support us, standing with us in the vision of who we are becoming. They also play the role of vision keeper by holding us accountable for the choices we make as we pursue our objectives. My two best

> Be really whole
> and all things
> will come to you.
> —Lao-Tzu

friends, Naomi and Jennifer, were absolutely invaluable allies in my quest for love.

Now, my birthday was a mere eight and a half months away. I had absolutely no prospects for any husband, let alone the ideal husband. However, I started acting as if my assertion were real. Within a month, just setting that intention turned my life upside down. Daniel and I had a very genuine talk; we laid it all out on the table. We discussed what each of us wanted in our lives and decided to break up, transitioning our relationship into a friendship. I had some very sincere heart-to-hearts with a couple of men who'd been my flirting buddies. The conversations brought clarity and, in one case, completion to our friendship. Like many of my relationships, it seemed founded upon the possibility of romance without his ever really being available to it. And I finally released and mourned a relationship that had taken five years to run its course.

During this time I was meditating each morning, which basically means that I was making a sincere attempt to sit in stillness for a few minutes before running off to the demands of my ridiculous schedule. I'd watch my mind rattle off its insistent "to do" list, settle into my body by paying attention to and then deepening my breathing, and try to get hold of some sense of center. Although entering the silence, as it is sometimes called, was not a new practice for me, I found myself receiving a level of inspiration, clarity, and intuitive instructions that I hadn't ever experienced before. I tentatively followed the guidance I was receiving, wondering all the while whether I was "just making it up" or if I really was being led to take certain actions and move in certain directions. Either way, upon reflection, the guidance I felt that I was receiving seemed sound enough, so I went with it. I spent Saturday nights at home alone going through my things, burning old love letters and deleting old e-mails that I'd saved for no reason other than to feel less lonely. I gave away jewelry given to me by former lovers. I put away poems that I'd inspired. I went through my apartment, removing any images that reflected loneliness, sorrow, or isolation, replacing them instead them with pictures that represented love, union, and joy. I wrote page after page after page in my by-now-tattered journal, getting to the bottom of my aloneness, reflecting upon all the ways in which it worked for me to live a solitary life and upon all of the things I did to ensure it, in spite of my protestations to the contrary.

It was uncomfortable to let go of my past before there was any evidence of something new. It was also disquieting to release the way I had always seen myself—my identity, so to speak. Getting rid of so many things that defined who I was left me with a tremendous void that danced in the pit of my stomach. However, I really believe that if you want to create something wonderful in your life, if you truly want to make a big change, you've got to learn to tolerate the "in-between" time. That's the period in which we let go of who we know ourselves to be in order to allow for the possibility of who we might become.

CALLING IN "THE ONE"

In February, thoughts of Mark began popping into my head again. Once more, I decided not to call him. It just didn't feel right. Then one Sunday in March, I attended services at a church I'd been going to for about ten years. In all of that time, I'd never once seen Mark there. As far as I knew, he wasn't even aware of the place. I was standing outside talking with a friend in a crowd of several hundred people who were milling about the parking lot. When I looked up, I saw Mark walking across the asphalt. Immediately I became timid and looked away, hesitating just long enough to lose sight of him. By the time I gathered enough courage to go look for him, he'd disappeared. "Oh, well, I guess it wasn't meant to be," I told myself, to mask my disappointment.

Two weeks later, I was talking to another friend on the phone. In spite of setting my intention and faithfully doing my inner work, I was complaining that I still wasn't even close to finding "The One." I was getting impatient. This was the end of March and I was on a deadline! My friend suggested that I log on to an Internet dating site where she'd been meeting some interesting people. I'd never been open to meeting men in this way before, but thought I'd finally give it a try.

She told me how to get to the site and what to do when I was there. When I turned on my computer, I was a little overwhelmed to find a quarter of a million people registered at this site, all of them looking for love in one form or another. After entering age, religion, and other logistic preferences, I was able to narrow down this impossible number to a mere eighty men. All of the profiles were anonymous, some with their pictures, but most without. No names were given and very few identifying characteristics were included.

As I read the profiles, one in particular captured my interest. The man who wrote it said that he believed we were all interconnected and, therefore, ultimately a part of one another—a conviction that I share. He went on to describe himself in a way that made me think that he was a well-rounded, happy, and successful man. I decided to respond to him. Feeling a little foolish and self-conscious, I quickly rattled off a brief and somewhat awkward e-mail about myself. I then continued scrolling through the other choices. One man's profile made me laugh out loud with his dry and urbane sense of humor; but when I began crafting a response to him, my computer froze. Having little patience with technical things, I turned it off and went to bed, losing the e-mail that I'd started.

The next evening, I turned on the computer and checked my e-mails. The one man I'd replied to had written back. Amazed, I stared at his name, which stood in parentheses next to his e-mail address. The man was Mark. "Of course," I thought, "how perfect." Since my identity was not obvious from my e-mail address, Mark did not know who I was and he wrote to me as he would to a stranger. I responded warmly, as though to an old friend, and revealed my identity. Weeks later, Mark would tell me that he was so stunned to hear from me this way that he literally fell off his chair when he read my e-mail. Soon after he received it, he collected himself and called to invite me out for coffee—a gesture, he later assured me, that he would never have made if it were not such an obviously meant-to-be encounter. Mark has a healthy amount of self-esteem and would not have asked me out again after my having turned him down twice before. As a matter of fact, he later confessed that he *had* seen me across the church parking lot that day and had deliberately left without speaking to me. So, you see, we needed a bit of a miracle to bring us together again.

Several days after hearing from him, I found myself sipping a large cup of decaf across from this handsome, bright, kind, and gentle man. I knew within one hour of being with him that he was the husband I'd been searching for. I was no longer afraid of love. I came home and excitedly e-mailed the two girlfriends who'd been supporting me, stating unequivocally that I'd just had a date with the man I was going to marry. And in fact, Mark proposed two months later, on the last day of May. Eight weeks *before* my birthday! As of this writing, Mark and I have been together for almost four years. We were blessed with a beautiful daughter shortly before Thanksgiving of 2000—my first child, at the age of forty-three.

THIS COURSE

There is a huge chasm between wanting to find your ideal partner and being truly available for that partner when he or she appears. This course is about bridging that chasm. It shows you how to set a strong intention to love and be loved, then outlines in clear, specific steps what you can do to make your intention become a reality.

I have used much of what I went through in my own journey to create the course outlined in this book. I've also taken many others successfully down this path. As a licensed psychotherapist, I have been able to bring to the table my years of experience with both psychological healing and spiritual transformation to structure an approach that is accessible, effective, and psychologically sound.

The road to finding love can be a long and arduous one. It can be fraught with wrong turns, dangerous potholes, and circuitous routes that sometimes feel as if they're leading you nowhere. But the very fact that you've been drawn to this book indicates that you are seriously searching for a change in your life. You are now being presented with an extraordinary opportunity. You are standing at the fork in the road. One path leads to more of the same. It's a safer journey, in many respects, but usually only leads to an all-too-familiar disappointment. The other path leads to freedom from the past and the very real possibility of love in the future. It is the unknown road. From this vantage point, it may seem somewhat intimidating and frightening. For this reason, it is the path less often traversed. However, this course will guide you down that road, leading you step by step to the fulfillment of love. I promise to give you daily support and direction, taking good care of you once you decide that you are ready for the journey. No matter how disappointed you've been in the past, no matter how weary and resigned you've become, I know that you can now choose a path that will enable you to find and welcome your beloved joyfully. For, truly, there *is* someone for everyone. Take heart and be not discouraged. Love belongs to all of us.

CALLING IN
"THE ONE"

INTRODUCTION

We are all born for love.

It is the principle of existence, and its only end.

—Benjamin Disraeli

As a society, we are outwardly focused. We want someone to tell us the rules of love. We want the manual on who says what, and who calls whom when. There is nothing wrong with this and there are many intelligent teachers out there who write about dating and finding love from that perspective. However, this course is *not* that. You will find no hard and fast rules on how you or others are supposed to behave in order to find and keep love. You will find no secret formulas for making someone love you and propose marriage within the year. What you *will* find, however, are the tools to transform your life from the inside out. What you *will* find is the very real possibility of the fulfillment of love.

Before we begin, there are three basic premises that I must ask you to consider. These premises are imperative to the success of your work, as they are the very foundation of the course.

PREMISE #1

Our lives are a creative work in progress. Most of us live as though there were a future "out there" somewhere and that all we need do to fulfill it is to live passively until we bump into it at some designated and preordained time. This is a fantasy, and a rather harmful one at that.

The first premise of this course is this:

Life is a creative process and our thoughts, beliefs, assumptions, choices, actions, and words are the tools that we use to invent our experiences and our circumstances.

In order to own that our lives are an act of invention, however, we have to give up the idea that we are victims. This may not be an easy one for many of us. We may have difficulty giving up the yoke of victimhood for several reasons. We may have built an entire identity around being victimized, knowing ourselves only through its burden. We may feel that being a victim brings us much desired love and compassion from others. Perhaps we are attached to punishing our perpetrators by making them witness our suffering year after year. Or we may not feel that anyone has truly heard and understood our pain as of yet, so we couldn't possibly just let it go. These are all understandable reasons to continue on under the weight of victimhood. Yet the price tag is incredibly high. Simply put, remaining a victim costs you love. Hopefully, we will be able to alter your relationship to this role by inspiring you to the wonderful possibilities that exist for you by giving it up.

PREMISE #2

We have a say in our own destiny through the intentions that we set. Although the lives we are living may seem headed in a particular direction, with a predictable outcome, we can, at any time, alter the likely course of our lives through setting a strong and clear intention.

The second premise, then, is:

We have the ability to create circumstances and opportunities in our lives by setting clear intentions and by committing to and living in alignment with these intentions.

Most of us live our lives not by setting intentions but rather by having expectations. These expectations go largely unfulfilled and often lead

---

Every moment of your life is infinitely creative and the universe is endlessly bountiful. Just put forth a clear enough request, and everything your heart desires must come to you.

—Shakti Gawain

There is little sense in attempting to change external conditions, you must first change inner beliefs, then outer conditions will change accordingly.

—Brian Adams

to feelings of disappointment and resignation. This is because we do not see ourselves as needing to be an active agent in the fulfillment of our dreams and desires.

PREMISE #3

The issues in our relationships are mirroring back to us our internal issues with ourselves. If we are having difficulty sustaining loving, nurturing, and committed relationships, the place to look is at your relationship with yourself. Ask yourself: In what ways are you failing to love, nurture, and commit to yourself?

The third premise, therefore, is:

**When you alter your relationship with yourself,
your external world will alter accordingly.**

Without changing our internal relationship with ourselves, we cannot create lasting change simply by altering external behaviors. When you alter your internal landscape, you effortlessly and authentically adjust your external behaviors, and life will begin occurring differently. Because you have dealt with the source of the difficulty, once you transform these internal conversations, your external world will forever be altered. And not just for as long as you remember to follow a set of rules and regulations that may feel forced and unnatural to you.

These three premises are very much the operative principles in this course. The definition of a premise is something that is to be taken without the need for proof. You may or may not agree with these three premises or you may not be sure, at this time, of their relevance to you. However, for the purpose of our work together, I ask that you try them on for size and at least give them a chance to work in your life. You can always discard them later if they are not helpful to you. Truth be told, once you master these premises in the service of bringing your beloved into your life, you can use them to create the fulfillment of your deepest and most treasured dreams in any area of your life.

Life consists of what a person is thinking about all day.
—Ralph Waldo Emerson

Every issue, belief, attitude, or assumption is precisely the issue that stands between you and your relationship to another human being; and between you and yourself.
—Gita Bellin

HOW TO DO THIS COURSE

When the word *God* is used … you may substitute the
thought *good orderly direction* or *flow*. It is not [my] intent …
to engage in explaining, debating, or defining that flow.
You do not need to understand electricity to use it.

—Julia Cameron, *The Artist's Way*

> The future is not
> there waiting for us.
> We create it by the
> power of imagination.
> —Pir Vilayat Khan

I define a "spiritual" person not as one who believes in a particular doctrine or religion, but rather as one who is actively pursuing the qualities
of character that constitute a life of goodness and love. I have met the
most devoted religious people who think little of examining their own
hearts authentically to ferret out selfishness and deceit. I have also met
those who profess to be atheist or agnostic and who go to great lengths to
cultivate the qualities of loving-kindness, compassion, and mercy in their
lives. Because of this, I have come to disregard those labels and credentials
that normally make up the definition of a "spiritual" person and grown to
appreciate profoundly the complexities and uniqueness of each person's
particular path.

COURSE SUPPLY LIST

Journal

Drawing paper

Cardboard and/or other backing
for collage

Drawing markers and/or crayons

Modeling clay (optional)

Scissors

Glue

Matches

Magazines and/or other resources
for pictures and images

Highlighter

As you go through the course, you may find yourself challenged by some basic spiritual principles that I employ and
invite you to embrace as well. If these moments occur for you,
I ask you to remain open-minded and willing to experiment
with ideas and practices that may be somewhat new and
unusual for you. I ask that you not become too distracted by
specific religious tenets but rather that you focus more on the
essence of the practice and the effect it is having upon you.

Those of you who remain steadfastly atheist or agnostic
throughout should have no more difficulty in successfully
navigating this course than anyone else. I promise you, I have
no interest in converting anyone. My experience of God is
very personal and, frankly, ever-evolving. I am much more
interested in continuing to discover my relationship with God

than in proselytizing who or what I believe God to be. I assume that you have your own understanding of spiritual matters and are growing yourself according to longings of your own heart. There are simply some things for which there really are no words.

This course integrates many spiritual traditions and healing methods, moving between meditations, physical activities, writing assignments, art projects, and suggested actions to take in your life. These practices, as they are called, are meant to engage you in a holistic process of growth and change. You cannot do this course effectively on the level of intellect. In other words, while it's fine to read through the course before going back to actually do the practices, I can promise you authentic movement in your life only to the extent that you are willing to *do* the course and not just *read* the course.

To those of you who would tell me that you've "already done this" (and I'm sure you have), I would suggest that doing this course is more in the realm of taking on a spiritual practice than it is experiencing a one-time event. Few of us would forgo prayer because we've prayed once before. Nor would we avoid going to the gym because we've worked out in the past. And while one can read volumes on the subject of meditation, there is simply no substitute for sitting down and spending twenty minutes or so giving it your best shot. This course is an on-the-court experience. It is designed to help you transform your life, which means that you must be willing to put your money where your mouth is by taking concrete actions and doing the work.

I suggest you get a special notebook that you dedicate specifically to doing the course. You may also wish to have a particular pen that you love writing with. Find a safe and private space to keep these items in. Your writings need to be kept confidential so that you feel safe enough to really tell the truth to yourself. You don't need to worry about the possibility of someone looking over your shoulder. Your work is for you and you alone, unless, of course, you choose to share it with someone. Many people have created a ritual such as lighting a scented candle or listening to meditative music each time they sat down to do the course. This is your time. Give it to yourself.

If you do the course as written, it will take you seven weeks to com-

If all you can do
is crawl,
start crawling.
—Rumi

If grass can grow through cement, love can find you at every time in your life.

—Cher

plete. I have a preference for doing it this way, straight through with one lesson a day for forty-nine days. If you do it like this, you should plan on setting aside twenty to forty-five minutes a day, preferably in the morning. While I understand that this might seem like a lot of time to some of you, consider the amount of time an intimate relationship is going to require of you and assume that commitment starts now.

I have discovered that some people prefer to work in a less linear way, perhaps reading a chapter at a time, which represents a whole week's worth of lessons. They then divvy up the practices so that they are doing a practice a day, or two one day and none the next, working in the context of the entire week. As each week focuses on one overall theme, this has proven to be quite effective. Another group of people will read through the book in its entirety before returning to Lesson One to actually *do* the practices. And then some will just amble along at their own pace, taking two or three days per lesson (or three to five months to complete the course).

It's important to keep in mind that there is no "wrong" way to do this course. This course is not an invitation to beat yourself up for not doing things perfectly. In fact, it's not possible to do the course perfectly and, if you try to, you should consider loosening up a little more in your life. This isn't about being perfect. This is about growing and stretching yourself. It's about discarding things that no longer work for you and embracing things that do. This is the bottom line. I wrote the book to be more than you could comfortably do in the course of seven weeks. I did that deliberately for those of you who might want to return and do it again, and maybe even again after that, getting all the juice out of it you can. The course is rich and succulent, and, frankly, you could feast on it several times through. So savor. Enjoy.

Having said all that, if you find that you are taking longer than six months to complete the course, you might want to seriously examine how much you actually want a relationship at this time. Too much delay could suggest a strong ambivalence about opening yourself up to the experience of intimate, romantic love. If you find that you are taking too long between lessons, procrastinating doing the practices, and/or getting stuck on various lessons, I recommend that you talk about your feelings with someone you trust, such as a therapist or spiritual adviser. They might be able to help you see more clearly what could be keeping you from completion.

If you find that, in general, you are moving forward but occasionally get "stuck" on a particular lesson because of its profound impact on you, there is nothing wrong with simply marking that lesson to return to once you've completed the entire forty-nine days. The course is comprehensive, traveling through an abundance of subjects. Some of these will be more relevant for you than others. The "hot" issues, the ones you discover you need to work on some more, should be notated and returned to later. Not everything is going to be healed in a day. You are engaged in a process. Please trust it. Much of the value of the course has to do with its ability to bring clarity regarding your particular blocks to love. Make note also of those practices that you find especially helpful, so that you can incorporate them into your life after you've completed the course.

A word of caution. The course can be intense at times. I will warn you as best I can when these times are coming up. However, if you've been the victim of abuse, which includes neglect and emotional mistreatment, as well as verbal, physical, and sexual abuse, you may find that you need extra support to move through the feelings of anxiety and fear that may arise as you expand your availability to love. Psychotherapy is a wonderful place to get this extra support, and if you are not in therapy at this time, I suggest that you pay attention to yourself and be willing to speak to a professional if you need to.

If you don't have a therapist and feel it might be helpful to speak with someone, don't be afraid to interview two to four people before choosing someone to work with. Choosing a therapist is a little like dating, in that it takes some time to find the right "match." Look for someone you respect, who shares your values and your philosophy of life, as well as someone you feel safe and comfortable with. For those of you who have financial considerations, know that local clinics often provide low-cost counseling in exchange for the training of graduate students who are studying to become therapists. Often, these students have a lot of talent and some excellent supervisors guiding them. What they lack in experience is often made up for in commitment and enthusiasm.

How much longer will you go on letting your energy sleep? How much longer are you going to stay oblivious of the immensity of yourself?
—Bhagwan Shree Rajneesh

Take heart, truth and
happiness will get
you in the end.
You can't lose in this
game. Have fun.

—John and Lyn St. Clair
Thomas

DOING THE COURSE WITH OTHERS

*We are meant to midwife dreams for one another …
Success occurs in clusters.*

—Julia Cameron, *The Artist's Way*

I encourage you to consider doing this course with a friend or a group of friends rather than by yourself, if at all possible. As you are doing this work in the hope of moving into a deeper and more profound experience of love, I can think of no better way to prepare yourself than by doing the course with others. Sharing with people who care about you and truly grasp the significance of the changes you are experiencing will serve as a demonstration of your willingness to create more love in your life, as well as help you to solidify the gains you are making all the more.

I've always loved that line of Scripture from the Book of James that admonishes us: "Confess your faults to one another and pray one for another that ye may be healed." When we are able to "tell on ourselves" and experience that it is safe to be our flawed and very vulnerable selves with others, it helps us to accept ourselves just as we are because, most often, we find that others accept us as we are. Yet, when we succumb to our insecurities, allowing ourselves to be dominated by the need to look good at the cost of our authenticity, we become alienated and isolated from others, thereby validating the very fears we are indulging.

It's important to let others in—to allow them to get to know the real you. It's important that you allow other people to hold the vision of the future you are creating along with you. It's too easy for self-doubt to undermine our efforts if and when we experience a disappointment or a setback. A strong circle of support can help us to stay in a place of antic-ipation and faith when these moments occur. There's a huge difference between trying to hold on to a vision by yourself, and doing so with the help of others who can sustain and steer that vision with you and even *for* you, during times of despair and discouragement. I believe this is the meaning of that passage in James, encouraging us to "pray one for another." The goodwill and support of others go a long way during moments of dissuasion.

Lastly, those in your support circle are able to bear witness to what it is that you are releasing and letting go of. This witnessing provides much needed understanding and compassion for the pain that you have been through, which, in turn, helps you to give it up. Many times, we have a difficult time letting go of the past simply because we haven't felt that the pain and suffering we've experienced has fully been understood and recognized by others.

If I've convinced you that doing this course with others is the way to go, here are a few guidelines that I would suggest for your group.

1. MEETINGS. As this is a seven-week course, I suggest you meet at least nine times—the same time each week for nine consecutive weeks (or ten, with a "breather" week off in the middle), with several scheduled follow-up meetings three to six months out. The nine-week structure allows for two extra meetings, a "Getting to Know You" introductory meeting and a "Closure" meeting. The dates of your meetings should be decided in advance so everyone coming into the group knows what they are signing on for.

2. MEMBERSHIP. I suggest that you make this a closed group. This means that you close it to newcomers after the first or second meeting. I suggest you look for members who are willing to commit to the entire life span of the group in advance. I will often allow someone into a group if they know in advance that they will have to miss just one meeting, as long as they commit to doing the work for the week that they miss. However, if they know that they'll need to miss more than one meeting, I ask them to wait and join another group.

3. CONFIDENTIALITY. I strongly suggest that you have a confidentiality agreement among members of the group. This means that you do not reveal the names of the other members to anyone outside the group. It also means that you do not repeat anything that is said during the meeting, even to other members of the group who may not have been in attendance. You do not gossip about one another or in any other way violate the trust and

> The only currency in this bankrupt world is what you share with someone else when you're uncool.
>
> —Philip Seymour Hoffman in *Almost Famous*

integrity of the group. This is of primary importance. Without establishing safety, the group's effectiveness is severely undermined and may actually sabotage it entirely.

4. TIME AND LOCATION. I suggest you establish a meeting place and a set time to begin and end the group each week so that people can plan in advance to be there. Group connection occurs because the same people show up on time and are ready to go consistently.

5. SHARING. The purpose of this group is to provide support and encouragement for all participants. Unless the group is being run by a professional, it is best to minimize feedback and cross-talk. Although it is difficult for some of us to refrain from "fixing" others and telling them how we think they should be living their lives, that is not the purpose of this group. It's important to remember that the simple act of caring listening is very helpful to those struggling to solve their problems. Sometimes it is more important to demonstrate confidence that others will find their way than it is to try to figure out how you yourself can help them out of their dilemmas. Bottom line: make sure that the word *I* is being used far more often than the word *you* (e.g., "I noticed I felt a little uncomfortable when you were talking," instead of "You really shouldn't feel that way."). Don't be afraid to hold your group accountable to keeping this principle in place. The ability of the group to be successful rests upon adherence to this principle. You may wish to divide the time evenly between members before the group begins so that all participants get the same amount of time and attention.

6. HOSTING. I suggest that you share the task of hosting the group, choosing the host for the next gathering at the end of each meeting. That host will be the one who brings water and snacks and also contacts everyone should there be any changes.

7. BUDDY SYSTEM. I suggest you call each other in between meetings for support. You may wish to choose buddies who rotate each time you meet, or you may wish to have a buddy whom you go through the entire course with. The important thing is to support each other, keep the faith for each other, and help each other stay focused and on track.

Essentially, we are talking about each of you taking on the role of "vision keeper" for one another. Be careful to not play prison guard for each other, or take on the role of critical parent. Don't try to play therapist by analyzing each other. Listening with compassion while occasionally asking simple questions about the motives behind certain actions and behaviors goes a long, long way in helping each other to grow.

If, after all of this, you still want to do the course alone, at least let your close friends know that you are doing it. It will be helpful for you to have at least one or two friends who know what you are up to. They can support you to live consistent with your commitment. In other words, if you begin behaving in ways that are inconsistent with the future of love fulfilled in your life (i.e., dating someone who is mean and abusive, becoming reclusive, acting in abusive ways yourself, etc.), your friends can help you stay on track by pointing out your inconsistency. Lovingly, of course.

You are now ready to begin an extraordinary journey. Allow yourself to undertake this journey exactly as you are. Be free to be your imperfect, messy, unenlightened self as well as your magnificent, extraordinary, fabulous self. I had one woman register for one of my workshops who almost canceled the day before because she hadn't "gotten rid" of her uncommitted, neglectful boyfriend before the course began. She thought she had to be perfect and have it all together before she took the course. I had to remind her that that was why she was coming in the first place! You don't need to clean the house before the cleaning lady comes. And you don't have to be perfect before, during, or after doing this course. Just stay authentic and risk telling the truth—first to yourself and then to others, because that's where the healing happens.

Blessings to you as you proceed on this wonderful, mystical pilgrimage to the fulfillment of love in your life.

Give sorrow words; the grief that does not speak whispers the o'er-fraught heart, and bids it break.
—William Shakespeare

One has just to be oneself. That's my basic message. The moment you accept yourself as you are, all burdens, all mountainous burdens simply disappear. Then life is a sheer joy, a festival of lights.
—Bhagwan Shree Rajneesh

PREPARING FOR LOVE

Someday, after we have mastered the winds, the waves, the tides and gravity, we shall harness for God the energies of love. Then for the second time in the history of the world, man will have discovered fire.

—Pierre Teilhard de Chardin

Too often, we believe our private agonies are ours alone to bear, forgetting that we are part of a vast collective where the majority of our concerns are shared in one form or another by many other people.

This week:

✳ We will explore the impact that the culture around us is having on our collective ability to create loving and meaningful relationships

✳ We will prepare ourselves for love by opening our hearts to those in our lives at a whole new level, exploring and expanding our capacity for healthy interdependence

✳ We will cultivate a vision of love fulfilled to begin anchoring and designing our lives around the realization of love

✳ We will begin taking specific actions that are consistent with, and supportive of, a future of love fulfilled

LESSON 1
Expanding Our Capacity to Love and Be Loved

If you want to learn to love, then you must start the process of
finding out what it is, what qualities make up a loving person and
how these are developed. Each person has the potential for love.
But potential is never realized without work.

—Leo Buscaglia, *Love*

One reason that so many of us do not have the love we are longing for is
that we have not yet become the people we will need to be in order to
attract and sustain that kind of love. Most of us have dramatically elevated
our standards of what we want from a partner far beyond what our parents expected from romantic union. Yet we may not have evolved our
level of maturity to the point where we can manifest and maintain the
love that we are hoping to create.

Romantic relationship today is a tentative and uncertain thing. No
longer is getting married the safe and secure way to go. Whereas once
upon a time people coupled up out of economic and social necessity, we
now seek to form such unions in an attempt to create soulful and meaningful lives. Yet, much of the time, falling in love means that we end up
standing by helplessly as we watch it all slip through our fingers. Why
can't we seem to hold on to the glorious transcendence of love? Why can't
we seem to harness passion, root it down, and make a home of it?

Some would say that romantic love is an illusion. A trick of nature
meant to entice us into procreation. In the aftermath of a devastating
breakup, we find ourselves asking, was he or was he not my soul mate?
Was it or was it not real love? The most beautiful moments of our lives
become reduced to their lowest common denominator: hormones, lust,
and those most dreaded of words—"It was just infatuation."

Yet many understand, if only intuitively, that romantic love holds a promise that we have yet to fully comprehend. Instinctively, we know it holds a key to our expansion. Because romantic love has such a profound capacity to bring out the best—and the worst—in us, we are beginning to see it as our newest frontier for spiritual growth and development.

Rather than calling us into seclusion, the spiritual path now beckons us deeper into the quality of our relationships. This premise is the very crux of the new term "spiritual partnership," which has recently emerged to describe the modern-day paradigm of marriage. What exactly is this new paradigm of marriage that everyone is speaking of? Well, if the concerns of the old paradigm were economic stability and morally sanctified sex, then the concerns of the new paradigm have to do with fulfilling our soul's destiny and actualizing our full potential. Spiritual partnership implies a goal of encouraging and supporting the unfolding of each other's soul's reasons for being here in the first place.

Not too long ago, being spiritual meant moving away from relationships by going off alone to the mountaintop or the monastery. However, it now means allowing ourselves to become fully immersed in knowing and being known fully by another human being. It means learning the terrain and the language of love through a commitment to the spiritual advancement of another person. It means learning to be completely vulnerable and undefended while at the same time being 100 percent authentic and true to ourselves. And it means going beyond the pervasive ideas of our parents' generation that romantic union was about compromise and sacrifice, and moving into an experience of romantic love as expansive and inclusive. In other words, those who still believe that romantic love and spiritual love are two different things understand little about the direction that either has taken.

This is not a book for those who wish to hide out. This is a book for those who aren't afraid of a challenge. It is designed to help you get from who you are today to who you need to be in order to bring in the best possible partner for you in this lifetime. For those of you who picked up this book because you "just wanted to get married," consider the possibility of what it would be like to find not just a mate, but a soul mate, not just a partner, but a spiritual partner.

Years ago, I heard Jack Canfield, coeditor of the *Chicken Soup* books,

> Each man lives love in his limited fashion and does not seem to relate the resultant confusion and loneliness to his lack of knowledge about love.
> —Leo Buscaglia

tell a moving story of a woman who'd had a near-death experience. She had had an accident and was pronounced dead soon after. While dead, she saw the tunnel of light that we so often hear about. She followed the light and soon came upon an Angelic Being who was radiating an enormous amount of love. The Being told her that it was not yet her time to die. However, before she was sent back into her body, she was asked two questions. The first was: "What wisdom have you gained in this lifetime?" and the second was: "How have you expanded your capacity to love?"

My husband and I wrote our wedding vows. One of the things I said was, "What I bring to you today are certain promises. I will endeavor always to live by these promises, knowing that they are larger than me and will require a growing and a maturing beyond that which I now possess." For those of us who just won't settle, life is always a stretch.

If you want to be ready to bring in "The One," you must be willing to grow yourself beyond the person that you are today. Because the person you are now is the person who has created the experiences that you have already had. As they say in the twelve-step programs, "Our best thinking got us here." As such, your task is to grow yourself healthier and stronger in order to create a space for a remarkable love to enter your life. As long as we are acting out the wounds of our childhood and in reaction to the disappointments of our past, we will most likely remain frustrated and unfulfilled in our attempts to actualize love in our lives. However, once we have done the work to heal ourselves, it then becomes possible for us to bring the best of who we are to others. In return, we will draw in those who are willing and able to bring the best of who they are to us. At the very least, we will be able to distinguish early on those who can't or won't do this, knowing that, although this person might have "great potential," he or she is no one to open our hearts to.

In order to attract an extraordinary love and then preserve a relationship distinguished by respect and kindness, we must first face our fears and come to terms with our woundedness. We must cultivate our ability to fluidly express the characteristics of love in all of our encounters. For without choosing to grow ourselves in this way, we will most likely have

> All our failures
> are ultimately
> failures in love.
> —Iris Murdoch

> In the orchard
> and rose garden
> I long to see
> your face.
> In the taste of
> Sweetness
> I long to kiss
> your lips.
> In the shadows
> of passion
> I long for your love.
> —Rumi

difficulty sustaining the love that does come into our lives. I invite you, therefore, to consciously take on expanding your capacity to love and be loved as a goal that you can call your own.

It's important to realize that we do not need to be with a partner in order to begin expanding our ability to give and receive love. We simply need the willingness to start by opening ourselves to the opportunities of love that surround us today.

> I was there in
> the beginning
> and I was
> the spirit of love.
> —Rumi

PRACTICE

In her book, *The Eight Human Talents,* yoga instructor Gurmukh, includes a simple yoga exercise meant to open the heart. The following is a modification of this exercise.

If you are able to, sit cross-legged on either the floor or a pillow to do this exercise. If you are unable to cross your legs in this way, simply sit up with a straight back, legs stretched out, and feet together on the floor in front of you, or try placing a pillow under you while sitting up on your knees.

Begin by stretching your arms out in front of you, palms together, elbows straight, with your arms parallel to the floor. As you inhale through your nose, open your arms widely to the sides, expansively bringing your shoulder blades as close together as possible. As you stretch, place your awareness on your heart. Imagine your heart opening and expanding as you fill your lungs with air by continuing to breathe in deeply. Feel your arms stretch out as though they were giant wings, while keeping your arms parallel to the ground.

When you've stretched your arms as far back as they can go, begin exhaling strongly through your nose, bringing your arms slowly back to the original position. Again, press your palms together, keeping your arms parallel to the ground the entire time.

Silently say to yourself with each expansion,

"I open myself fully to give and receive love."

If you are able to, repeat this movement twenty-six times, with your eyes closed and slightly rolled up and focused just above and between the eyebrows (your "third eye" point).

Do this exercise at a moderate pace. Allow yourself to relax between expansions, if necessary, by bringing your arms down to rest upon your knees.

BONUS: PRACTICE IN ACTION

Throughout the day, whenever you think of it, breathe deeply into your heart, repeating silently to yourself,

"I open myself fully to give and receive love."

LESSON 2
Looking Through Laura's Eyes

A human being is a part of the whole....He experiences
himself, his thoughts and feelings, as something separated from
the rest, a kind of optical delusion of...consciousness.
This delusion is a kind of prison for us, restricting us to our
personal desires and to affection for a few persons nearest to us.

—Albert Einstein

A friend of mine who was born and raised in India used to confide in me
how desperately lonely he felt in the United States. "There is so much isolation here," he'd say. "How do you Americans stand it?" As a psychotherapist, I'm more privy than most to the inner world of those I come
into contact with. And, after thinking about his question for quite some
time now, I'd have to answer him by saying, "Not very well, my friend.
Not very well at all."

Too many of us feel isolated and alone in life. In our materially
advanced and technologically sophisticated society, we've done little to
advance a collective sense of love and relatedness. As a culture we are well
versed in growing ourselves in material value but terribly undernourished
in recognizing the opportunities we have to give and receive love. These
opportunities come our way constantly. Yet we often do not even
acknowledge them, let alone allow ourselves to seize upon them. If we
did, we would walk through life with a profound experience of connectedness and well-being.

A couple of years ago, I lost my dear friend Laura to breast cancer. Two
days before she died, my soon-to-be-husband, Mark, and I went to see her
in the hospital. Laura had never met Mark and she burst into tears at the
sight of us together. She said that she could see the love between us as

though it were a physical entity, and it filled her with joy. She was glowing with pure delight and looked lovingly at us as she spoke.

Sometimes, when someone is dying, they become almost radiant right before they leave their bodies. This was the case with Laura. She saw love in every interaction as a beautiful and very tangible force field that moved from others to her and back again. In the excited voice of a child, she told us of the love she saw when her nurses walked in the room to care for her and even when the janitor came by with his broom to sweep the hallway. In her heightened state of awareness, she could see love in each and every gesture as she prepared herself for death.

I sometimes wonder what life would be like if we were all able to see even partially what Laura could see on that day. As it is, we must consciously choose to cultivate the qualities of love and compassion, hoping in our hearts that one day the veil will be lifted. At times, cultivating an awareness of our interconnectedness with those around us will put us in direct opposition to our current cultural values and social mores. While we might be moved to give away a valuable possession to a friend in need, common wisdom may suggest that we'd best hoard our possessions and let others fend for themselves. For though it may seem that we Westerners place a high priority on love, in truth, we don't. In spite of our plethora of love songs, romantic comedies, and romance novels, we're basically a "me first, you later" society. I would even suggest that our preoccupation with romantic love is a symptom of our inner poverty. In *Gila: Life and Death of an American River,* author Gregory McNamee writes

> An anthropologist once asked a Hopi why so many of his people's songs were about rain. The Hopi replied, "Because water is so scarce. Is that why so many of your songs are about love?"

Our fascination with romantic love tends to focus on the finding of such a love and not the substance of what truly makes up a loving relationship. Rarely do our movies or our songs deal with the day in, day out minutiae of what true love actually requires of us. But the experience of loving for the long haul, of generously extending oneself day after day after day, while receiving the kind of constancy and kindness that weaves

In the modern world we also tend to see everything as if it were a machine, including our most precious relationships.

—Thomas Moore

one's broken heart back together again, is about as high drama as we'll ever hope to find in this lifetime. It always amazes me that we tend to skip that part in the movies. For truly, it is the absolute best part of love and yet most of us have no idea what it even looks like. Being consumed with falling in love as opposed to the sustaining of love is a little like stopping at foreplay.

We tend to distinguish romantic love as separate from *agape,* or neighborly love. Perhaps this is one reason that the divorce rate is so high. And while romantic love does have the benefit of hormones and biological urges to enhance its allure, the qualities that make up a loving relationship are the same whether we love our friend, our sister, our student, or our husband. Compassion, generosity, and kindness transcend gender, title, or the form of a relationship.

> The biggest disease today is not leprosy or tuberculosis, but rather the feeling of being unwanted, uncared for and deserted by everybody.
> —Mother Teresa

Often, in a materialistic culture such as ours, a person is valued in terms of their net worth and an encounter is valued in terms of its networking potential. This creates a vast void in the hearts of those of us who are living in this society. For we are relating to one another as though people were objects. Our disconnectedness from one another is no small matter and must be considered when we look at how alone many of us feel and how desperately we are longing for love.

In his book *Ethics for the New Millennium,* the Dalai Lama speaks extensively about the connection between Western culture and feelings of alienation and loneliness that are so pervasive today.

In place of our dependence on one another for support, today, wherever possible, we tend to rely on machines and services. Whereas formerly farmers would call in all their family members to help with the harvest, today they simply telephone a contractor. We find modern living organized so that it demands the least possible direct dependence on others. The more or less universal ambition seems to be for everyone to own their own house, their own car, their own computer, and so on in order to be as independent as possible. This is natural and understandable. The increasing autonomy that people enjoy as a result of advances in science and technology has its good points. In fact, it is possible today to be far more independent of others than ever before.

Our cities with their
swollen populations
and cliff dwelling
high - rise buildings
are breeding places
for loneliness.... In a
world of wheels, old
and comfortable
groupings of people
have disappeared.

—Allan Fromme

But with these developments, there has arisen a sense that my future is not dependent on my neighbor but rather on my job or, at most, my employer. This in turn encourages us to suppose that because others are not important for my happiness, their happiness is not important to me.

George Bernard Shaw once said that our ". . . worst sin toward our fellow creatures is not to hate them, but to be indifferent to them." Most of us don't walk around harboring strong negative emotions such as loathing or rage. Yet, the challenge for many is to overcome the apathy and indifference we have toward one another: to be available and attentive to those we pass in the aisles at the market, the coworkers we see daily in the hallways of our offices, and those acquaintances we regularly notice in our social and/or spiritual circles.

Our sense of community is fostered readily in the aftermath of any tragedy. Yet, a sense of belonging must be cultivated and valued in and of itself for us to feel truly fulfilled in our lives. As Einstein suggests, in order for us to transcend the "delusion of separateness," we must learn to "free ourselves from this prison by widening our circle of compassion to embrace all living creatures and to the whole of nature in all its beauty."

PRACTICE

Today we are going to concentrate our efforts on developing an awareness of the interconnectedness that binds us all together always. I invite you to begin the day with a simple meditation designed to open you to an awareness of love and connection. I suggest that you read through the meditation once or twice and then just do it by memory. Do the best you can in recalling the meditation but don't worry if you don't do it exactly as written.

I recommend that you don't try to meditate lying down as it is too easy to fall asleep, particularly first thing in the morning. If you can, sit up straight and cross your legs in front of you. Rest your hands gently on your thighs and close your eyes. (Note: For some of you, sitting still like this presents an immense challenge. If this is true for you, I'd rather you try a walking meditation than skip the meditations included in this book entirely. Take a mindful walk around the block, while doing the assigned meditations as best you can.)

Notice if there is any tension in your body. If so, release it and allow yourself to feel relaxed. Focus on your breathing, allowing your breath to fill up your belly and then your heart. Imagine a beautiful light expanding the energy around your heart with each breath. Next, think of your neighbors. Notice that there is vibrant energy that connects your heart to their hearts and back again from them to you. Say to yourself

"I am connected to everyone and everything."

Now think of your coworkers or those you come into contact with on a daily basis. Again, notice that beautiful force fields of energy connect you with each person you see. Whether you know the person by name or not, repeat the phrase to yourself with each person you think of. Now, imagine that you are walking down a street. Again, see energy connecting you to everyone you pass. Continue to repeat the phrase.

Next, think of those people who you are estranged from. Maybe it's because there is unresolved anger between you. Perhaps it's because time has passed and you've lost touch. Whoever comes to mind is fine. As you repeat the phrase with each person who comes to mind, imagine a beautiful energy passing between your heart and theirs, connecting you in love.

Spend at least three minutes doing this exercise. If you are able to sit for a longer period, I encourage you to do so but you need not do it for longer than three minutes.

BONUS: PRACTICE IN ACTION

Today, I invite you to spend the day looking through Laura's eyes. Frequently throughout your day, connect with your own heart and repeat silently to yourself

In a social environment that is ever crowded and impersonal, it is becoming increasingly important to reconsider the value of close personal relationships before we are driven to ask the forlorn question, "Whatever happened to love?"
—Desmond Morris

A strange passion is
moving in my head.
My heart has
become a bird
Which searches
in the sky.
Every part of me
goes in different
directions.
Is it really so
That the one I love
is everywhere?

—Rumi

"I am connected to everyone and everything."

Consciously relate to those around you, looking to discover the connection between yourself and others. Make eye contact, speak to someone you would not ordinarily speak to, smile at someone you might normally look away from, ask someone how they are and pause long enough to listen to their response. Note if any of this makes you uncomfortable and just breathe through your discomfort. Do not allow your discomfort to stop you from doing the exercise throughout the day.

At the end of the day, take out your journal and write down the moments where you experienced a sense of connection, relatedness, and belonging that passed between you and another person, whether or not you knew them. It could be that a stranger looked at you and smiled. Perhaps you opened the door for an elderly person or someone called you for business purposes. Remember, we are looking through Laura's eyes, so look for love everywhere.

LESSON 3
Honoring Our Need for Others

We are each of us angels with only one wing.
And we can only fly embracing each other.

—Luciano De Crescenzo

A friend, Stuart, and I had lunch a while back. We met at a small restaurant overlooking the bay in Marina del Rey on a beautiful, clear afternoon. As I bit into an overstuffed turkey burger, Stuart leaned in and asked me a question. "Do you know the difference between heaven and hell?" he inquired.

"I'm not sure," I replied. "Why don't you explain it to me."

"Well," he said, leaning back in his chair, "hell is like this. You enter a beautiful dining hall, decorated with the finest linens and china. Over in the corner, an orchestra plays exquisite music. You look around and see that everyone is dressed in elegant clothes and draped in splendid jewels. They are all sitting around tables abundant with fine food and drink. You think you've arrived.

"But slowly you begin to see that there is something wrong. The people do not look happy. As a matter of fact, they look rather sad and confused. In spite of the magnificent array of food laid out before them, they cannot partake of it because the utensils they have are too large. Although they can manage to get the food onto their forks, they cannot get it into their mouths. The handles on their silverware are simply too long. You notice that they are starving to death." He sat quietly.

"And heaven?" I asked, taking the bait. "Oh, heaven," he replied, with a mischievous smile. "You walk into the same scenario. Same fine linen and china, same exquisite music, same magnificent food, even the same utensils. Only this time the people are flourishing, laughing, smiling, and having a wonderful time. And the only difference is that, while the people still cannot feed themselves with their large forks, they have learned how to use their utensils to feed one another."

This story touches us because we know, intuitively, that most of us are living a little bit too close to hell. We've become confused about when and how much we should be feeding others and/or allowing them to feed us back. In our therapeutically hip and savvy culture, we have collapsed codependence with interdependence, no longer able to distinguish between the two. In our confusion, we have stopped giving much of ourselves to others. We have stopped allowing others to give much of themselves to us. For we have come to think of needing others as a negative thing. Our misguided goal has become total independence and self-sufficiency, lest we be thought of as "too needy." And we've become all the sadder for it.

My friend Aviva got lung cancer while only in her mid-thirties. She had two beautiful children, a boy who was five and a girl who was three, a loving husband and a wonderful career ahead of her to live for. When she first heard the news, she called together a healing circle, inviting everyone in her community to come be with her and her family. About sixty of us showed up bearing gifts, poems, prayers, and offers of help. One woman brought a gold ring that her mother had given her on her wedding day. She laid it down at Aviva's feet, telling her that she was giving it to her so that she could give it to her daughter on her wedding day. No one was without tears that day.

Aviva's illness allowed us all to band together in a way that is uncommon in our culture. Her best friend, Rachael, put all of us on a schedule. Some people did the grocery shopping. Some cleaned the house. Others babysat one day a week and some took her back and forth to the doctor's office. You would think that this community would be morose and heavy with sorrow, but nothing could be farther from the truth. People were so happy to be needed in this way. They wanted to contribute to Aviva and her family in a way that made a difference for them. There was always laughter and joy coming from that house. Ultimately, Aviva surrendered to death. But even on her deathbed, people were helping out, praying, talking to her and reassuring her that all was well and that she was safe to go. One of the saddest things for me about Aviva's death is that we all had to return to our own isolated, little lives. She used to confide in me how embarrassed she was that so many people "had to go out of their way" to help her. I tried to tell her many times what a gift she was giving to others. Most likely, she understands now.

The simple truth is that human beings need other human beings. And while men and women may not need one another for economic survival any longer, we do need one another for nurturing and for emotional well-being.[1] We all need to feel connected, valued, cared for, and respected. These experiences do not exist in a vacuum. They exist in relationship to one another. We've become so afraid of appearing too needy that many of us have given up a healthy sense of entitlement. I frequently counsel women who are afraid to insist that they be treated well, tolerating all sorts of dismissive, disrespectful behavior from those they date simply because they don't want to appear "too demanding" or "too needy." Many of us have given up entirely on expressing our needs to others. But we've thrown the baby out with the bathwater. It's appropriate for us to go into a relationship with the intention of caring for the needs of another, with the anticipation that our needs for love, connection, and belonging will be cared for in return. It's part of what it is to be human.

Love requires that we give up a certain degree of autonomy and allow ourselves to become unguarded and accessible. Love is about feeding one another. It is about coming to rely on this exchange and to depend upon it for our health and well-being. Loving relationships must include the ability to be vulnerable enough to depend upon someone.

Often, when my clients complain that they are too needy, I discover that the people whom they are spending time with are unwilling or unable to provide support, consistency, and love to them. I assure them that it may not necessarily be that they are too needy. Rather, they may be choosing people who, for whatever reason, aren't taking their needs into consideration. Of course, this then leads us to explore how willing they are to take their own needs seriously.

Love comforteth like sunshine after rain.
—William Shakespeare

---

[1] I realize and respect that many women choose other women and many men choose other men as their intimate partners. This book is for those in the gay community just as much as it is for those in the straight community. Please be gracious with me for failing to acknowledge homosexual love as often as I do heterosexual love, knowing that I've held those of you who are gay in my heart as I wrote, as well.

The bird a nest,
the spider a web,
man friendship.
—William Blake

I become so disheartened sometimes listening to women telling me why they don't need a man in their lives. It's as though needing a man were akin to needing a wheelchair. The truth is that I will come to rely upon anyone I let into my inner circle. That's how it should be. I need many things from the people in my life and, hopefully, they trust me enough to need many things back from me.

Now, I understand that many of us are carrying around unhealed wounds from the past that occur in the present as neediness. We feel as though we have to hide our needs, fearing that they will engulf anyone who gets too close. Yet in our efforts not to appear inappropriately needy, many of us have tried to shut down our needs entirely. The appropriate needs get thrown together with the inappropriate ones and we swallow them all. Yet this, in turn, only creates more hunger because it's simply not normal for us to not have needs in our relationships with others. When we try to pretend that our needs don't exist, or treat them as though they were pathological, we only feed the hunger in our hearts that much more intensely.

Human beings are not meant to live in isolation. We are here to have relationships. Nothing much gets accomplished in life outside of a connection to other people. Rather than trying to get rid of your need for love, kindness, respect, and belonging, consider instead, taking your needs seriously. Begin cultivating relationships with people who are able and willing to respond lovingly toward you when you ask for what you need, instead of staying with people who don't and hoping that they will change.

Men and women, in general, have somewhat different needs. A woman needs to feel heard and tended to in a relationship. Ideally, she needs to be noticed, wanted, and adored. She needs to feel treasured by her man and she needs a partner who demonstrates that he cares about her feelings. She needs someone who will anticipate her wishes and take action to fulfill them, even before she thinks to ask. She needs her partner to keep his word to her. She needs him to be someone she can count on, someone who will do his best to make her feel secure.

Men, on the other hand, need to feel needed. A man will thrive when he feels appreciated by his partner and when he is acknowledged for his accomplishments. Too often, women remember to acknowledge a man for his big accomplishments but forget the little things that he does each day to make her happy. He needs to be acknowledged for these little things, too. He needs to be accepted just the way he is. He will thrive if he feels admired, authentically liked, and respected. A loving partner who encourages and inspires him will bring out the best in him.

It's important to identify what we need so that we can adequately assess who we should, or should not, open our hearts to. It's important that we don't judge ourselves or make ourselves wrong for having the needs that we have. Until you can take full responsibility for what you want and need in a relationship, you may waste a lot of your time with people who either don't have what you want or, for whatever reason, simply aren't interested in giving it to you.

> The great question... which I have not been able to answer, despite my thirty years of research into the feminine soul, is "What does a woman want?"
> —Sigmund Freud

PRACTICE

In your journal, write a list of five things or more you need in order to be happy in a relationship. Allow yourself to be authentic. Your list might include things like:

> **I need to feel valued and respected.**
> **I need to be told that I am beautiful.**
> **I need to be inspired.**

Now, close your eyes and, one statement at a time, grant yourself each item on your list by speaking it to yourself silently or out loud. For example:

I need to feel valued and respected	*becomes*	**I value and respect myself.**
I need to be told that I am beautiful	*becomes*	**I acknowledge how beautiful I am.**
I need to be inspired	*becomes*	**I inspire myself constantly.**

Now, write out your statements of affirmation ten or more times each. As you write, feel it to be so in your heart.

What makes a
happy marriage?
It is a question which
all men and women
ask one another...
The answer is to be
found, I think, in the
mutual discovery,
by two who marry,
of the deepest need
of the other's
personality, and
the satisfaction of
that need.

—Pearl Buck

BONUS: PRACTICE IN ACTION

Carve out some quiet time today so you can privately craft a letter to yourself, written to you from your ideal lover. Imagine what he might say to you as he whispers softly in your ear in a moment of great tenderness and love. What is it that your heart has longed to hear your lover say to you?

For example: "You are the most beautiful woman I have ever known. I will always love you and I will do everything in my power to make you happy. Your heart is safe with me—I will dedicate myself to loving you and caring for you all the days of my life."

When you are finished, reread your letter and again allow yourself to imagine these words being spoken to you with great kindness and care. Now, place your hand upon your heart. Silently or aloud, lovingly say your name to yourself. Slowly and with great meaning, read your letter to yourself, from yourself. Allow your heart to open and receive the sweet sentiments that you have written.

LESSON 4
Love for Love's Sake

When human relationships fail … they fail because they were entered into for the wrong reason.

—Neale Donald Walsch, *Conversations with God, Book 1*

For the past hundred and some odd years, psychologists have been trying to figure out what motivates human beings to do the things we do. Sigmund Freud believed it was our unconscious drive for pleasure, Alfred Adler thought it to be our need for esteem among our peers, Abraham Maslow considered it to be the necessity of self-actualization, and Viktor Frankl believed it could be found in our constant quest for meaning. Perhaps they each had hold of one small piece of the pie. When it all boils down to the very heart of the matter: we each have to decide what it's all about for us. We each have to ultimately choose what makes sense to us and then reflect that choice in the ways in which we approach bringing in a mate.

One reason that so many relationships fail is that we are going into them for reasons that can't sustain us. We're afraid to be alone. We want someone to give us what our parents did not. We are hoping to be taken care of financially. Whereas, at one time, these reasons were perfectly acceptable ones for choosing a life-partner, they are no longer sufficient. For truthfully, most of us want the best that love has to offer and we will settle for nothing less. And so, whenever we create a relationship that is based on anything less than the motivation to truly love and be loved, it's only a matter of time before we become restless and discontented. Then we'll begin kicking the relationship around, poking holes in it, tearing it apart and eventually going into therapy to try to fix what never really worked for us in the first place. We can no longer get away with creating loving relationships inside of a context of fear and deprivation. Love itself

We are what we think. All that we are arises with our thought. With our thoughts we make the world.

—The Dhammapada

is demanding more from us. As author Daphne Rose Kingma says, "Love is trying to find us." Love is insisting that we up the ante. Love works these days only when entered into for loving reasons—to extend and expand, to give and to grow, to bless and be blessed.

We're either surviving or thriving in life. To survive indicates that we are operating under the assumption that life is dangerous, that it's set up for us to not get what we need, that others are out to get us and that, if we stopped manipulating and cajoling, we would soon go under. To thrive means that we have chosen a new foundation. We've stepped into an awareness that the possibilities for love in our lives are unlimited, that abundance is ours for the asking, that what we have to bring to the table is very much welcomed, and that, if we just open ourselves up and start trusting both ourselves and others more, goodness and love will flow toward us always.

I'm inviting you to continue in your quest for romantic union from a foundation of love rather than fear. Most likely, many of you picked up this book out of fear. "I'm afraid that love will pass me by," "I'm afraid that I'm not good enough, healthy enough, smart enough to find love," "I'm afraid I've missed my chance for love," etc. You thought if you bought this book and did this course that I would straighten you out, fix what's wrong with you and tell you what you need to do to find someone who will take care of you. But I don't think you need straightening out. I don't think you need fixing. And I don't think you need anyone to take care of you.

What I do hope to inspire you to do, however, is to release all that is not love in your lives so that the bright and beautiful sun that you already are can come out from behind the clouds. As Marianne Williamson suggests in her book *A Return to Love,* "Love is within us. It cannot be destroyed, but can only be hidden." You already have all the love you need in your lives. It's locked inside your own magnificent heart. I'm just offering to help you to rediscover it and begin sharing it boldly with others.

Life is an unceasingly creative process. So often, I hear people go on about how uncreative they are, unaware that we are all creating our very lives in every moment of every day. Most of us are living as though life were happening *to* us rather than *through* us. We are not present to the fact that we are constantly generating our lives, as though they were great works of art. The tools we are given from which to create are our thoughts, beliefs, assumptions, actions, decisions, and words.

Often, when we want to create something that we do not yet possess, we stand inside of fear, rather than come from a place of possibility. Instead of owning our own readiness to expand into love, we are contracted and anxious. Even the idea of moving into a consciousness of possibility can feel scary. We don't want to be disappointed. We're afraid that if we ask for what we want, we may be denied and then we'll feel even more deprived. We're terrified that we'll find out that our worst fear is true—that we really are unworthy of love.

We do not want to do this course motivated by fear. Having fear as the foundation of our work just sets us up for failure because we tend to create that which we focus on. So, it's important that we don't allow fear to dominate our search for love. It's much more effective to say, "I am ready and available for love" than "I can't stand being alone anymore." If you do this course motivated mainly by fear, such as an anxiety that you'll never be loved, you may find that you generate that very thing you fear the most. That's because it's the thing you are focused on and it's the thing that has the most energy around it. A good indication that your foundation is fear is the feeling of desperation. If you are feeling desperate, you can be sure that you're rooted in fear. If you do this course to escape those things that you most fear, you may, unfortunately, create more of that which you most dread. As the saying goes, "What you resist, persists."

Therefore, as we embark on this journey of creation together, I invite you first to choose a particular Essence Quality(ies) to be the foundation of your quest for love. An Essence Quality is a property of love. I'm inviting you to anchor yourself in love as the foundation for doing the course. If you have been deeply betrayed in the past, you might wish to anchor yourself in Healing and Courage as you again open yourself to love. If you have been abandoned, you might want to take on cultivating Trust and Openness as your new foundation for creating loving relationships. It is from this place of doing your own inner healing work that it is most powerful, and most appropriate, to call in true love.

Love is letting go
of fear.
—Gerald Jampolsky

Love is the
wrecking ball that
is pulverizing
every relationship
of record that isn't
wide enough or
brave enough
to let real love in.
—Daphne Rose Kingma

PRACTICE

We have often heard that love is more powerful than fear. Fear might be present, but we put love in charge of this quest. I invite you to create a foundation of love for your work by choosing one or more Essence Qualities from which to create.

Simply close your eyes for a moment, go within your heart and see which quality or qualities speak to you the most. The following suggested Essence Qualities may be helpful. I suggest that you trust the ones that come to you, whether they are on this list or not.

Abundance	Acceptance	Appreciation
Awe	Beauty	Celebration
Compassion	Completion	Confidence
Courage	Creativity	Curiosity
Divine Love	Ease	Faith
Forgiveness	Freedom	Fulfillment
Fun	Generosity	Grace
Gratitude	Healing	Health
Honesty	Hope	Humor
Integrity	Intimacy	Joy
Kindness	Laughter	Lightness
Love	Loveliness	Openness
Optimism	Passion	Peace
Play	Rejoicing	Rejuvenation
Self-Love	Serenity	Success
Surrender	Synchronicity	Tenderness
Trust	Truth	Unconditional Love
Wonder		

For each of the Essence Qualities you chose, create a statement of affirmation to anchor and ground you in that quality (e.g., for Abundance: "My life is abundant and overflowing with love.").

Write your statements of affirmation ten or more times each in your journal. As you write, feel it to be so in your heart. Then write them on small cards and/or Post-its and place them strategically where you can see them often as you do this course.

BONUS: PRACTICE IN ACTION

Do at least one thing today that demonstrates the Essence Quality(ies) you chose this morning. For example, if your Essence Quality is Freedom, write a letter to the person you have felt bound by, claiming your freedom, and either send it or burn it. If your Essence Quality is Openness, ask a stranger for directions or for a favor. If your Essence Quality is Wonder, take some time to walk in the garden.

LESSON 5
A Vision of Love Fulfilled

Like a great athlete, we must have a very clear vision of what
we want to accomplish before we make a move. Vision, in
preparation for an action, is as important as the action itself.

—Marianne Williamson, *Healing the Soul of America*

I've met many people who simply can't envision having a loving relationship. Yet it's hard to create something that you can't even allow yourself to imagine having. I met Susan at a recent Calling In "The One" workshop that was sponsored through a local church. She's an attractive woman in her mid to late thirties with long, red hair that hangs deliciously down her back. Within the first hour, Susan admitted that she could not even conceive of actually having a loving and lasting romantic relationship. When pressed, all she can say is that she can see it for other women but just not for herself. I asked her, "So, you believe that God singled you out as the one and only woman who is destined to be alone and suffer with terrible loneliness your entire life?" She laughs because, although it is what she believes, it sounds so silly when I say it out loud. "I guess so," she admits sheepishly. "So, who is this God that you serve?" I ask. "Because He or She sounds pretty cold and heartless to me."

Before I reconnected with my husband, I had a conversation with a minister friend of mine, Nirvana Gayle. It was a conversation that altered my life forever. I was upset because I was feeling lonely. I didn't understand why I couldn't seem to find the right relationship. Over forty, I was beyond a ticking clock, figuring that, at this point, my batteries were probably dead.

Nirvana asked me if I'd ever made any promises to God in my life. I thought about it for a moment before remembering that, when I was nineteen, I went through a period of about six months where I spent a lot of time in prayer and meditation. At the time, I was studying to become a minister and trying my best to live according to Christian principles, as I understood them. I was a bit of a puritan back then. In my heartfelt idealism and fervor, I gave away most of my material possessions and lived a very austere life. It was during this period that I dedicated my life to God, asking God to use me throughout my life for good. Basically, I "married" God. As I was talking, it became clear to both of us that the life I was living in my forties was a reflection of that which I had imagined when I was nineteen—I was working as a clinical director at a center for the homeless, making a difference but very little money and living alone in a tiny one-bedroom apartment with my fifteen-year-old cat, Clover.

Nirvana commented that I seemed to have "married me a God of poverty"—a God who valued a strict adherence to an austere life. I will always love him for the audacity of what he said next. "If I were you, I'd divorce that God and marry you a new one!"

When I went into meditation later that day, I considered his advice and decided to take it. It felt a little like jumping off a cliff. But within a matter of months, I had re-created a vision of my life that included love and material abundance in addition to serving people and contributing to their lives in a way that felt meaningful to me. As I was able to re-create a vision for my life that was more consistent with what I truly wanted, almost immediately my life began to open up to include these very things.

When I relayed this story to Susan, she said that she identified with it. She, too, had always been a deeply spiritual person and her spirituality had a sort of reclusive, nun (as in "none") like quality to it. In her current vision of her life, she was unable to imagine a future where love was abundantly fulfilled. She saw herself alone, living a simple and unadorned life of devotion and service to others. So there was a core conflict in what she felt to be her life path, which was resolvable only when she determined to do what I had done—re-create a vision of her life as inclusive of both spiritual *and* romantic fulfillment.

Until you are able to *see* yourself living the life that you truly want, it will be difficult for you to create it. So, we are going to be doing a lot of work in the next few weeks to enhance your ability to imagine your life

I am enough of an artist to draw freely upon my imagination. Imagination is more important than knowledge. Knowledge is limited. Imagination encircles the world.

—Albert Einstein

Hope is ... an orientation of the heart; it transcends the world that is immediately experienced, and is anchored somewhere beyond its horizons.

—Václav Havel

abundantly fulfilled in love, inclusive of the other things that you want for yourself as well.

A while back, a lovely woman, Kimberly, attended my workshop. She is a first-rate singer by profession and travels all over the world performing her music. On the way to the workshop, she got lost, which caused her to be about a half hour late. She apologized to everyone, saying how happy she was to be in the workshop, as finding her life-partner was of high priority to her. However, as the afternoon wore on, it became clear that Kimberly was terrified of making a commitment. She was very attached to her singing career and feared that a relationship would prevent her from achieving her professional goals. She had a belief that she had to choose between finding a husband or becoming successful as a singer. Kimberly ended up leaving the workshop early because she got a singing job. She promised me that she'd enroll in the next workshop to complete the course. To date, she has never returned to a workshop and the last time I ran into her, she was still single.

Many of us see our desires as mutually exclusive. Either I get to have a meaningful career or I get to have love. I get to be famous or I get to have a relationship. I get to serve God or I get to have a happy family. Does your current vision of your life have this either/or quality? If so, I would say that your vision is way too small. We need first to begin cultivating a much larger vision of what is possible for you. I invite you to begin creating a vision for your life that allows you to have *all* of what you want, instead of having to settle for only part of what is possible.

PRACTICE

Take out your journal. Write a list of your goals—all of the things you feel are important for you to accomplish in this lifetime. I invite you to begin a collage today that you can work on at your own pace throughout the course. If you wish to spend the day doing this project to complete it, that's great. However, if the most you can do today is simply begin the collage by locating one picture or phrase that you want to include, that's fine.

Look for images and/or words that represent the fulfillment of love in your life. Make sure that you include images of *all* of the various parts of yourself and your life that are important to you, including those needs that you identified yesterday. It's important that you create a portrait of your life in which romantic love coexists with other things that you love and need in your life in order to feel fulfilled. You might look in a magazine or in a bookstore for images created by masters or unknown artists that inspire you and touch your heart. You may even wish to draw or paint your own images into the collage. Find or create at least one image today that fills your heart with the possibility of love and deep connection. Make sure that you choose an image to which you have a strong emotional response.

Allow yourself to be creative and unconventional. As you collect pictures and words to include, you may want to keep them in a special folder or box so that they are treated with reverence and respect. You may gather them all together before you begin gluing them onto a piece of cardboard, canvas, or wood, or you may create your masterpiece as you go.

Place your images where you can see them often. Whenever you look at the images, say to yourself, "Yes. This is for me. Thank you, God."

> It's easy to enjoy each other while on a vacation in Maui. The key is to find someone you can have fun with during the six-hour flight over there.
> —Tom Arnold

BONUS: PRACTICE IN ACTION

Today, I invite you to write about your quest for love by turning your life and all you've been through into your own personalized fairy tale. Allow yourself to write about your life as though you were standing outside of yourself. Be creative, expressing your setbacks and failures as the obstacles you need to overcome. See the people in your life—yourself included—as mythological characters. See parts of yourself in all of your main archetypal characters—the "damsel in distress" who longs for someone to rescue her; the "knight in shining armor" who heroically goes to many lengths to save her from her sorrows; and the critical, tyrannical parent who would have her settle for less than her ideal love. Write about the challenges you are facing as the dragons that need to be slayed before love can be realized. Begin your fairy tale with "Once upon a time . . ." and end it with a happy ending where love and all the important goals of your life are abundantly fulfilled.

> This or something better now manifests for me in totally satisfying and harmonious ways, for the highest good of all concerned.
> —Shakti Gawain

LESSON 6
The Nature of a Soul Connection

*Our soulmates seldom appeal to our personality—our ego.
That's why they are called soulmates rather than egomates.*

—Carolyn G. Miller, *Soulmates*

Not long ago, a study was done at Rutgers University in which a group of single people between the ages of twenty and twenty-nine were asked to agree or disagree with the statement "When you marry, you want your spouse to be your soul mate first and foremost." A whopping 94 percent agreed. Most of us aren't really looking for just "someone." We're looking for "The One."

In his book *Soul Mates,* author Thomas Moore defines a soul mate as ". . . someone to whom we feel profoundly connected, as though the communicating and communing that take place between us were not the product of intentional efforts, but rather a divine grace." A soul connection is a profound gift and can be found in *many* different kinds of relationships—friends, family members, coworkers, or neighbors. In our ever-present desire for romance, however, we tend to focus all our yearning for connection on a lover with whom we can share this experience. We try to imagine what he or she will be like and can muse for hours on the many qualities that we might hope for in an intimate partner.

I've always felt a little uncomfortable with the popular practice of writing out a list of the qualities we want in a partner. Attractive, successful, ambitious, wealthy, college educated, etc., etc. While I agree that we should be clear about what we want in our lives, some of the lists I've seen have been so detailed as to specify what he or she does for a living ("I really want to fall in love with a writer"), where the person lives ("I want a guy who lives in Beverly Hills"), and what kind of car they drive ("I need someone fun who drives a sports car"). But bringing in a mate isn't like ordering a meal—I'll have the dressing on the side, extra tomatoes, and hold the cheese, please. The external attributes that we think are so important actually have little to do with the heart of a person or the tone of a relationship, those things that reflect what we call soul.

Rarely will the love of your life look the way you think he or she should look. Because we are so attached to our mental fantasies of love, we'll often pass right over what could be an extraordinary love experience, enhanced exactly because the person *doesn't* look the way we think that he or she should. If you've read in the preface about how my husband and I met, you'll notice that I turned him down twice before I finally recognized him as "The One" some six years later. I often wonder about the choices I made back then. If you had asked me at the time, I would have sworn that I was looking for the man I was going to marry. I was in my mid-thirties, wanted a child, and thought I was ready. Looking back, I had to ask myself, How could I have missed him?

Right before I ran across Mark for the third time, I was meditating one night when I heard an inner voice tell me loud and clear, "He is not going to look the way that you think that he should." It startled me right out of meditation. I thought about it for all of ten seconds before I spoke back saying, "Well, OK, then. Thanks for the warning."

Through my mother's side of the family, I am part Sicilian and part English. My father is a Scandinavian Jew, although he didn't raise me. I grew up with my mom and my adoptive father, a man of German descent, in the suburbs of Long Island. We lived in a very homogeneous neighborhood. We had just two black kids at our high school and, although I was friendly with them both, my upbringing was pretty segregated. I was a difficult kid—self-destructive, impulsive, and rebellious. I felt compelled to do everything and anything that was just the opposite of how everyone else was doing it. In response, my mother felt the need to caution me about many things. On more than one occasion she told me, "Whatever you do, do not bring home a black man." In hindsight, I'm sure this was her attempt to protect me from my wild and reckless nature. At the time, however, I heard it as the one edict to which I must adhere in order to not push her right off the deep end. Since dating black men wasn't a "thing" for me, it didn't seem like much of an issue

Soulful marriages
are often odd on
the surface.
—Thomas Moore

> Vision is not
> necessarily
> attachment to
> a picture.
> —Shakti Gawain

at the time. I simply filed the information away in the recesses of my mind.

Well, you may have guessed by now that my husband, Mark, is a black man. Hindsight now tells me that I felt connected with Mark right from the start, but *he didn't look the way I thought he should and so I dismissed him.* The first two times we went out, I wasn't really ready to deal with the possible consequences of choosing him as my husband. I was liberal enough not to worry about any stigma that might be attached to dating a man of another race, but marrying him was a whole different matter. It wasn't until I was in my early forties that I felt confident enough in my own judgment to risk alienating my family by choosing him. As an aside, the story wouldn't be complete if I did not let you know that my mother has not only accepted Mark into our family but has genuinely grown to love and appreciate him. And she most certainly adores her first grandchild.

Too often, we mistake "chemistry" for a soul mate connection, when in fact we may have very little in common with the person we feel instantly attracted to. Rather than being about excitement and lust, a soul mate relationship is characterized by such things as a shared life path, a sense of comfort and ease, and a genuine liking of each other. And while you may very well experience times of excitement and lust with your soul mate, the relationship is not defined by these moments. Dr. Carolyn Miller, in her book *Soulmates,* describes it this way

> Our soul . . . [tries] to direct us to individuals who share our purpose in life, complement our strengths, and supplement our weaknesses. But there is no guarantee that these ideal mates are going to look the way we expect, or be of our own background. That's only one of the reasons why they are so easy to miss if we are not listening *(to our inner voice)* for guidance. [Italics mine]

The relationship you are looking for simply cannot be reduced to a checklist. I dated a guy once who had all the attributes I thought I wanted. He, too, thought that I had all the attributes that he believed he wanted. It took us a full six months to finally admit that, although it *looked* like it should be right, it wasn't. The truth was, we just didn't love each other. There was no real substance, no deep and meaningful connection between us. I thank God that we had the wisdom to part ways.

You must look for "The One" with your heart and not with your expectations or your hormones. As such, we are called to move into our heart center when relating to others. Rather than being so captured by the judgments and assessments of our very busy minds, we need to practice being with people from a more open-hearted and curious space. This means that we must strip ourselves of our more defended stance in life and soften into a more receptive, more welcoming way of being.

> The soul selects
> her own society.
> —Emily Dickinson

PRACTICE

This morning, we are going to do a simple meditation. Read the instructions once through and then do the meditation from memory to the best of your ability.

Sit up straight with arms uncrossed and resting easily. Close your eyes and relax your entire body. Starting at the bottom of your feet and working your way up through the body—your toes, your ankles, calves, knees, thighs, until you reach the top of your head, release any tension you find. Breath in and out normally, without any effort, with your mouth slightly open and at rest. Feel yourself breathing but do not try to regulate your breath in any way.

Now imagine what a relationship with "The One" might feel like. Don't try to picture what your partner looks like or who they are in the world. Instead, try to imagine what it might *feel* like to actually have this relationship. Imagine this person sitting in front of you, breathing in unison with your breath, his heart beating in unison with your heartbeat. Imagine laughing freely, crying freely, and telling him a secret about yourself, knowing that you will not be judged but only valued and loved. Imagine what it is like to know that you are this safe, this appreciated, and this cherished.

This is what you are looking for. This is what you are opening yourself to.

> A soul mate is…
> someone whose
> way of viewing life
> is not necessarily
> the same as yours
> but complements
> yours, so that
> there is not a
> compromise, there
> is a complement.
> —Paul Robear

Magazines and talk shows are filled with people who say that a successful marriage is hard and requires a lot of work. But to soulmates, their harmony often feels effortless, as though it is the most natural thing in the world to be completely at ease in a relationship.

—Rosemary Ellen Guiley

BONUS: PRACTICE IN ACTION

Throughout the day, instead of assessing people primarily with your mind, try dropping down into your heart by asking yourself how they actually *feel* to you. Warm and welcoming? Intimidating and angry? Sad and lonely? Joyful and fun? Use your feelings and your intuition to assess the connection that is between you and those you come into contact with. Is this person someone you could be friends with? Laugh with? Trust with a secret? Is he or she someone you feel safe with? Judged by? Who seems to genuinely like you for who you are? Who doesn't?

Tonight, before bed, take out your journal and write down your thoughts and impressions on your interactions with others. Assess the connections you made with others not from external things about them like sex, race, age, education, financial status, or position, but from the way that the relationship between the two of you actually *felt* to you.

LESSON 7
Making the Space for Love

Make room for love and it always comes. Make a nest
for love and it always settles. Make a home for the beloved
and he will find his way there.

—Marianne Williamson, *A Woman's Worth*

One gray night, I was traveling with a group of about fifty on a large, chartered bus. We were inspired and relaxed after an exciting conference that had ended several hours earlier. People were sharing snacks and songs, telling silly jokes and simply enjoying one another's company. I found myself sitting across the aisle from a man I'd never met before, and I began a conversation with him.

Jeffrey was in his late thirties and he had just gotten engaged for the first time. He was beaming with contentment. I asked him how he'd met his wife-to-be. With a great smile of satisfaction on his face, he told me that she was nothing like he'd pictured his wife would be. For years, he had a list of qualifications that he was looking for that he now described as his "rigid criteria." He said that "The One" hadn't shown up in his life until he'd given up the attachment of what he thought she should look like. The real work, he confided, was that he needed to open himself to love and be loved. When I asked him how he did this, he smiled sheepishly and leaned in to tell me his secret. "I cleaned out my closets," he confessed. "I literally created a space in my bedroom closet and cleared out a drawer so that when she showed up, she'd have a place to put her things."

If you want a great love to come to you, you must make sure that your environment is an open and welcoming space for that person to show up in. Even if your home is too small for two people and you are certain that you will move when you find him or her, it is important to have room for this person where you are right now, if even symbolically. There's a lot of wisdom in the age-old advice: If you want a relationship, go out and buy a double bed.

The best room to begin with is, of course, the bedroom. The purpose of the bedroom is twofold: rest and intimacy. If you have your office set up in your bedroom or if any other activities go on there, you may wish to move these to another part of your home or at least screen off that area at night. Your bedroom is your personal space and it is important to dedicate this one room to the exchange of love, warmth, affection, and rejuvenation.

If your bedroom is filled with stuffed animals left over from childhood, pictures of your parents, relics from former love affairs, or framed copies of your advanced graduate degrees, I invite you to reconsider how you are using this room. One woman I worked with complained to me of depression and exhaustion. She was having difficulty separating herself emotionally from her ex-husband and often found herself sleepless, irritable, and upset. During the course of our conversation, I discovered that, in her attempt to avoid looking at the mounds of paperwork that were being generated from her difficult and ongoing divorce proceedings, she was storing all of the legal documents underneath her bed. I was stunned. No wonder she was unable to get a good night's sleep. Needless to say, I advised her to get them out of there at once and to store them appropriately in another part of the house. She immediately began to sleep better at night.

When I began designing my environment to support calling in "The One," one of the first things I noticed was my bed. Although it was queen-size, it was pushed up against the wall so that it could only be gotten into from one side. It was not a big adjustment to turn the bed cater-cornered so that it could be entered from both sides.

So many of us, when single, tolerate living in environments that have little meaning for us. Too often, we procrastinate creating a loving and nurturing space until we have the right partner, only to find that our dissatisfaction with our lives is aggravated by a home that feels temporary, empty, and undernourishing. Worse yet, many people are living in homes that hold reminders of a former relationship, thereby keeping it alive in

> Our lives will mirror our surroundings. Choose thoughtfully.
> —Karen Ann Tompkins

their space. If any of these describe you, I suggest you begin creating an environment that reflects and supports the future you are calling in.

Feng shui is an ancient Chinese art and science first developed some six thousand years ago. Very simply, feng shui is about the energy flow in a given space, concerning itself with how the placement of objects affects how people feel when they are in that environment. In feng shui, using pairs of items accentuates the possibility of romantic union. Pairs of pillows, pairs of pictures, pairs of candlesticks all bring forth the feeling of a harmonious relationship and evoke a feeling of intimacy. When calling in romantic partnership, feng shui also encourages one to reflect both the male and the female aspects of a relationship in the environment. If you are a woman with lots of puffy, lacy, flowery things throughout your home, you may wish to balance this with more masculine motifs, colors, and lines, and vice versa. The desire for a balance of yin and yang holds true for same-sex relationships as well.

While driving to a recent Calling In "The One" workshop, Cynthia, a charismatic woman in her early forties, shared that she found herself becoming irritated at the very thought of sharing her bedroom with anyone. She described the room to us, noting that she had a different nightstand on each side of the bed. One nightstand had shelves for her books and a nice-size lamp so she could read at night. The other had no shelves and was too small to hold a lamp. When she met her man, she assumed that she would feel compelled to give him the nicer of the two, thereby leaving her with a nightstand that was inadequate for her needs. Already she was a martyr, resenting a man she hadn't even met. At least she could laugh at herself. The group encouraged her to purchase another nightstand to match the one that she liked, and to get rid of the smaller one entirely, a suggestion that she took.

Creating space for the love of your life isn't always about the physical environment. Make sure that you have breathing room in your schedule so that you have the time to explore relationships and let new people into your life. You may feel particularly driven to fill your life with constant activity in an effort to create a sense of meaning and purpose. Many people I know make themselves excessively busy in an effort to avoid the pain of coming home to an empty house.

If a home doesn't make sense, nothing does.
—Henrietta Ripperger

Above all, love your home.... You cannot expect love to come and stay in a place that is unloved. A place that is loved for being home will invite more love in.

—Rosemary Ellen Guiley

Tolerating the void is not for the faint of heart. It's for the warriors, those ready to do battle with those fears that might speak up, if given half the chance. Whether you are seeking a greater sense of meaning in your life, have difficulty saying no, or are simply inspired and enthusiastic about life, you may need to let some things go. We all must master the ability to release who we are for the possibility of who we might become. As the saying goes, "In order to fly, you have to give up the ground you are standing on."

Make sure you give yourself some unstructured downtime as you go through this course. This time will ensure that you have room for another person to come into your life. It will also support you to grow in your ability to cultivate loving solitude, which is quite a different experience from the feeling of loneliness.

PRACTICE

Go through your home and notice whether or not it is a welcoming place for another person. Is it a place that you would feel comfortable inviting someone into? Does your home have room for another? Could you make space for the person you are inviting into your life?

Notice the artwork on your walls, the way that you've placed the furniture, and the number of items that you have in your home. Do you only have one table next to the bed? Only one mug for morning coffee? If so, begin gathering pairs of items to bring into your home, representing the future you are creating for yourself.

Take out your notebook. Make a list of at least five things you could alter in your home to create a more welcoming environment for an intimate partner. Add to that one or two things you could do to alter your schedule so that there is some breathing room in your life to explore new relationships.

BONUS: PRACTICE IN ACTION

Make one or more changes in your home today to reflect a more welcoming environment for the romance that you are inviting into your life (e.g., purchase a pair of pillows for your bed; take down any pictures that evoke a feeling of loneliness or sorrow; make space in your closet for someone else to put their things). Also make one or more plans that create possibilities for you to meet new people (e.g., make a date to go out dancing with a friend, ask a coworker to set you up on a blind date, schedule some downtime in your day to go outside for a walk, read the newspaper at a coffee shop, or just window-shop at the local mall).

SUGGESTED STUDY GUIDE
FOR GROUP DISCUSSION

1. How connected and/or disconnected do you feel to the people in your life and in what ways do you perpetuate this?

2. What do you need in your most intimate relationships and how do you go about getting your needs met?

3. What Essence Qualities did you choose and what affirmations did you create for yourself?

4. Share your vision of love fulfilled in your life.

5. What specific changes did you make this week to create space for love in your life?

COMPLETIONS

Your task is not to seek for love, but merely to seek and find
all of the barriers within yourself that you have built against it.

—*A Course in Miracles*

Now is the time to roll up our shirtsleeves and get down to the nitty-gritty work of actualizing love in our lives, as we begin a two-week process of identifying and releasing all that is in its way.

This week:

* We will challenge ourselves to undergo the necessary losses of those things that thwart the development of love in our lives

* We will explore the ingredients of true forgiveness to complete and release the past

* We will examine the toxic ties that are preventing other, healthier relationships from taking root in our lives

* We will let go of agreements and patterns that no longer serve us

* We will redefine who we are in relationship to the wounds we have suffered in order to create an opening for love

LESSON 8
Allowing Loss

To give oneself over to love and marriage is to say yes to death.

—Thomas Moore, *Care of the Soul*

Most of us want something for nothing. We want to be thin without exerting ourselves, successful without taking a risk, and loved without losing anything. This "all blessings, no burdens" idea of how life should be is very American, since America is the only culture in the world that seems to expect life to be comfortable and relatively pain free. However, in most spiritual traditions, we find countless examples of the inevitable relationship between joy and despair, fullness and emptiness, life and death. Philosopher Alan Watts said, "Good without evil is like up without down, and . . . to make an ideal of pursuing the good is like trying to get rid of the left by turning constantly to the right."

The first time I considered the possibility that finding "The One" might entail some losses was the day I asked my happily married hairdresser, Carrie, about her courtship with her husband. She recognized him as the man she wanted to be with almost immediately: she felt both a great respect and an intense attraction the moment they met. Although she was overjoyed that they had committed their lives to each other, their engagement was actually a very difficult time for her. As the date of their wedding grew closer, the reality of joining her life with this man compelled her to examine certain habits and patterns she'd had for years. She discovered that her image of herself as strong and independent was actually counterproductive to creating an enduring bond with him. She had to allow herself to give up the emotional armor she'd grown so used to, becoming more vulnerable and undefended than ever before. She also had to give up a fantasy she'd had since childhood that she would please her father by marrying a man just like him. Her fiancé was nothing like her father, and the two men, although polite and respectful, were actually a bit uncomfortable with each other. Little by little, Carrie was compelled to give up that which was incongruent with the life she was committing herself to creating. Thus, their courtship was a major adjustment period that included many losses and much maturing on Carrie's part.

We are so captivated by our collective myth of the happy ending, that we rarely acknowledge the amount of loss that can be involved in getting there. The truth is, each gain in life represents the loss of something else. We simply never move forward in life without losing something. No wonder most of us are resistant to change, even when those changes promise to be positive. Surrendering to change means letting go of being in control. Yet, as much as we want our lives to be different, the truth is, we don't like it much when our illusion of being in control is challenged. The feeling that we are in charge of our lives gives us leverage in our attempts to avoid the experience of loss. Yet, these efforts to circumvent loss are the very foundation of our excessive anxiety and worry. Many of us are suffering severe levels of angst in an attempt to avoid the natural order of life, which always includes periods of endings and passing away.

No matter how much we profess to the contrary, the truth is, many of us would secretly rather stay the same, even if that means we continue to suffer. Better that than actually undergo the necessary losses of life. But life isn't really set up to allow for standing still. When we refuse to move forward, it becomes clear within a relatively short period of time that, in fact, we've begun to move backwards. Refusing to risk the next step, we discover a loss of vitality. We become uninspired, depressed, and resigned. Not the best states of mind to attract in love, although it might make the longing for love even more acute, since life is so devoid of its spark.

One of the most important skills we can acquire in life is the ability to respond well to loss and disappointment. The first step in doing so is to give up the assumption that, when we suffer a loss, that something is "wrong." Nothing is wrong. Loss is a part of life. Sometimes there is a sadness, a silence, a despair, or a loneliness that just needs to be listened to. The ancient Sufi poet Rumi, says it best

Like the moth longing for the flame, insane for the light that will extinguish its very life, the lover longs for the beloved partner.
—Connie Zweig

This being human is a guest house.
Every morning a new arrival.
A joy, a depression, a meanness,
Some momentary awareness comes
As an unexpected visitor.
Welcome and attend them all!
Even if they're a crowd of sorrows,
Who violently sweep your house
Empty of its furniture.
Still, treat each guest honorably.
He may be clearing you out for some new delight.

Our lives are always in motion. As such, we will continually be asked to give up the life we have for the life we are creating. For those of us who've suffered traumatic losses, particularly ones that occurred in early childhood, the feelings that we associate with loss, such as sorrow, fear, and frustration, can be unsettling and frightening. However, it's important to learn how to feel these feelings without needing to numb out or act in ways that are hurtful and destructive.

When you decide to improve your life, the first thing you will experience is loss. I see it all the time. You begin therapy or join a spiritual group because you see a possibility for yourself that you want to realize. You think that, because you've taken positive action, things should start to look up. Instead, very often, something strange happens. Things actually begin to get worse. That is because you have made a decision to grow yourself into a wiser, more-loving version of yourself. And that means that the "old" you has to die so that the "new" you can be born. The first act of creation is always destruction.

Just before my husband came into my life, I initiated the death of three relationships. The first was with my ex-boyfriend, whom I was still hanging on to, both through the desperate hope that he'd change and a fierce resentment that he hadn't. The second was with the man I'd been dating, Daniel, who was very clear with me that he had no interest in creating a family. Although Daniel is still my friend, the form of our relationship as "girlfriend, boyfriend" had to be surrendered so that we could each be true to ourselves. And lastly, I let go of a friendship with a man who'd been flirting with me for over two years, dangling the carrot of "maybe someday" he'd leave his live-in girlfriend and we would build a life together. These relationships had to be released before I could receive Mark into my life. More accurate, the me that had created these relationships in the first place had to die and be replaced with the me who was open and available to attract in her beloved. That old me used to believe that I was "inferior to other women," that I was "too old to find someone" and "too difficult" for anyone to want to deal with me. No wonder I compromised myself by hanging on to unavailable men. On some level I thought that my choice was either that or be alone entirely.

In order to live rich and meaningful lives, we must learn to undergo the necessary losses of life without having to distract ourselves with drama, or be rescued from the unknown. We must learn to move forward even when we are afraid, embracing the very losses that we have been trying to avoid. For that is how we will transform our disappointments, our defeats, and our sad tales into something valuable—a deepening of the soul, a growing in compassion, a leveling of false pride. These are the experiences that have the capacity to help us expand our ability to give and receive love.

There is a Chinese proverb that I find very beautiful.

> My barn having burned to the ground,
> I can now see the moon.

Loss is like that. Our job is to simply surrender those things that block the experience of love, trusting the promise of the Psalmist that "weeping may endure for a night but joy cometh in the morning."

Every day a
little death.
—Stephen Sondheim

If there is one thing
to bear in mind
until the truth of its
words eases the
heart troubled by
apparent failure
and loss, it is this:
*The new life is
always greater
than the old.*
—Ralph Blum

PRACTICE

Take out your journal. Make a list of three or more losses that you suffered (and thought you wouldn't survive) and your subsequent gain. For example:

LOSS #1

Harold broke up with me right before what was to be our dream vacation. I cried for three days before I decided to go anyway.

SUBSEQUENT GAIN

Discovered that I could make friends anywhere. Opened up a whole new world for me to know that I could travel alone and have a great time. Now I vacation alone at least once a year.

Now, write on this question:

**What necessary losses and/or potential disappointments
have I been trying to avoid?**

One may not reach
the dawn save by the
path of the night.
—Kahlil Gibran

Hint: Look to see where you've been feeling excessively worried and anxious (i.e., I've been trying to avoid giving up my ex-boyfriend even though I know the relationship is bad for me; I've been trying to avoid getting rejected so I've not been putting myself out there to meet new people; I've been avoiding getting hurt again by not opening my heart up to anyone.).

BONUS: PRACTICE IN ACTION

Take one or more actions today to initiate a loss that you have been trying to avoid (for example, end a friendship that clearly isn't working for you anymore, burn an old love letter from an ex that you've been holding onto through prolonged grief, go through your closets and get rid of everything that you haven't worn for a year or more).

LESSON 9
Letting Go of the Past

Pause at the word: "for - give." "For - to - give." Forgiveness is such a
gift that "give" lives in the word. Christian tradition has tried
to make it a meek and passive word; turn the other cheek. But the
word contains the active word "give," which reveals its truth.

—Michael Ventura, *Meeting the Shadow*

Each year, I try to get away for a three-day silent-meditation retreat. There
are usually about fifty or sixty participants, all of us convening around 9
A.M. and continuing together in silence until about 9 or 10 P.M., with very
little eye contact so as not to distract our attention outward.

This particular retreat was difficult for me. I had made the assertion
that I would be engaged by my birthday a few weeks earlier and I was in
the early stage of my process. I was dealing with intense feelings of rage
and a desire for revenge toward my ex-boyfriend, who was already in love
with another woman. I struggled the entire weekend to let go of the angry
feelings I was having, to no avail. I was completely consumed by the
agony of unresolved anger.

I had every right to be angry. From my perspective, my ex had
wronged me deeply. I had brought an idea to him several years before to
run workshops with professional songwriters and people who had, at one
time, been homeless. I wanted to help these men, women, and children
tell their stories of hope and renewal through music, thereby solidifying
and celebrating the gains they had made while also highlighting solutions
to homelessness. My ex loved the idea and, together, for five years we ran
these very special workshops between those in recovery from homelessness and some of the best songwriters in the world. I was completely in
love with the difference we were making in people's lives and the music
we were helping to create. The workshops were sheer magic and the first

What! Must I hold a
candle to my shames?
—William Shakespeare

time I felt that I was having a real impact on the world around me. Yet the relationship between my ex and myself was troubled and unfulfilling for both of us. I couldn't figure out, however, how to leave the relationship but keep the project since, at that point, it really belonged to both of us. It was as though we had birthed a child together. When I finally did leave the relationship, my worst fears occurred. The project stayed with him and I ended up leaving them both.

I was furious. I simply could not talk myself out of the victim position on *this* one: *I* was the one who'd had the original vision! I was the one who'd invited him to participate and now I was the one who had to give it up. It just wasn't fair. To make matters worse, I didn't believe the project would even survive losing me, and it seemed that I was right. After we broke up, the project looked like it was dying from lack of activity. Not one workshop had been produced, not one song written or recorded. So, not only did he "steal" the project by refusing to relinquish any and all control of the organization, but now he was neglecting (and thereby destroying) it as well.

For two days I wrestled in the silence with the ideal of forgiveness, unable to release the resentment I felt toward him. I knew that, in order to be a clear space for a loving relationship to enter my life, I would have to let go of this bitterness.

Late at night, at the end of the second day, I had what might be called an epiphany or a spiritually transcendent experience. I was standing outside on a bluff, looking up at a large, bright, and perfectly round moon as it shone through the bare branches of an old gnarly tree. Suddenly, the moon became illuminated and I was transported into another realm of awareness. I sensed the presence of a multitude of ethereal beings who spoke to me, not as an external voice but as an internal knowing, saying, "We understand your suffering and know well of your loss. You are right that you are owed a great debt. However, we have now incurred that debt and are the ones holding it. We will make sure that all that is due you will be paid above and beyond that which you can even imagine. But in order for us to do this, you must first release him, for your attachment to getting restitution from him is preventing us from being able to give you your due." In that moment, I let go of my resentment toward him completely, never again to be plagued by feelings of bitterness or rage. In place of hostility, I suddenly found compassion, acceptance, and understanding.

Not surprisingly, the next day, I began to understand my part in our relationship much more clearly. It seems that when I was finally able to quiet the constant internal tirade against my ex, I was available to see how I myself had created this difficult situation. I saw that I had actually given away my power five years before when we set up the original structure of the organization. Instead of giving my ex an executive position and delegating parts of my vision to him, I had made him a full-fledged owner and partner right off the bat. What made me do that? I barely knew him at the time. I had to confess to myself that the only reason I had done that was because I didn't believe in my abilities to bring my vision forth in the world. I didn't value my idea as being special and unique. As I thought more about it, I remembered feeling uneasy about the partnership right from the start. My intuition was trying to speak to me but I had been too insecure to listen.

I began to see that throughout my entire life, I had consistently devalued and doubted my ideas. I saw how I'd suffered because of a lack of belief in myself. Yet, the project we created was extraordinary. Hundreds of people throughout the Los Angeles music community had happily participated in the songwriting workshops we had set up. The songs written were inspiring, uplifting, and just plain great music. We'd held a nationally televised concert and made a CD with star artists that had been sold in record stores throughout the country. I had the time of my life doing that project—the project that I had been afraid to believe in—an idea that I feared was foolish and insignificant and consequently gave away.

What I learned is this: that I had paid too high a price for the self-doubts I had carried since childhood; that I was through with giving away my brilliance and creativity because I thought my ideas were worthless. In that moment, I gave up being willing to allow self-judgment and self-criticism to stop me in life.

Even more important, I learned how to truly love someone. Not because I loved my ex so well but because, in anger toward him, I withheld love from him. We were engaged in such a severe power struggle that whatever potential for love there was between us, was pretty much starved

> In this life-creative adventure the criterion of achievement will be…the courage to let go of the past, with its truths, its goals, its dogmas of "meaning," and its gifts: to die to the world and come to birth from within.
>
> —Joseph Campbell

to death. Because of that relationship, I came to understand that there are certain lines you don't cross when you are building a trusting, loving connection with another person. Now, that may seem simple enough but I honestly didn't know that before. I experienced, firsthand, that being right often costs us being loved. Never again would I have to learn that lesson.

A lot of us think that we have to wait until feelings of hurt and anger are resolved before we can forgive someone. However, this is not always so. Forgiveness is actually a deliberate and intentional act. It is a decision that restores vitality, possibility, and integrity to your life. As such, magnanimous feelings of appreciation and benevolence are often the last things to fall into place, if they ever do at all. Realize that you are only resentful to the extent that you have given away your personal power. If you are in full possession of your personal power, you can afford to be generous when someone else is behaving poorly. It's only when you don't own your power fully that it shows up as resentment.

Ultimately, to forgive someone means to cancel the debt you feel they owe you. It is a surrender and release of the hurt that has passed between you. That doesn't mean that you agree with what the person did, condone their behavior, or ever invite them back into your life again—often, it is unwise to do so.

Sometimes we hang on to resentment because our anger is all that we have left. We are afraid to tolerate the void associated with letting go. However, when this is the case, we usually end up creating even more emptiness and loneliness, because we so thoroughly block any new possibilities of love.

Many of us must also give up needing to have the person who hurt us understand the agony that they have caused. It's great to get an apology, but it's not really necessary. The real value in these situations is to see our own part and to grow ourselves wiser and more whole.

Soon after that night when I'd had the transcendent experience looking up at the moon, blessing upon blessing began coming into my life— meeting Mark, effortlessly getting pregnant with my daughter at the age of forty-two, coming into a large sum of money, moving into a home that I had wanted to live in for years, etc. When I forgave my ex by taking responsibility for my actions, I opened up a space for love and abundance to come toward me, and come it did.

The antidote to resentment is acceptance. The truth is, I had to accept the loss of my beloved organization. I had to accept a situation that, at first glance, did not seem at all just. I had to accept that the years I spent buried in the intensely hard work of creating that organization had turned to dust in my hands because I hadn't bothered to protect what I had built properly. Most important, I had to accept full responsibility for how I, and I alone, had caused the pain that I was in.

It was also very important to assess the gains I'd made during that time of my life. When I was able to let go of being a victim, I could finally acknowledge my ex for having brought my seeds of a vision into a bona fide reality. Because I hadn't believed in myself, I can't imagine that I would have done what was necessary to bring the project anywhere near the level of success that it achieved. That was the tenacity of my ex—the same tenacity that I called stubbornness, which drove me bananas and that I constantly complained about. This was the same man who'd made my dream come true and ultimately demonstrated to me that my ideas were valuable and worthwhile.

You'll know that you have really completed your relationship with someone when you don't have a lot of energy in it anymore—when you can acknowledge the relationship from the perspective of being 100 percent responsible for having created it, if even by just being able to locate exactly when, where, and how you gave your power away, and when you are able to recognize the lessons you learned and truly appreciate the gifts that you received from that encounter. While that may, at first, appear to be a tall order, nothing short of complete neutrality toward those we've resented will do. When it comes to creating more love in our lives, we stand ready, like samurai warriors, to release all that is not love from our hearts.

Forgiveness is...the means for correcting our misperceptions.
—Gerald Jampolsky

PRACTICE

Take out your journal and make a list of those you resent.

Who am I carrying a resentment toward?

Go through your list and choose the person who feels the most "hot" to you. Write out an answer to each of the following questions for that person. When you have the time, return to this list and complete the following questions with everyone you've listed.

What do I resent this person for?

What can I be responsible for in this situation?

**In what ways can this experience help me
to become a more mature person?**

What lessons did I learn?

What good can come of this situation?

What have I been unwilling to accept about this situation?

What can I now let go of so the situation is complete?

BONUS: PRACTICE IN ACTION

Write a letter to someone you are ready to forgive. In the letter, write about the resentment you felt from the perspective of what *you* can be responsible for. How did you yourself create the situation? How did the situation help you to grow and mature? What lessons did you learn? What good came out of the situation? Declare the situation complete by stating your willingness to forgive this person and release them from the debt you've thought they've owed you.

You can send the letter to this person, or you can burn it or rip it up as a ceremonial release. If you are uncertain whether or not to mail the letter, you may keep it so that you can consider sending it in the future. You may, however, wish to keep the letter as a reminder to yourself of the stand that you have taken to let go and release the debt you have felt that this person owed you.

LESSON 10
Releasing Toxic Ties

If you have been operating in the dark, there is now enough
light to see that the patient on the operating table is yourself.

—Ralph Blum, *The Book of Runes*

All relationships are an energy exchange. Each connection either feeds us power or sucks it away, i.e., "draining" our energy. If we saw all of our relationships from this perspective, we would see that "toxic ties" are those attachments that cause us to lose personal power.

The associations we form have the capacity to nurture and inspire our growth, catapulting us into being the best that we can possibly be. However, the flip side is also true. Sometimes, we form attachments that can, and do, block the experience and expression of love in our lives. The most obvious example of this is, of course, a romantic attachment to a person who, for whatever reason, is unwilling or unable to love us.

Paul came to see me because he was in deep emotional pain over his relationship with his business partner of four years, Susan. Paul and Susan, both songwriters and music producers, were lovers for a few weeks shortly before they formed their business, a small recording studio. He had been trying to get back together with her for the duration of their business relationship. He sheepishly admitted that this was one of the reasons he had wanted to go into business with her in the first place.

Paul and Susan call each other often, speaking up to ten times a day by phone. They spend countless hours together working on producing her songs and trying to get her a record deal. Susan has some unhealed childhood wounds that cause her to be an excessively insecure and frightened person. Paul spends many, many hours of his day talking to her about her problems and encouraging her to believe in herself. His own recording projects have fallen by the wayside. Paul reports that Susan says she "loves him as a friend," yet she is uninterested in him as a sexual partner. She is now seeing another man and he is outraged and obsessed with "getting her back."

Although Paul is only thirty-five, he confides that a recent doctor's visit determined he's an imminent candidate for a heart attack and he was immediately put on medication. He is about thirty pounds overweight because, he explains, he is overeating out of anger and sexual frustration. And, he admits, he is broke, as he and Susan are entangled in a huge debt that they jointly incurred while launching her career. He also mentions offhandedly that all of their joint debt is actually in *his* name, since she has problems with her credit.

Much of my work with Paul has been to help him accept Susan's lack of romantic interest, to give up blaming her for failing to love him, and to be responsible for the many attempts he has made to manipulate her through his excessive "helpfulness." I encourage Paul to examine what his relationship with Susan reflects in his relationship with himself. He is able to acknowledge that her lack of sexual attraction to him mirrors his own disgust with his body, as he is furious with himself for being "too fat." His resistance to taking care of himself, even with the threat of a heart attack, makes it clear that he is trying to get Susan to love him while he is adamantly refusing to love himself. In fact, Paul can see that he has actually succeeded in getting Susan to reject him in exactly the same way that he rejects himself.

Even the most sagacious of us may be tempted to behave destructively in an effort to avoid facing the disappointment of unrequited love. However, try as we might, the truth is, we have absolutely no power to sway another person when they have decided to close their heart to us. It is one of life's great paradoxes that, though we are the authors of our own experience, we have no ability to superimpose our will onto another person. An unwillingness to accept this will be the source of great suffering. For even if we are successful at maneuvering ourselves into a "significant-other" position, the relationship itself will most likely be characterized by resentment, excessive dependency, disappointment, and power struggles, thereby making it a toxic tie.

Perhaps you're on the other end of the spectrum, having succumbed to the efforts of another to entice you into loving them for all the wrong reasons. Many of us have made choices out of the most needy, dependent parts of ourselves and then suffered the consequences of feeling the dreadful, dull ache of being stuck in a relationship that has absolutely no chance of a future.

I once had a client who was quite beautiful but, unfortunately, quite insecure and secretly self-loathing. Like Narcissus, she spent vast amounts of time looking in the mirror, fussing with her clothes, her hair, and her makeup. She dressed in sexy, seductive clothing that brought her lots of attention from men and spent an inordinate amount of time and money in an effort to enhance her beauty. It was not surprising to me, then, when she confided in me that she was deeply entangled in a relationship with a man whom she actually didn't even like, let alone love. When we explored how this happened, we discovered that she was so captured by his constant admiration of her beauty, that she just allowed herself to become entangled with him. Now she felt trapped and frightened by his ever-increasing possessive behavior toward her. She hadn't seen the warning signs at the beginning, because his obsessive preoccupation with her had simply mirrored her own. Her excessive neediness had attracted in a man who intuitively knew her weakness and had used it to his advantage.

Susan Forward, author of *Emotional Blackmail,* talks about the "blinding FOG—Fear, Obligation, and Guilt"—that characterizes most "toxic tie" relationships. Unbridled fears that we are unlovable, that we will never find anyone to really love us, or that we will be abandoned, and therefore annihilated, by someone we desperately need, top the list of anxieties that can entice us into giving away more and more of our personal power. Often, due to an undeveloped ability to set healthy emotional boundaries, we will feel overly responsible for another's feelings, and allow an inappropriate sense of obligation to dominate how we make choices regarding the relationship. Or we'll feel consumed by feelings of guilt and shame, as though we owe another our very life force for things we have allegedly done to them in the past.

When someone capitalizes on these vulnerabilities, they are simply

> The best advice for people who can't seem to end an unsatisfying relationship might be to stop waiting for something from the other person. Probably what it is will never come.
> —Thomas Moore

exerting a manipulative effort at getting what they want at your expense. Real love will never use fear, obligation, or guilt to influence you. Until you clear your life of these "*un*true" loves, you will block "true" love from being able to come to you, and you will always know, in your heart of hearts, that you are settling.

These types of relationships suck the life force right out of us, draining much of our creativity and personal power, thereby reducing us to the least of who we are. Unfortunately, when we are in these kinds of relationships, many of us will justify all sorts of poor behavior, by convincing ourselves that, over time, the other person will change. However, people aren't projects. They generally don't respond well when we try to "improve" them. And, the truth is, we are always training people how they need to be with us by how we respond to their behavior. What you tolerate *will* happen again . . . and again . . . and again.

If you find yourself engaged in a toxic tie, it's not the other person's fault. If you are allowing someone to use you, manipulate you, and treat you poorly, then you must ask yourself what the relationship is reflecting in your relationship with yourself.

Toxic ties undermine and weaken our vision of what is possible in our lives. We perpetuate them because we think it's better to hold on to someone who loves us a little rather than risk being without anyone at all. Or we are captured by the dramatic pull of the person who seems to love us a lot, in spite of how destructive and hurtful they are. The truth is, we hold on to these unhealthy relationships because we're afraid it's the best we can do and because we don't believe we deserve real love. Releasing them requires the courage that comes only when one's commitment to love is greater than one's fear of being alone.

If you are operating under the illusion that you can continue to hold on to people who you know are not good for you, and still create an extraordinary life filled with love and fulfillment, then you are fooling yourself. Toxic ties cost us and they cost us big time. If you are feeling stuck in your life, look to see who or what it is that you are stuck to.

PRACTICE

Take out your journal and answer the following questions. (Note: Don't limit your answers to those you've had romantic encounters with. Include anyone who comes to mind, be it friends, family, coworkers, etc.)

**What relationship(s), if any, do I suspect
may qualify as a "toxic tie"?**

Choose one of these relationships to work on today by completing the following questions. When you can, return to this list and complete the following questions with everyone you've listed.

What fear(s) are dominating me in this relationship?

What obligations do I feel compelled to fulfill?

**In what ways am I allowing myself to be manipulated through
feelings of guilt and shame?**

What does this relationship reflect in my relationship to myself?

**What can I give up in order to restore my own sense of personal
power? (For example, avoiding having that person be angry with
me, doing for that person what he won't do for himself, etc.)**

**What boundaries could I set that would increase health and
wellness in this relationship?**

Relationships are not
sporting events. Stop
wrestling for control.
No one ever wins
this kind of match
except divorce
lawyers.
—Leo Buscaglia

BONUS: PRACTICE IN ACTION

Make a promise to yourself to give up participating in all toxic-tie dynamics, by righting your relationship to yourself first. Take at least one action to right your relationship to yourself (e.g., if you've discovered that the abuse you've been tolerating from someone is a reflection of how you've been mistreating yourself, take an action that represents a willingness to give up one way that you are being harmful or disrespectful toward yourself). In addition, take at least one action today to set a healthy boundary with someone you've been engaged in a toxic-tie relationship with.

LESSON 11
Renegotiating Old Agreements

We must be willing to get rid of the life we've planned,
so as to have the life that is waiting for us.

—Joseph Campbell

The first time I was in love, I was fifteen. Frank was kind and thoughtful, frequently going out of his way to make me happy. When with him, I felt protected and loved. When I was seventeen he asked me to marry him. My mother was beside herself. She insisted that I go to college and get a life before committing to someone whom I met when I was just a sophomore in high school. It became a war between us. The harder she tried to separate us, the harder I fought to keep him. At one point, she even threatened to call the police if he so much as stepped foot in our driveway.

You can imagine the heightened sense of drama that surrounded the relationship amidst such an onslaught of protest. However, my mother's concerns proved all too true when, in our last year together, we began fighting about the choices I was facing as I turned eighteen. I wanted to go to college. Frank, however, had decided against college in favor of going into his family's business. He was dead-set against me pursuing an education when he hadn't. No discussion, end of story, and, sadly enough, end of relationship.

Our breakup wrenched my heart and sent me reeling into an anguished grief. One of the ways I dealt with my overwhelming sorrow was to make a promise. Since I couldn't bear the thought that I would never see him again, I told Frank that I would find him when I was in my sixties. At that point, I thought, I would have lived my life and made all my choices. As an older woman, I would finally be available to be with him and love him completely.

The old skin has to be shed before the new one can come.
—Joseph Campbell

Twenty-plus years later, I had all but forgotten this promise. One night, about a month into my quest for "The One," it dawned on me that this agreement was always in the background of my life. Those words, spoken so long ago in a moment of complete desperation and sorrow, were still hanging out there somewhere, waiting to be fulfilled.

I decided that, although I'd not spoken to him in well over twenty years, I needed to contact Frank directly to undo this promise. I tried finding him by calling information. When that didn't work, I checked the Internet. In the end, I settled for calling him, figuratively, into my meditation practice. I sat quietly for a long time before calling his name several times in my mind and imagining him sitting there in front of me. When I could see his face in my mind's eye, I told him how sorry I was for the ways I might have hurt him all those years ago. I let him know how much I'd missed him in my life and that I appreciated all the love he'd given me at a time when I needed it so much. Then I told him that I couldn't keep the promise I'd made to him and why. It was holding me up from finding someone else that I could be happy with and preventing me from creating a life where I might not be free when I was in my sixties. I asked him to let me go if he'd been holding on to that promise and to please forgive me for not being able to keep it. And then I let him go, freeing myself from the contract I'd made so many years before.

All relationships have their agreements. Actually, it could be said that the very definition of *relationship* is to enter into a covenant with another. As such, relationships are determined by a series of pacts and promises that are sometimes spoken out loud, as mine was, but most times are not. Those agreements that are made without words—often matters of loyalty and expectations—will usually remain covert in nature while exercising a strong pull over decisions made and paths taken. Covert agreements can even influence us to violate our own values and beliefs, gaining leverage through our innate need to be a part of a tribal community.

I have a client, Tara, who desperately wanted to get an education. However, no one in her family had ever gotten an education before and they felt threatened by her aspirations. They ridiculed her desire and succeeded in thwarting her efforts to go to college through a thinly veiled threat to withdraw their love and support from her should she try to "make herself better than them."

Although Tara's case sounds extreme, in truth, many of us make covert agreements with our parents to not be more successful than they were. Therefore, forming a loving, happy partnership when no one in your family has been able to do so, can feel nothing short of disloyal. It is not uncommon for us to sacrifice ourselves out of a fear that our success will cause pain for our parents, or at least aggravate the parts of them that are unhappy and unfulfilled.

Consider Donna, a beautiful and bright woman in her late thirties who attended a recent Calling In "The One" workshop. Like many of the women I work with, it appeared as though she should have no problem finding the right man. Yet there she was, complaining about being close to forty and husbandless, with no prospects in sight. She seemed somewhat confused about her single status.

During the workshop it became clear that Donna adored her father, describing their relationship as "very close." In fact, her father played a very active and dominant presence in her life; he lived close by and they spoke almost daily on the phone. She confessed that she felt safe, particularly as a single woman, due to his "overprotectiveness" of her. However, what began to disturb the group but unfortunately not her, was the way that her father weeded out the men who got too close to her. She saw this as part of his protectiveness and, therefore, an expression of his love for her. The more she shared with us, however, the more obvious it became that Donna would actually choose men who were a little dangerous so that her father could rescue her from them, thereby proving his love for her and reinforcing their bond.

Underneath this dynamic was an unspoken agreement that Donna had made with her father that she was able to identify. When she was a little girl, she witnessed the deterioration of her parents' troubled marriage. Her mother seemed to handle this well, but her father became more and more depressed and despondent as the years went on. She recalls feeling a tremendous and persistent sorrow for him. So she made a decision. Although her mother did not seem to love him, she would make sure that

Life is full and overflowing with the new. But it is necessary to empty out the old to make room for the new to enter.
—Eileen Caddy

Seek to discover
what it is you are
holding onto that
keeps this condition
in effect, and let go.
Shed, release,
cleanse away the old.
That will bring on
the thaw.
—Ralph Blum

her father always knew that *she* did. He would always be the most important person in the world to her. And in fact she did become "the light of Daddy's life."

Donna resisted seeing the impact that this type of unspoken agreement might be having on her relationships with other men. As she left the workshop, she was still justifying and rationalizing that this wasn't that big of a deal. Actually, she simply wasn't ready to give it up yet and so she didn't. Yet truthfully, I doubt that she will be available to love another man until she renegotiates this unspoken agreement with her father either in person or simply within herself.

Our need to be a part of something larger than ourselves is one of our most primal instincts, and we will go to great lengths to protect our sense of tribal belonging. Margo was the third generation in a lineage of strong, smart, and powerful firstborn females. Her primary sense of identity is with her matriarchal ancestry—her mother and her mother's mother before her. The three of them all look alike and are ambitious, educated, and accomplished. They've also all had their share of difficulties with the men in their lives. So it's no wonder that, as a way to survive their disappointments, they've developed a "humorous" little banter that "just slightly" diminishes the men in their lives. It's a covert thing—a roll of the eyes, a sideways snicker and glance, a subtle shake of the head. They have formed their own little matriarchal club and the membership dues are to scorn any man who gets too close. In a recent workshop, Margo was able to see the absurdity of trying to find a man to love and be loved by, while, at the same time, keeping her covert agreement with her mother and grandmother to disrespect and disdain all men.

Recently I heard about a woman whose stepfather incestuously pursued her when she was a preteen. The girl was so distraught by his advances that she made him a desperate promise. If you leave me alone now, she assured him, when I turn twenty-five, if you still want me, then I will marry you. It worked and he stopped his unwanted advances. Somewhere along the way, he divorced her mother but stayed in contact with her. She repressed her unpleasant memories of his advances and completely forgot about her promise to him. When she was twenty-four, she received a proposal from a decent man whom she did not love. She promptly accepted and married him right before her twenty-fifth birthday. Years later, when getting a divorce, she couldn't understand why she had married a man she did not love. After many hours of self-examination she finally remembered the horrible pledge she'd made in her youth, and she understood. She married her ex-husband as a way to avoid keeping the dreaded promise to her stepfather.

There's one more type of agreement that is important to mention: the agreements we make with ourselves in an attempt to deal with an emotional injury that we've suffered. Nancy is a fifty-something year old friend of mine. When Nancy was a child, not more than two, she had to have a lifesaving operation on her throat. When Nancy was little, many doctors believed that young children did not really know the difference between their mother and any other caregiver. The hospital Nancy was admitted to did not allow the parents to visit their children when they were in the intensive care unit. It was believed that the nurses could do a better job if their efforts went uninterrupted and unchallenged by the parents.

So, there was little Nancy, subjected to a terrifying operation at the hands of strangers. And, although these strangers were most likely competent and kind, they were not people whom Nancy felt bonded to. They were, therefore, unable to comfort her the way her parents could have. Nancy spent the entire week at the hospital without seeing a single member of her family.

Although Nancy was just a young child, to this day, she remembers being furious at her mother for leaving her at a time when she most needed her. And the thing she remembers most profoundly is that she made a decision at that time to never trust anyone again. Her mother validated Nancy's recollection by admitting, many years later, that their relationship was never the same after that week. She reports that Nancy became distant and detached from her and others in their family from that time on, unwilling to bond with and depend upon them to the same extent that she did before the operation. Nancy had made an agreement with herself to never trust anyone again. As you can imagine, this decision was causing her much difficulty in her adult life. It was a resolve that desperately needed to be renegotiated.

The agreements we make, both consciously and unconsciously, have a

We learn wisdom from failure much more than from success: we often discover what will do by finding out what will not do: and probably he who never made a mistake never made a discovery.
—Samuel Smiles

To every thing
there is a season,
and a time
to every purpose
under the heaven.

—Ecclesiastes 3:1

profound impact upon our lives, for they serve as intentions that we set. These intentions have weight and authority in the universe to affect that which comes our way—and that which doesn't. Never underestimate the power of your agreements to influence your life.

PRACTICE

Today, we will examine the agreements, both spoken and unspoken, that you've made with others and with yourself. We will also identify whom, if anyone, you are protecting by being alone.

Take out your journal and complete the following sentences, answering as many times as you wish for each sentence stem. Don't censor yourself. Write whatever comes to mind even if it initially does not seem to make sense.

**The agreements, both spoken and unspoken,
I made with my mother were:**

**The agreements, both spoken and unspoken,
I made with my father were:**

**The agreements, both spoken and unspoken,
I made with _____ (any other significant person in your life,
such as a stepmother, stepfather, exboyfriend, sibling, etc.) were:**

By being in the situation I'm in, I am keeping my agreements to:

**The agreements I made with myself regarding
closeness and love are:**

By being in the situation I'm in, I am protecting:

These agreements are affecting me by:

In order to renegotiate these agreements, I would have to let go of:

The new agreements I could make instead are:

BONUS: PRACTICE IN ACTION

Complete and/or renegotiate at least one agreement that no longer serves you. You can do this by writing a letter, calling someone, e-mailing them, or by bringing the person into your meditation for an imaginary conversation. However you choose to do it, tell the person what agreement you wish to renegotiate and why. Let the person know exactly how you want to renegotiate the agreement(s) so that it works for you.

If you decided to write a letter, you can choose to keep it as a reminder of your commitment to release the agreement, or you can send it to the person. If you like, you can put the letter in an envelope with a stamp and write only the first name of the person on the envelope with a silly address like Main Street, Anytown, USA 00000 and enjoy the satisfaction of placing the letter in the mailbox without actually giving them the letter. Or you may simply wish to burn it, rip it up, and/or throw it away.

LESSON 12
Sacred Wounds

What do sad people have in common? It seems they
have all built a shrine to the past and often go there and
do a strange wail and worship. What is the beginning of
happiness? It is to stop being so religious like that.

—Hafiz, translated by Daniel Ladinsky

Our unhealed wounds are invisible prisons—capturing us with their iron
bars just as surely as if we were locked inside cold, gray, concrete walls.
Sometimes it seems, no matter how hard we try to escape, that we will
forever be prisoners of our own sad stories, doomed to repeat painful
dynamics over and over and over again, in spite of our wishes to the contrary.

Elizabeth sat hunched over, rocking herself back and forth, staring
down at the floor in front of her. The other women, gathered together for
a Calling In "The One" workshop, sat quietly in the circle, waiting for her
to speak. "I can't get past the belief that I'm dirty!" she spoke in a strained,
frustrated voice. "I'm damaged goods and I can't seem to forget it even for
a moment. And every single relationship I've ever had ends up just as broken and damaged as I am. When do I get rid of this ugliness inside of me?
When do I get to be free? When do I get to have love in my life?" By now
tears were streaming down her face as she recalled being sexually molested
by her father when she was a mere four years old.

"Elizabeth, do you really believe that you are dirty, as if that is a core
truth about who you are?" I asked softly. "Yes!" she replied without needing to think about it. "It always comes down to the truth: I am a dirty,
dirty person."

I invited Elizabeth, as she is now, an adult woman who of forty-one,
to imagine that she was looking at herself as a four-year-old girl. I asked

her to picture a grown man, her father—a man who, we would hope, would protect and love her—instead trying to have sex with her. "What do you think of this little girl?" I asked. "Would you look at her and say to yourself, 'What a dirty, dirty little girl. No wonder that man is sexually abusing her.'?"

Elizabeth burst into tears as, for the first time, she actually understood her blamelessness. The foolishness of the belief that she was dirty was finally evident to her. At last she felt a deep compassion for herself, claiming her innocence as the real truth about who she was.

"I am so sick of being wounded," she sighed. "Why do I have to carry this burden around with me? When can I get rid of it?" she asked me with complete trust and simplicity. "Well," I replied carefully, "I don't know that we ever 'get rid' of our woundedness. Our wounding experiences are a part of our history. We can, however, give up defining ourselves by what happened to us in the past. We can stop identifying ourselves with the pain that we have suffered. This is not a denial of what we've been through but, rather, an awareness that the essence of who we are is far, far beyond it."

As Elizabeth pondered my words, I continued. "Our woundedness is actually an opportunity for enlightenment—for, truthfully, apart from a lifetime of victimization, there really is no other option. I always think of those of us who've been born into a deeply troubled situation to be like samurai warriors—the ones who are profoundly committed and dedicated to evolving spiritually—because you almost can't *not* do that, with woundings that are as severe as the one you've just described. These difficult wounds call us to be the best that we can be, and often will serve as a catalyst for us to discover what it is that we have to offer to others. In this way our wounding actually transforms into what we call our 'Sacred Wound'—because wherever you've suffered the most is where you have the opportunity to contribute the greatest amount."

My comments startled Elizabeth, who had always seen the goal of her healing work as getting rid of the abuse—forgetting it and distancing herself forever from the impact it had had upon her life. Remnants of a smile appeared on her face as she comprehended, for the first time, that this wound had had a tremendous bearing upon the kind of woman she had

> People want you
> to be happy.
> Don't keep serving
> them your pain!
> —Rumi

From suffering
I have learned this:
that whoever is sore
wounded by love will
never be made whole
unless she embrace
the very same love
that wounded her.

—Mechtilde of
Magdeburg

become—a fighter, who was devoted to personal and spiritual growth both for herself and for others. In fact, Elizabeth's life was largely defined by her desire to give generously of herself to others. Her rigorous candor and authentic sharing that weekend served to move the entire group of women to a much deeper level than they would have gone had she not been there.

As much as we profess to hate our brokenness, we'll often set up camp, root down, and build our entire identities around our tales of woe. In her book *Why People Don't Heal and How They Can,* Caroline Myss writes, "The sharing of wounds [has] become the new language of intimacy, a shortcut to developing trust and understanding." Consider the friendships we form based upon what Dr. Myss calls our "woundology," where we bond with another through complaining about our victimization and the sad state of our lives. What happens then, when one person, out of a commitment to heal, suddenly decides to give up being in the victim position? Oftentimes, such a friendship will not survive a "betrayal" of this sort, since the silent agreement is to reinforce the oppression of each other.

Many of us even choose our significant others based upon their ability to understand our wounds and their willingness to dance around them and not expect too much from us. This usually works for a time. But what happens if and when the "wounded" party decides to get better? Relationships whose currency is "woundology" don't have room for people to thrive and become their best selves, because the covert agreement is: If one person is "broken," then the other gets to prop up their self-esteem either by (1) caretaking them, or (2) being superior to them.

Many people have a difficult time bringing in a loving relationship, because they are still too invested in being damaged to allow their tragedies to transform into something beautiful. These people will usually continue to attract romantic partners who are also very attached to being damaged and are, therefore, not healthy enough to be suitable life partners.

We have to ask ourselves how attached we are to our pain. What is driving us to cling so fiercely to our sorrow? Sometimes, we women will hold on to our victimization because we are acting out our collective myth of "damsel in distress." However, as long as we hold on to the pain of the past, it continues to live—and it continues to hurt us. When we do this, we are behaving as though the past were more powerful and more prominent than the present. The truth is, it's never what happens to us that matters as much as what we *do* with what happens to us. Those who hurt you in the past have no authority to determine whether or not you will live a life of love and fulfillment. *You* are the only one holding that power.

We can't "get rid" of our wounds, but we do have to find a way to make them meaningful. In his book *Man's Search for Meaning,* Viktor Frankl, a prominent Jewish psychiatrist who survived the camps of Auschwitz and Dachau, writes of an elderly man who came to him two years after the death of his beloved wife. The man was severely depressed, as he was unable to overcome his loss. In the face of such suffering, Dr. Frankl was wise enough to sit quietly, listening intently as the man poured out his grief and his sorrow. When the man was finished, Dr. Frankl asked him the following question: "What would have happened if you had died first, and your wife would have had to survive you?" "Oh," the man answered, "for her this would have been terrible; how she would have suffered!" To this, Dr. Frankl replied, "You see, such a suffering has been spared her, and it was you who have spared her this suffering—to be sure, at the price that now you have to survive and mourn her." The man was so moved by Dr. Frankl's words, that he simply stood up, shook his hand, and left, never to return again. Dr. Frankl concludes this story by writing, "In some way, suffering ceases to be suffering at the moment it finds a meaning."

In his book *The Power of Now,* spiritual teacher Eckhart Tolle writes, "If you are trapped in a nightmare you will probably be more strongly motivated to awaken than someone who is just caught in the ups and downs of an ordinary dream." For those of us who have had to endure incredible losses and sorrows, life demands an awakening of a much more profound nature than those who have not. We must find lessons and weave meaning out of the sorrows we've had to bear. For many of us have been challenged to live out circumstances in which our hearts have been splintered and broken in two. Our task is to find our way through the ruins so that we may, as the Zen saying goes, "allow our hearts to break open." It is here that one not only comes to love again, but actually comes to love in a way that heals the entire world.

PRACTICE

Write a brief "woundology" biography, not from the perspective of your victimization but, rather, from the perspective of your strength to overcome adversity and your courage in the face of hardship. Identify the wounding that has since become your "Sacred Wound"—the wounding that is now your greatest strength and your contribution to others. Write about your Sacred Wound.

BONUS: PRACTICE IN ACTION

Call at least one trusted confidant today and share your "woundology" biography from the perspective of your strength and resilience. Share your heroism in the face of challenge, your bravery in response to profound disappointment. Share with this person what your Sacred Wound is—the contribution that you now have to offer others as a result of the wounding that you endured.

I invite you to begin speaking your life story from this perspective from now on, as it will help you to create relationships where you are encouraged to be strong and which support you to grow yourself healthy and happy.

LESSON 13
Mirror, Mirror, on the Wall

An ordinary man behaves like a dog which,
upon entering a hall of mirrors, barks at all the other dogs.
The sage, entering the hall of mirrors, sees only himself.

—Gurunathan

Often, upon hearing the heartening story of how I hooked up with my husband, I am asked by others how they, too, can manifest their deepest, most heartfelt desires. To these people, I always say, "But you already know how to manifest. Look at your life. What you have is a reflection of what you believe you can have, and your relationships are a perfect mirror of your relationship to yourself. Manifesting is not reserved for those who've reached a certain spiritual pinnacle. Manifesting is the natural order of life—both as commonplace and as miraculous as breathing. We do it all the time without even thinking."

Love attracts love. When you are filled with love within, you tend to draw in experiences and relationships that are loving and nurturing. That's because whatever we think of and emotionally resonate with the most, is that which comes to us. We don't necessarily get what we *want* in life—we do, however, get what we give our attention to. We get what we believe we *can* and *should* have. Not what we *think* we believe, or that which we'd *like* to believe, but, rather, that which we really *do* believe.

Thirty-six-year-old Margaret has recently started therapy. When she was a young girl, Margaret lived in a small town that allowed dogs to run free in the streets. Margaret was a small and feisty girl, and several of the neighborhood dogs seemed to enjoy chasing after her. Several times these episodes turned terrifying, as Margaret was just barely able to avoid being bitten while pedaling her bicycle as fast as she could to get away. One time she was even chased several times around a parked car by a Doberman

I drew them…
with bands of love.
—Hosea 11:4

pinscher who easily could have hurt her quite badly. To this day, Margaret remains terrified of all dogs, both big and small.

What is of great interest to me about Margaret's story, however, is what happens to her today. Although she now lives in a city where the dogs tend to be small and kept vigilantly on leashes, Margaret continues to be chased by them on a fairly regular basis. When she sees a dog—any dog at all—she becomes paralyzed with fear. The dogs must find this titillating, because they will go to great lengths to run after her—suddenly breaking free from their owners to chase her while she darts for safety through a crowded metropolitan street. The intense amount of energy Margaret has on dogs "manifests" their intense attraction for her as well.

Ellen, another client of mine, is a forty-something physician who was divorced from her ex-husband over ten years ago. Although she desperately wants to get married again, Ellen complains that all the men she meets find her sexually unattractive and say those awful, dreaded words: They "just want to be friends." Because she is slightly overweight, she believes that the extra pounds she is carrying is the sole reason that men find her unappealing. However, I have personally known several women who were much bigger than Ellen who have met wonderful men, fallen in love, and are now quite happily married; and so I am suspicious. When I inquire about Ellen's own relationship to her sexuality, she replies in a venomous tone that she absolutely loathes her body and considers it to be her enemy, given her tendency to gain weight easily and lose it so slowly. To this, I reply, "Well, if you *yourself* don't want to be in your body, why would you think that anyone *else* would want to be there?" Ellen's self-loathing is being reflected back to her by the men she is dating. Until she can fully accept and appreciate her body for the miraculous machine that it is, I tell her, she will most likely continue to have difficulty finding a satisfying relationship.

Rachael, a petite, pretty woman in her early thirties, has been coming to see me for the past two years. She wants very much to be in an intimate relationship, and it seems that she has plenty of opportunities, as men find her very attractive. However, she is not satisfied with any of her suitors, clear that she is unwilling to "settle" in her selection of a mate. And while this sounds good to me, there is something "off" about it.

When I explore her criteria for "The One," Rachael describes someone charismatic, creative, inspiring, and very much engaged in following his "dream," whatever that may be. However, Rachael herself has been "stuck" for many years in a career she doesn't really like. She has a sense of what she'd like to do instead; but every time I ask her about taking the risk to pursue her own dreams, she has one excuse after another. Finally, I suggest to Rachael that the reason that the only men who are showing up in her life are ones she'd have to "settle" for, is that she herself is "settling" for a life that doesn't inspire her. Consequently, Rachael is now willing to explore the possibility of living her life more fully, in the hope that she will become more able to attract in the kind of man she is looking for.

Before we understood, or even contemplated, the Law of Gravity, it existed as a constant and pervasive phenomenon in our experience. Although not yet scientifically proven, so too, the Law of Attraction is in full and continual operation. The Law of Attraction is simply this: the more intense your feelings around something, the sooner it will come to you. That is why it is more important to talk and think about what it is that we want in our lives as opposed to what it is that we don't. In other words, if you are consumed with fear that you will not have what you desire, then you will tend to *not* have it even if you try to push to make something happen in reaction to this fear. It also means, however, that if you cultivate and nurture a state of excited anticipation and gratitude for the impending arrival of what you want, you will draw it toward you that much faster.

We often have more faith in the act of assertion than we do in the Law of Attraction—trusting more in trying to make things happen by taking actions than we do in drawing things toward us and allowing them to happen. This doing-ness could be called the masculine aspect of the creative process; that part that goes out and gets what it wants. It is the hunter in all of us, both male and female. The masculine creative principle is largely how our Western culture works. It is the principle that we are most familiar with and the one that we trust in the most.

The feminine aspect of the creative principle, however, draws toward itself that which it is actively creating from within. We often mistake this stillness as passive and static. Women, who are usually cast in this inactive

I no longer try to change outer things. They are simply a reflection. I change my inner perception and the outer reveals the beauty so long obscured by my own attitude. I concentrate on my inner vision and find my outer view transformed.

—Daily Word

role, are often frustrated by the "sit and wait by the phone" thing. However, this is a misunderstanding of the power of the feminine creative process, which conceives by cultivating a strong inner vision and then working internally to draw that vision in. Feminine creative energy is like a barber pole. It alternates between the red and the white with no beginning and no end. The internal vision is the magnet for the external condition and they dance fluidly and in harmony with one another constantly.

Just because something is called "masculine" or "feminine" does not mean that men need one type and women need the other. In order to live balanced and fulfilled lives, we all need to be adept at causing results in our lives both by being empowered to take actions and also through the ability to draw toward us those things that we truly want.

Many of us feel so desperate and driven to find love. But the feeling of desperation is really a panicked response to an inner belief that you will not get what you want. This belief then causes an anxious ambition to have this *not be so,* and we start trying to push, manipulate, and cajole the events of our lives in reaction. But there's absolutely nothing you can do externally to prove that your own internal belief is wrong. Because it's neither right nor wrong. It's simply your belief. As such, it has the power to magnetize that which does—and that which does not—come into your life.

I'm reminded of that old Henry Ford quote "If you think you can't do something, you're right." If you believe that you are unlovable, then you'll be right and no one will love you. If they try to, you'll either talk them out of it, or you'll get rid of them completely. If you believe that you're worthless, then you'll be right then, too, and you'll find that others will treat you poorly. And if you believe you're destined to be alone in life, then, guess what? You'll be alone no matter how much you pine for love and affection. As King Solomon, author of the book of Proverbs, said thousands of years ago, "For as [a man] thinketh in his heart, so is he."

If you find that others treat you with disrespect, instead of complaining and making them wrong, ask yourself in what ways you are disrespecting yourself. If you pull in people who are unavailable, have the courage to ask yourself in what ways you are unavailable to yourself. If

you end up involved with people who can't seem to commit, look to discover whether or not you are committed to yourself. I once worked with
a gifted spiritual teacher, Georgina Lindsey, who constantly reminded us
of the Buddhist philosophy that "there is no one out there."

What can't come through you, can't come to you. If you want to
attract in the people, situations, and circumstances that support the manifestation of love in your life, then you must feel love, believe that it is
possible for you, and claim it as your own. Because we draw toward us
that which is most compelling within us, believing with all your heart that
you *can* and *will* have love is the single most important thing that you can
do on this quest for fulfillment. If you get nothing else out of this course
but that, I would say that you did just fine.

Jesus said, "All things whatsoever ye ask in prayer, *believing,* ye shall
receive." The more intensely you can do this, the more quickly those
things that support the fulfillment of love can—and will—come to you.

> A loving person lives
> in a loving world.
> A hostile person
> lives in a
> hostile world.
> Everyone you meet
> is your mirror.
> —Ken Keyes Jr.

PRACTICE

Take out your journal and write down your answer to the following question:

> **On a scale of 0 to 10, 0 meaning that absolutely no part of you
> believes you can or ever will have love in your life,
> and 10 meaning that you absolutely know for sure in your heart
> that you will, where are you?**

(*Note:* If you answered 0, I suggest that you speak with a wise and caring
adviser as soon as possible about your inability to believe that you can have
what you want.)

Now, complete the following sentences, answering as many times as
you wish for each sentence stem:

> **I believe that I can and will find love because:**

I see these beliefs mirrored back at me when:

I fear that I can't and won't find love because:

I see these beliefs mirrored back at me when:

Others relate to me the same way I relate to myself when they:

**The beliefs that no longer serve me that I'd be willing to
let go of are:**

**The beliefs that do serve me that I wish to strengthen and
bolster up are:**

Write those beliefs that you have that you wish to strengthen and bolster up ten or more times each in your journal. As you write, feel it to be so in your heart.

BONUS: PRACTICE IN ACTION

Repeat those beliefs that you wish to bolster and strengthen silently to yourself throughout the day. Notice if other people respond to you differently as you move about your day in this way, mirroring back to you your own more empowering and honoring way of relating to yourself.

At some point today, find some time to do the following meditation: Sit quietly, centering yourself with your breath and stilling your body by releasing any tension you may find. Become present to "The One" who is soon to come to you. Feel him sitting in front of you, giving you love. Allow your heart to open up to receive the love that he is pouring into you. Allow yourself to sink deeply into the feeling of this experience, celebrating the joy of this union as though it were already here. Give thanks to the Universe for blessing you with such a beautiful love. Repeat this experience often throughout the rest of the course.

LESSON 14
Relinquishing Unconscious Patterns

That which we do not bring to consciousness
appears in our lives as fate.

—Carl G. Jung

Patterns are about being unconscious. They are about thinking, feeling, and behaving in ways that are repetitive and automatic—thoughtless and conditioned by others who were also unconscious, and affected by forces they did not understand. There is no choice when one is engaged in acting out this imprinting. We are simply re-creating that which we know. It provides us with a sense of continuity, cohesion, and control.

While we tend to blame ourselves for "doing these things to myself over and over," we must try to understand that patterns have a life of their own. They are like vortices of energy. They have their own pull, which is like a force field. The only way to resist their magnetism is to become fully conscious and thus activate the power of choice.

For years I suffered with mild depression, which I likened to a low-grade fever. Although I rarely experience depression at all anymore, I will occasionally go through periods in which this low-level malaise returns. Recently this happened, and after several days, I had a conversation with myself as I was driving my car. "Katherine," I said, "you really don't have to suffer this way. You can shift this feeling right now if you want to. You know how to do that." What I saw next helped me to understand the magnitude of the gravitational pull that these patterns can have on us. Even though I *knew* that I could alter how I was feeling, and even though I didn't like how I felt at all, I recognized that *I didn't want to let it go.* I was in a Svengali-like trance, completely mesmerized by the feeling of melancholy. Of course, just the process of observing my attachment to the pain changed my relationship to it and within minutes, I was able to let

Destruction
before creation.
—Joseph Campbell

it go. This is not to suggest that all depressions and/or anxieties can so easily be released. It does, however, imply that often times we actually become attached to and invested in these negative feeling states, making them much more difficult, if not impossible, to overcome.

Much of healing ourselves is trying to become clear about what energy patterns we are running and then finding a way to make a different choice. I usually start out a Calling In "The One" workshop by going around the room and having people share who they are, and what their patterns are in relationship. This helps break the ice, because we can usually start to see parts of ourselves in one another. Frequently, people are upset and exacerbated when talking about the patterns they run because they can't seem to do anything differently. There is a general feeling of frustration and resignation, laced with moments of comic relief upon recognizing the absolute lunacy of some of the things we do. By the end of the day, workshop participants usually have more of a grasp on how they themselves are causing what seems to be just happening to them.

Lena, an attractive, professionally accomplished woman, was a recent workshop participant. When it was her turn, she spoke sadly and slowly. "I don't understand why it is but every man that I am with ends up telling me exactly the same thing. 'I like you. I respect you. I enjoy being with you. But I do not love you.' They all leave me for this reason." Lena seemed baffled. She could not understand how each one of her relationships ended in exactly the same way. Later on, however, when we began to explore specific ways in which we ourselves were the cause of our experience, Lena had a breakthrough. "I am never vulnerable with a man," she was telling the group. "Ever since my mother died when I was a little girl, and my father made it clear to me that I had to be strong and never cry, I have been unwilling to let a man see how I truly feel." "Lena," I asked her, "do you understand the connection between your unwillingness to be vulnerable and the pattern of men not falling in love with you?" She looked at me curiously. "It's like this," I continued. "People will usually like us for being nice. They will admire and respect us for having our act together. But they can only love us when we allow them to see our vulnerabilities and our flaws." She was shocked. She'd been trying for years to hide her feelings and her flaws in order to be loved and here I was telling her that she had to do exactly the opposite.

Lena was responding to all men as though they were her father, who she believed would love her only if she were emotionally self-contained and "strong." Even though it had been horribly isolating for her to not be allowed to openly grieve her mother's death, she also grew comfortable with withholding herself from others. She even came to rely upon her ability to shut down emotionally as the perfect way to protect herself from ever being as hurt as she was after her mother died and left her so alone.

Once Lena understood herself as the source of the pattern, the power of choice was restored. She could give up generalizing that all men would be like her father, and she could give up protecting herself from the possibility that someone else she dared to open her heart to might also die. The first new possibility—that the men she dated would probably be very different from her father—was not so difficult. It was the second that presented the greater challenge and one that she might have to work with for some time to come. But at least now she could give up being a victim of the pattern, and start to deal with her ambivalence about surrendering to love.

Thirty-six-year-old Yolanda, another client, works for herself and owns her own home. She has a powerful, take-care-of-business approach to life that has worked for her for years, both personally and professionally. However, after living with Steve for three years, she was not sure that he was "The One" and she came to me to help her sort it out. Steve is a kind man who enjoys spiritual retreats and hanging out with friends. He does not, however, enjoy focusing too much on the tasks of daily living such as managing a schedule or earning a living. While he does OK financially, his ambitions simply lie elsewhere. For a time this was fine with Yolanda, who truly appreciated having a boyfriend who was sensitive to spiritual matters. She was used to being the one in the relationship who had the "male energy." In fact, she confided, she found herself playing this role in every single one of her close relationships. She was the friend whom others came to when they needed money or advice on how to manage their business affairs. The problem, however, was that she wanted to

> Take a moment and think about the personality traits of the people that you have seriously considered as mates. If you were to make a list of their predominant personality traits, you would discover a lot of similarities, including, surprisingly, their negative traits.
> —Harville Hendrix

be able to be the "female" sometimes. She wanted someone who could take care of her, too. She wanted to be the receiver as well as the giver. Because of this Yolanda decided not to make a lifetime commitment to Steve, and they amicably parted ways.

Within weeks, Aaron—a longtime business associate—expressed romantic interest in Yolanda. Since Aaron lived in another part of the country, they wrote frequent e-mails to each other as he began to court her. They were scheduled to meet in another city the following week on business. Aaron began making plans for the two of them, casually e-mailing Yolanda asking her if she had any preferences regarding their agenda. Yolanda wrote back a very detailed response. She preferred a particular restaurant because it was known for its fish dishes and she loved fish; she liked a certain hotel because they had a reputation for excellent service, etc., etc. Before she sent it, however, she had a thought that it might be a good idea to call me and run her reply by me. After hearing it, I laughed at her. "Oh, boy, not having an easy time letting go of male energy, are you?" I had to coach her on how to respond with female energy. "If you want to experience being taken care of, you have to let yourself give up being in control. Throw that e-mail out and write something simple, like 'I'm sure you are handling everything beautifully. I'm looking forward to seeing you.'"

Two weeks later she called me to thank me. She'd had a wonderful time. She was surprised at how vulnerable she felt to place herself so completely in Aaron's hands, but was delighted to discover how nurturing it was to receive his loving care. So delighted, in fact, that both she and Aaron were actively exploring the possibility of a larger, more substantial commitment.

Later, Yolanda shared with me the challenge it presented to her to let go of being in the "male" position. In her family, the one in power appeared to be her father. Her mother, who was a traditional woman, was terribly unhappy and frustrated. She seemed to have few options, as she was so completely dependent upon her husband for financial survival. In contrast, Yolanda's father dominated and controlled the entire family. She decided early on that he was the one she should identify with, and she unconsciously took on his energy patterns.

Because we grow attached to that which is familiar, we often develop strong bonds with the patterns that were acted out by one or both of our parents when we were growing up. Hence, if one or both of our parents were alcoholic, there is a high likelihood that we will either be addicted to something, or display patterns of codependent behavior. If one or both of our parents were chronic worriers, we ourselves will probably also struggle with anxiety. If they were shy and apprehensive about life, we, too, may suffer from a debilitating sense of insecurity.

Because we are creatures of habit, if we, or someone in our family, have a history of depression, we will have an energetic tie with that particular frequency—the thoughts, body movements, and feelings associated with depression will occur as both seductive and inviting. As much as we may hate it, depression may be as comforting as putting on an old sweater or visiting an old friend to whom we have grown attached.

Breaking a pattern is much like breaking any addiction—difficult but certainly not impossible. It will, however, require of you an advanced level of self-awareness regarding the connection between what it is that you are doing and the results that you are getting. The alternative—to continue on in the same unconscious fashion, creating the same disappointing results—is simply unacceptable. Kierkegaard wrote, "To cheat oneself out of love is the most terrible deception; it is an eternal loss for which there is no reparation, either in time or in eternity." Let us be fearless, then, in examining ourselves as the cause of that which is happening in our lives, so that the possibility of love is thereby restored.

> It's much easier to fall into old habits than to take the time to establish new ones. But once they're established, they're established. And then they replace and become as constant as the old ones.
> —Geneen Roth

PRACTICE

Take out your journal and write for several minutes each on the following questions:

What is the pattern(s) I've experienced over and over again in my romantic relationships?

What specifically am I doing to create the results that I am getting?

In what ways, if any, was this pattern(s) acted out by one or
both of my parents?

Which of these patterns, if any, do I want to release from
my life?

What specifically would I have to give up in order to do this?

BONUS: PRACTICE IN ACTION

Do at least one thing today that breaks up the pattern of what the "normal" you is like by taking at least one action that demonstrates a complete departure from your usual way of doing things. For example, if your style is normally quiet and passive, then speak up at a meeting in a bold and assertive way; if you are usually a "beige" person, wear a bright color like orange or red; if you are slow and sedentary, go for a run or a fast walk.

SUGGESTED STUDY GUIDE
FOR GROUP DISCUSSION

1. What losses have you been avoiding and how is this costing you love?

2. Whom, if anyone, have you forgiven this week, and what did you have to take responsibility for in order to do so?

3. In which relationship(s) have fear, obligation, and guilt been determining your actions and what, if anything, have you done to alter this?

4. What outdated agreements did you complete this week and what new agreements, if any, have you replaced them with?

5. Share about your "Sacred Wound." What do you now have to offer others as a result of what you've been through in life?

6. What in your relationship with yourself is being mirrored back to you in your relationships with others?

7. What patterns are you hoping to release from your life? What would you have to give up in order to do this?

HEALING CORE WOUNDS

The world breaks everyone and afterwards
many are strong at the broken places.

—Ernest Hemingway

The inner work we embark upon this week is work that, truthfully, we could spend months, if not years, doing. And while it's impossible to do the Cliff Notes version of healing ourselves of our core wounds, it's important to remember that the purpose of healing work is not so much to do it perfectly, but to restore the power of choice to our lives.

These next few days will be the most challenging and provocative ones that we will encounter. They represent that part of the race where endurance, courage, and persistence are very much needed in order to secure a safe and successful passage to the next level.

This week:

* We will examine the impact that your early childhood experiences are having upon your intimate relationships today

* We will identify and explore core beliefs you hold about yourself that are affecting your ability to create and sustain loving relationships

* We will explore the ways in which you are needy and look at alternative ways of responding to this insistent hunger of the heart

✳ We will reclaim formerly disowned aspects of self as the means to fully embrace our wholeness, and our strong, autonomous selves

✳ We will end this period of intense self-examination with a release ceremony to cleanse away all blocks to the fulfillment of love

LESSON 15
Early Childhood Woundings

I've learned…that love, not time, heals all wounds.

—Andy Rooney

Imagine, for a moment, your experience as a newborn. Unable to satisfy your hunger, change into dry clothes, quench an unpleasant thirst, move into a more comfortable position, or escape a frightening situation, you were completely at the mercy of others. How these people felt about this responsibility and how well they were able to perform it was your initiation into the world of relationships. Their capacity to respond to your limited ability to express what you needed in any given moment determined whether the world was a safe and loving place, or an unpredictable and dangerous one. Psychologically, the first year of life has but one primary task: we must learn to trust.

Bob was born into an alcoholic and abusive home. There were frequent fights and fits of rage as his parents sat for hours in the living room drinking, ignoring the cries from his room. Even now, at the age of forty-two, Bob complains of a panicky feeling that has "always been with him" that he won't get what he needs. He has little trust that good things will come his way in life. His desperation becomes so great at times that, although he considers himself to be a good person, he admits to some white-collar criminal activity on and off throughout his adult life. Bob pines for romantic love but becomes so anxious and demanding when he meets someone that he likes, that he's just decided he can't handle it. He's been celibate for several years now.

Samuel began therapy with me when he was in his late forties. He is handsome, fit, exceptionally bright, and vastly talented as a comedian and as a writer. However, his inability to trust others was so severe that one might have characterized him as an eccentric recluse. As an infant, Samuel suffered from his mother's bizarre and destructive methods of parenting him, including her regular practice of masturbating him "to help calm him down." Various forms of emotional and psychological abuse continued throughout his entire childhood, as his mother continued to behave both in seductive and sadistic ways toward him.

Trust was not an easy thing to establish with Samuel, but over time, our relationship became an important one in his life. His belief that others would most certainly abuse him should he ever dare to let them in began to be discredited. The connection that we developed, which was characterized by respect, constancy, care, and healthy boundaries, has given Samuel the opportunity to consider that perhaps the world is not a completely dangerous and hostile place, after all. Through that experience, Samuel allowed himself, for the first time in his life, to open up to the experience of love. And, in spite of being a "confirmed bachelor" for many years, Samuel and his beloved, Lianna, were recently married.

Most of us have not suffered the burden of such severe abuse. Yet almost all of us, to one degree or another, do carry scars and hurts from our childhoods that diminish our ability to love and be loved. To face these hurts head on, as we do in this chapter, may occur for some of you as the dreaded dark passage, forcing you to face demons and forces heretofore unnamed, and untamed. For others, it will be a welcome relief. And for a blessed few, a simple review. Regardless of which category you fall into, I assure you that the task of healing core woundedness is always, always worth its weight in gold, as the agony of acting out destructive dynamics over and over again is finally abated.

By giving ourselves the gift of identifying those things that have driven us to destroy the seeds of love in our lives, we have a profound opportunity to overcome them. Samuel found his way to Lianna because, as his ability to name the fears and false beliefs that had kept him separate and alone for all of those years grew, he could finally choose to take a risk on love. Bob, on the other hand, is still in reaction to the wounding he suffered. Although he yearns for love, the ability to choose love still, as of this writing, eludes him. The question becomes, really, do you have the wound or does the wound have you?

Recently I had the good fortune of hearing psychotherapist and bestselling author Thomas Moore speak at a conference. He reminded us that it has only been in the past hundred years or so that human beings have begun defining themselves so exclusively according to the experiences of their childhoods. As a therapist, it was good to hear that perspective, lest I forget how vast and glorious we are, in spite of our sad stories and unmet needs of childhood. We are more than the hurts we have suffered. Our woundedness is not the sum total of who and what we are. I think it's important to remember this as we delve into this inquiry. Because few of us had the good fortune of being born to those who had themselves so mastered their own evolution, that they were able to ensure our successful passage through the thorny terrain of personality development.

According to development psychologist Erik Erikson, there are several psychosocial stages that we must successfully navigate in childhood in order to arrive at adulthood fully prepared for life. These tasks include: (1) learning to trust others, as well as in the overall goodness of our lives; (2) learning to operate as a separate, autonomous being; (3) learning to take appropriate risks that demonstrate initiative and ingenuity; (4) gaining a sense of competence and mastery regarding the basic challenges of life; and (5) developing a consistent personal identity. As long as we remain incomplete on any of these tasks, the development of a cohesive and solid sense of self is thwarted.

In his book *Search for the Real Self,* psychotherapist James Masterson describes this much-desired "solid sense of self." It includes:

1. The capacity to experience a wide variety of feelings, as well as an ability to soothe painful feelings in a positive way;

2. The ability to express your thoughts and feelings authentically to another person without too much fear of either being engulfed or abandoned;

3. The capacity to tolerate your own aloneness;

4. A healthy sense of entitlement that life holds good things for you and that you deserve to have them;

5. The ability to assert your individuality and authenticity in the world; and

6. A stability of self, meaning that you are always aware that you are

> Children's talent to endure stems from their ignorance of alternatives.
> —Maya Angelou

You fell in love
because your old
brain had your
partner confused
with your parents!
Your old brain
believed that it had
finally found the
ideal antidote to
make up for the
psychological and
emotional damage
you experienced
in childhood.
—Harville Hendrix

the same person regardless of who you are with, what you are doing, or the current circumstances (both good and bad) of your life.

Put simply, core wounds are those things that interfere with the successful establishment of a solid self. And, since solid relationships require solid selves, until we go back and finish what was left incomplete in our own development, we run the risk of experiencing chronic and painful problems in our most intimate relationships.

Many times people come to psychotherapy only to confess in the first few sessions that they feel "guilty" pampering themselves with such an extravagant "self-indulgence" as therapy. But what could possibly be worth your time and efforts as much as investing in yourself and your ability to having joyful, harmonious relationships in your life? Making more money (with no one to share it with)? Buying more land (with no one to live there with)? Getting another degree (with no one to come to your graduation and applaud your efforts)? Creating more meaningful work (and coming home each night to an empty apartment)? Unless you have children, there really is nothing more important than investing yourself in your ability to be close to others and to richly give and receive love.

The point of this journey is to find our way to love. We don't do it because we are fascinated with our own pain. In her book *Sacred Contracts,* Caroline Myss writes, "I am forever reminding people that their spiritual life should not be only about trying to figure out why bad things have happened to them and finding the right prayers to get out of their dark nights. The emphasis in too many people's lives has more to do with healing than with enjoying life." We do this, therefore, as part of a commitment to actualize a life of joy and fulfillment. We are seeking to make the connections between what we've been through and who we are today, as a means of opening up and restoring the possibility of choice in our lives. Because, as author Ken Keyes Jr. said, "To see your drama clearly is to be liberated from it."

PRACTICE

Take out your journal and complete the following sentences, answering as many times as you wish for each sentence stem. Don't censor yourself. Use your imagination and write whatever comes to mind even if it initially does not make seem to make sense.

The caregiving I received as an infant was:

How my mother felt about being my mother was:

How my father felt about being my father was:

In response, I felt:

The ways in which these feelings affect me today are:

I am able to trust others when:

I am unable to trust others when:

My last romantic partner was like my initial caregiver(s) in:

My last romantic partner was different from my initial caregiver(s) in:

The similarities between the care I received as a child and my relationships today are:

NOTE: If you had a significant relationship with an older sibling, foster parents, stepparent, or significant older relative, please do this exercise with that person as well. If you were adopted, you may wish to do the exercise on your biological parents, even if you never met them and/or don't know who they are. Just use your imagination and trust your instincts about what was going on for them at the time. The point of this particular exercise is to access how you internalized your experiences, and not necessarily to uncover the exact facts of what actually occurred.

BONUS: PRACTICE IN ACTION

Take a risk today by making at least one uncharacteristically trusting gesture (for example, confess a vulnerability to a coworker; confide your true feelings to an acquaintance; ask a friend for a bigger favor than you ordinarily would). Don't worry about whether or not you get the response you were hoping for. The point is, simply, to take a risk to trust others beyond your comfort zone. Risk implies that it might not work out, so don't be too attached to the outcome. Notice, however, that, in taking a risk, you have expanded your repertoire of what is possible for you in relationship to others.

NOTE: If you believe that you may be suffering from severe woundings around attachment and fundamental trust, like Samuel was, I suggest that you seek the support and guidance of a competent therapist, as these wounds do best when worked out in relationship with another human being who is able to be there for you consistently.

LESSON 16
Core Beliefs and Other Distortions of Reality

How do you take your woundings, your betrayals, your 'holes,' and
make yourself holy instead of battered? This process
involves the dramatic remythologizing of yourself and your life…
the gaining of a very different perspective…

—Jean Houston, *The Search for the Beloved*

At a conference I attended recently, author/psychologist Dr. Ty Colbert
told a story of a schizophrenic man who could be found rocking back and
forth, in one continuous motion, for hours. A doctor asked the man why
he was bowing.

"I don't bow."
"But you do this."
"That's not bowing."
"What is it?"
"It's balancing."
"What are you balancing?"
"Emotions."
"What emotions?"
"Fear and loneliness."

We are all balancing fear and loneliness to one degree or another. We
move back and forth between the fear of getting too close to another—
the alarming likelihood of becoming too entangled, too vulnerable, too
dependent upon another person (i.e., "engulfed" and/or "trapped"), and
the fear of isolation—the loneliness that can occur as a result of being
deserted or from pushing others away in an attempt to "protect" ourselves
from this horrifying prospect (i.e., "abandoned"). In lay terms, it's what

It is in the nature
of things to be
drawn to the very
experiences that
will spoil
our innocence,
transform our
lives, and give
us necessary
complexity
and depth.

—Thomas Moore

we call the "push-pull" relationship. Many of us find ourselves bouncing between the two extremes, over and over again, forever balancing these polarized positions. For some of us, this is the central drama of our lives, particularly of our romantic lives.

Henry and Amanda have been dating for five years now. Amanda has been excessively uncertain whether or not Henry is the right man for her, although Henry has "just known" all along that they are right for each other. Amanda has been uncommitted and ambivalent throughout the majority of their relationship, which has vacillated between whirlwind, romantic encounters and disruptive, explosive arguments that have generally been followed by cooling-off periods lasting anywhere from a day to a week. Henry's been bounced back and forth between hope and despair more times than he cares to admit. However, when Amanda finally tells him that she is ready to commit herself to the relationship, it is Henry who suddenly becomes ambivalent. Out of the blue, he meets another woman at work and begins dating her while continuing to see Amanda as well, thereby continuing their unstable push-pull dynamic.

The failure to successfully navigate the first task of childhood, to develop a strong capacity for trust, can cause profound difficulties in the ability to form secure and stable bonds with others throughout adulthood. The reluctance to allow oneself to depend upon an inner circle of "others" might indicate that one's worldview is skewed by the belief that it is somehow unsafe to do so. Studies have shown that, as far back as in the womb, we make decisions regarding who we are, and the nature of the world around us. Conclusions like "The world is dangerous," "I am unlovable," or "I am unimportant" are often the assumptions of children far too young to understand that it is their caregivers, and not they themselves, who are in some way inadequate and deficient in their abilities.

Tammy was born to a Mexican father and an Italian mother. Her father, a heavy drinker, regularly beat her mother until they were finally able to escape when Tammy was four. She and Tammy moved in with her mother's parents, who, according to her, were "basically good people." However, Tammy remembers frequent comments about her Mexican blood, as her grandparents expressed their covert and, at times, overt racism toward her. At the age of five, Tammy did not know anything about racism. She did not know that her grandparents were being small-minded. She did not understand that there are many good people in the world who believe destructive and foolish things. All she knew was that, somehow, she was a "bad seed." She grew up feeling different, and inferior to other kids in the neighborhood. For many years, she struggled with deep feelings of inferiority and shame for who she was.

Because these decisions are made so early in our lives, sometimes before we can even talk, they become pervasive in our experience of who we are, and what we could expect from life. This is not so much because these decisions were *true* as much as, given that we are in a constant state of creating our lives out of our words, thoughts, feelings, and actions, they became true for us because we believed it to be so. For example, if, in response to the constant uncaring behavior of my primary caregivers over a significant period of time, I decide, at the age of two, that I am worthless, then I will tend to do one of two things. Either I will bring in experiences that validate the truth of this statement (for example: never having much money; going out with people who treat me like dirt; driving a beat-up old car, etc.), *or* I will be compelled to prove otherwise by being driven to make money, buy the most expensive items, or find the richest of lovers. However, because the latter is an attempt to compensate for a perceived deficit, no matter how much material wealth I accumulate, or how many accolades I receive that tout my value, it will never be enough to convince me of my own true worth. I will constantly hunger for and compulsively attempt to get more.

As you might imagine, the beliefs we hold, particularly when they are unconscious and unidentified, can wreak absolute havoc with our love lives. For not only do we live our lives in reaction to these beliefs (e.g., the woman who secretly believes she's worthless and marries a man she doesn't love for his wealth), but also because we are constantly finding ways to validate and confirm these beliefs, in spite of ourselves.

Ann grew up in Beverly Hills, one of the richest and, arguably, most pretentious places in America. Her mother was a single mom raising two daughters on a modest salary. From the time she entered grade school, Ann was self-conscious about her economic status, embarrassed by her "cheap" clothes, her "ugly little" apartment, and her mother's "hideously old" car. By the second grade she'd stopped having friends over, and was mortified whenever her mother came to the school to pick her up. Ann decided, at the age of seven, that, try as she might to hide it, she was inferior to the other girls. She lived her entire childhood cloaked in a sense of shame and humiliation over this "fact."

Today Ann has her own "ugly little" apartment in Beverly Hills. She is completely embarrassed to bring a man she is dating to her home, because she believes it to be inferior to where she "should" be living by now. Although she is beautiful, she thinks she is "barely average." She is a perfect size six but often complains about how fat and flabby she is. Although she earns close to a six-figure salary, she is sure that her salary is inadequate to purchase the things that would make her feel good about herself and her life. Ann is tortured by how inferior she feels to be "still single," at the ripe old age of thirty-four. She is often the only single woman at the frequent parties she attends, and she struggles through these interminable evenings with deep feelings of humiliation and shame that she does her best to hide. Worst of all, however, is that whenever Ann meets a man she likes, he inevitably ends up rejecting her for being not good enough for him somehow. Predictably, the men who do like her and want to be with her, she finds inadequate and lacking in some substantial way. In Ann's world, someone is always inferior.

The beliefs that we operate out of become the building blocks to how we conceptualize our lives and who we are in the world. They become our identity. We don't just think that maybe, sometimes we behave badly. No—we believe that we *are* bad (and are therefore compelled to treat others "badly," or to choose others who will appropriately punish us for how "bad" we really are). And while it can feel downright depressing to identify the worst-case scenarios we secretly harbor in our hearts about ourselves, it's also a relief just to finally say it out loud. It's like taking the first step in Alcoholics Anonymous. "Hi, I'm Jane and I believe that I'm ugly and alone in life." Whew.

One reason I had such difficulty finding lasting love for the first forty years or so of my life, was my belief that I was worthless and inferior. I crafted those two "truths" about myself from an experience of being "left" by my father in childhood (so I must be worthless) and of having a mother who was so beautiful, smart, and competent that I didn't believe

I could ever live up to her (so I must be inferior). These were the mere musings of a child far too young to understand the dynamics of what was transpiring around me. Yet, those two beliefs affected absolutely every relationship I ever had. If someone was attracted to me, I would generally treat him or her as though their ardor were something to toy with, and to dismiss without much regard (oh, God, I pray they all forgive me!). When I was attracted to someone, that person usually responded with an indifference and a disregard for me, as though I were too worthless and inferior to bother with. And round and round we go.

> I hate all that
> don't love me, and
> slight all that do.
> —George Farquhar

Children constantly look to others to discover who and what they are. The whole world is their mirror; and for someone under the age of four or five, that world basically consists of one's parents, siblings, and other primary caregiver(s). As we are purely egocentric as children (i.e., absolutely everything that happens around me is about me), we make frequent misinterpretations and come to many erroneous conclusions. For example: My mother became ill because I made her sick ("I'm guilty"); my parents divorced because I misbehaved ("I'm bad"); I was given up for adoption because I wasn't important enough to keep around ("I'm insignificant and disposable").

It is our task to consciously review the way we internalized our experiences as children. Once we can see the meaning we crafted out of the circumstances we endured, we then have to consciously "remythologize our lives," as author Jean Houston suggests, by considering more appropriate, healthy interpretations of these events. Otherwise, we spend our entire lives living out of a two-, three-, or four-year-old's account of who we are, and what's possible for us. And, while the magic and enchantment of childhood is certainly worth defending, our destructive, distorted illusions are not.

PRACTICE

Today we are going to distinguish the beliefs and subsequent identity you've been crafting and cultivating since childhood. Take out your journal and write on the following questions:

What was a significant disappointment
that I endured in childhood?

What did I make this disappointment mean about me and my life?

NOTE: Use the following list as a guideline.

I am alone. I am bad. I am a brat. I am a disappointment. I am dirt. I am disposable. I don't matter. I am a failure. I am fat. I am gross. I am incapable. I am inferior. I am insignificant. I am a loser. I am a mess. I'm not enough. I am unlovable. I am unimportant. I am sad. I am a screw-up. I am selfish. I am sneaky. I am smelly. I am stupid. I am uncreative. I am unworthy. I am ugly. I am unlikable. I am unwanted. I am worthless. . . .

What did I make this disappointment mean
about the world and other people?

NOTE: Use the following list as a guideline.

The world is dangerous. No one can be trusted. Everyone is out for themselves. There's not enough to go around. No relationship is safe. You can only count on yourself. I never get a break. "The sky is falling." The rug will always be pulled out from under you. No one cares. Bad things always happen. Life is hard and then you die. I'm just waiting for the other shoe to drop. . . .

What is an alternative interpretation of this experience?

NOTE: Use the following list as a guideline.

My parents were exhausted from working so much and had little attention to give. My mother was grieving and couldn't tolerate opening her heart to me. My father was too intimidated by my mother to protect me from her. My teacher had way too many students in her class and consequently made frequent mistakes. . . .

What messages (verbal and nonverbal) did I receive from others about myself in childhood (i.e., parents, siblings, other caregivers, teachers, peers, etc.)?

What beliefs did my mother have about herself and/or the world that I adopted?

What beliefs did my father have about himself and/or the world that I adopted?

What do I make it mean about myself that I am single?

Finish the following sentences with as many answers as you can. Don't censor yourself. Just write whatever comes to mind whether or not it initially makes sense.

I am:

Life is:

The world is:

Men are:

Women are:

What evidence can you find that suggests that your negative beliefs about yourself may not be true?

What evidence can you find that suggests that your negative beliefs about the world and others may not be true?

BONUS: PRACTICE IN ACTION

Today is about increasing self-awareness regarding the core beliefs that you operate from. As you move through the day, at any given time, ask yourself what beliefs you are operating out of in this moment.

Before you go to bed, write in your journal on any insights you received today regarding your core beliefs and how much or how little you are operating out of them. Write down alternative beliefs that you would prefer to nurture and cultivate in your life. Write the new, more empowering beliefs ten or more times each in your journal. As you write, feel it to be so in your heart.

LESSON 17
Transforming an Identity

Transform does not mean to fix or make go away whatever trauma
and scars you may be carrying from childhood; instead, you
slowly develop a new relationship with your difficulty, such that it
is no longer a controlling factor in your life.

—Phillip Moffitt, *Yoga Journal*

Tanya, a young woman in her mid-twenties, came to me to help her heal
an eating disorder that she'd developed as a teenager. We worked for
months, to no avail. Week after week Tanya would return with tales of
more late-night eating binges followed by several days of starvation. It
wasn't until Tanya had the following dream that things began to improve
for her. "I walked down a long corridor before entering a room with a
large rectangular table in the center. It appeared to be a boardroom of
some sort, and there were several people in positions of authority sitting
around the table talking. I took a gun out from under my jacket and
began shooting. I shot and killed my mother's daughter. I then left, satisfied."

Tanya's dream symbolized a profound shift that was taking place
within her. Before this dream, Tanya's sense of herself was very much tied
to her mother's perception of her (i.e., she was her "mother's daughter").
In response to the impossible demands made upon her by her mother that
she be "perfect," "the most talented," and "the most beautiful girl in the
room," Tanya was compelled to behave flawlessly in all areas of her life.
However, her ultimate inability to be a perfect human being was all too
evident, and she secretly began to believe that she was a failure—and a
complete disgrace to her mother, who seemed to somehow desperately
need her daughter to be picture-perfect in a variety of ways.

The pressure and shame that Tanya secretly felt manifested itself as an

Daughter am I in
my mother's house,
But mistress
in my own.
—Rudyard Kipling

eating disorder that began when she was eight years old and went on her first diet. For years, Tanya would try her best to eat "perfectly" in order to have the "perfect" body. When she ate one "bad" thing, she would completely lose control and eat everything in sight. The terror that she would make a bad food choice led to days of starvation, since she found it easier simply not to eat at all. This starve-binge pattern lasted for years. It was not until Tanya began to deconstruct (i.e., "shoot and kill") that part of herself that believed she *had* to be the most perfect girl in the room— the thinnest, the most beautiful, and the most talented, (i.e., her mother's daughter) that she began to get better.

Tanya could not overcome her pervasive and compelling conviction that she was a failure by simply creating an affirmation that opposed such a belief. Saying over and over to herself, "I am a success, I am a success" without also challenging the validity of the belief that she was a failure to begin with would be like pulling the flower off the dandelion. While affirmations can be enormously helpful, we will forever be enslaved as long as we hold these mistaken self-concepts to be shameful *truths* about who and what we are. We can't fix that which was never broken to begin with. We actually have to begin to understand these beliefs to be the creative musings of a child under duress. Although they became the foundation upon which we built our entire identities, they were actually just the constructs of a child trying to make sense of a senseless world. Since we, as children, had little capacity to understand that our caregivers had problems that had *nothing* to do with us, we created erroneous meaning out of the experiences we had.

Too often we assume that, merely because we think something, or because someone such as a parent, an older sibling, or a teacher said something, that it must be true. We don't even question the toxic thought. We just try to compensate for it and/or try to hide it from others, so they will like us. Life becomes about proving that we are *not* that—the doctor who is motivated to keep earning more degrees only because, when she was little, she had an older sister who teased her, telling her over and over that she was stupid; or the beautiful woman who spends inordinate amounts of time and money enhancing her physical appearance because she was a "plain Jane" all through school and overlooked by all the boys. These are people who are trying to compensate for something that they believe is wrong with them. Perhaps, though, all that is "wrong" was the original assumption.

Tanya could not contend the validity of her belief that she was a failure by being in reaction to it, trying to prove it wrong. If she could, then winning a beauty contest and getting invited to join a world-renowned dance company would have been sufficient to disprove her beliefs once and for all. But they weren't. On the contrary: these two events actually made things worse for Tanya. Now, the expectations that she felt from her mother were coming from others, as well. In the end, every situation she found herself in had the potential to validate the worst about herself because, after all, try as she might, she simply could not continue being the most perfect, the most beautiful, and the most talented girl everywhere she went.

While Tanya was in reaction to her belief that she was a failure, she did not take too many risks when it came to love. She rarely told the truth about her feelings to anyone she dated, and she monitored every gesture with great care. She wasn't about to let anyone close enough to see the real her, given that she feared the real her was utterly unacceptable. It wasn't until she learned that it was OK to mess up, dress down, fall short, bomb out, cut off all her hair and—the ultimate—disappoint Mom, that things began to change. It was when she finally got that it really was up to her to figure out how successful *or how unsuccessful* she felt like being, that she allowed herself to fall in love with someone who was just as sweet and imperfect as she was.

Many of us cannot allow ourselves to form loving, happy unions because it is outside of our identity to be truly loved and valued by another. Our whole sense of self may have formed itself in reaction to a wounding or an event that suggested that we were unlovable, unworthy of love, or simply alone in life. In order to bring love into our lives, these constructs of self must be revealed for being just that—constructs—and not the truth of who we are. We must remember that who we are is often times far more vast than our *ideas* of who we are. In short, in order to allow love into our lives, we often must shed our old ways of defining who we are.

Notice the difference between what happens when a man says to himself, "I have failed three times," and what happens when he says, "I am a failure."

—S. I. Hayakawa

Leaving our identities behind like this is like leaving home for the very first time. These identities are created inside of the context of our initial environments. To deconstruct them, therefore, is akin to challenging the gods. Just because your stepfather told you over and over again that you'd never amount to anything, *does not mean that this statement bears any resemblance to the truth.* In this shedding, our parents are revealed for the mere mortals that they are. So revealed, in fact, that we might even find it in our hearts to respond with pity and compassion to how difficult it must have been for them to try to give us what we needed when they themselves were so severely lacking.

Let me break it to you gently. Your parents, siblings, teachers, neighbors, and peers were very often quite off the mark in their assessment of you. They may have undervalued you, overpressured you, neglected to notice your strengths, ignored your unique abilities, failed to understand the blessed quirkiness of what it is to be you, or criticized you mercilessly for what they secretly feared was errant about themselves. That is no excuse, however, for you to then continue to shoulder the burden of their inadequacies. You must stop perpetrating the abuse against yourself that they originated by indulging these errant beliefs, day after day, year after year. For you are doing just that whenever you persist in treating yourself in the same destructive ways that you complain your caregivers treated you. We can lament for years about the way our fathers neglected us, but until we stop neglecting ourselves it won't make one bit of difference.

When Tanya finally put her foot down by refusing to perform, and refusing to be perfect (and believe me, her mother tested her again and again), it was fascinating to watch her mother begin to blossom. For the first time in Tanya's memory, her mother began to take dance lessons. It seems that her constant pushing of Tanya was sourced from an inner frustration that she herself had always wanted to be a dancer. *She* wanted to be the one who did the steps perfectly, who sailed across the room with grace and beauty. Her mother, who was nearing sixty years old at the time, even began entering dance contests in Las Vegas and, lo and behold, winning them. And while it was agony for Tanya to tolerate disappointing her mother initially, they all lived through it and, ultimately, prospered because of it.

Today, Tanya watches when the internal "I'm a failure" dialogue kicks in. Usually it's when she's nervous or uncertain of herself, or trying something new. She's learned to take risks in spite of this inner bully. She's even begun to talk back to it.

"You're such a failure," it will say.

"Well, everyone fails sometimes. It's not so bad to fail."

"No, it's horrible to fail."

"Oh, this is just fear talking. That's OK. I admire myself for taking risks even when I'm scared."

And the bully is usually appeased, much like a small child who was simply having a tantrum.

Our goal is not so much to get rid of the false beliefs we have about ourselves as it is to transform the relationships we have with them. They may never go away entirely. Yet we must learn to give up relating to them as though they were the dreaded truth about who and what we are. Rather than allow these beliefs to bully us with their incessant chatter, eat away at our confidence, and devour years of our lives, we simply have to watch them, listen to them, and even give up our resistance to their constant and predictable drone. "Ah," we say, "that's 'I'm not good enough' talking again. Well, now, 'I'm not good enough,' what have you to say to me today?"

We have to take the charge off these inner conversations, listening to them much as we might to a child tell us of a boogeyman under the bed, reassuring her that these very distressing and threatening "monsters" are not even real. For when we operate as though the core beliefs we harbor in our hearts are true, we tend to behave in ways that end up validating their existence. Either that, or we'll feel driven to find love in an attempt to prove that they are not. We'll impose upon our lover the taxing responsibility of reassuring us that we are lovable, worthy, important, sexy, and wanted, all the while covertly doing all we can to convince him or her that we are anything but. We really don't want to burden our intimate relationships with this impossible task. For no one can repair that which was never broken to begin with.

When Zusya, a Hasidic rabbi, was criticized for unorthodox behavior, he replied, "In the next world I will not be asked why in this life I was not Moses but rather why I was not Zusya."

—Hasidic tale

The bottom line for
everyone is "I'm not
good enough."
It's only a thought,
and a thought
can be changed.
—Louise L. Hay

PRACTICE

Take out your art supplies. You may do the following project using either drawing paper and markers, or modeling clay, which you can shape with your hands.

I'd like to invite you to create two figures. The first embodies and represents an erroneous belief that has been haunting your life. Draw or shape the actual belief itself. Obviously this cannot be a literal interpretation of the belief, but simply a representation of what the belief *feels* like as it attempts to dominate and control your life. When you are finished, I invite you to name your figure.

The second figure you are invited to create is a representation of your true self—a figure that represents you as larger and more powerful than the erroneous belief that you just created. Create a figure that is capable of usurping the power that your other figure holds. Use this as an opportunity to see yourself as having dominion and jurisdiction over the belief, rather than the other way around. Again, name your figure.

Do these figures without concerning yourself with the artistic merit of your designs. Use your emotions to craft these two figures, allowing your feelings to lead the way.

BONUS: PRACTICE IN ACTION

As you move through your day, notice the erroneous beliefs that speak to you in your mind's eye. Notice when these beliefs tempt you to act in ways that are self-diminishing or self-defeating. See if you can get yourself to talk back to the beliefs, offering correction and a more balanced perspective, much like you might speak to a frightened child. Alter your course of action accordingly.

LESSON 18
Healing the Hungry Heart

I dreamt last night oh marvelous error that there were honeybees in my heart making honey out of my old failures.

—Antonio Machado

David, a thirty-something gay man who works as a freelance writer, can't understand why, whenever he begins dating someone he likes, he starts obsessively acting out in possessive and overly dependent ways. In spite of his best efforts to the contrary, he becomes neurotic, needy, and insecure the moment he meets someone he believes he could have a relationship with. Like David, many of us who are functioning well in life, with good jobs and good friends, suddenly begin behaving as though we are starving and desperate for love at the first signs of possible romantic union.

"Falling" in love is a regressive state. It brings us straight to the heart of our hunger—our hunger for meaning, for comfort, for satisfaction, for safety. The sexual bonding we long for—the disappearance of all boundaries and borders, the complete state of union and primal bliss—is a connection similar to the one an infant ideally has with a mother. The act of lovemaking is a merging, as two people become one energy. We are no longer alone. Our defenses are down. We are revealed beyond our well-defined, autonomous selves. We are fused, once again visitors to our native land—that time and place where we knew not the concepts of separateness, identity, and autonomy. If we have adapted ourselves in life, rather than healed—if we have coped rather than cured, so to speak—it will show up when we fall in love, or even, sometimes, simply begin dating. Even before engaging in sex, we may find ourselves regressing, becoming needy and possessive, just in the anticipation of having sex or from experiencing the sexual feelings that someone might arouse.

"Neediness" is a state of inner deprivation based upon unmet dependency needs in early childhood. When we are needy, we are trying to get from others what was denied us in the past. Unfortunately, though, many of these childhood needs cannot adequately be met in present-time, and particularly not with people we barely know. No one can ever really make up for the fact that, for many of us, our parents simply couldn't love us the way we needed them to. No one can take on how drastically they failed us.

What a queer cosmic joke, then, that, in spite of our best intentions, we seem to attract those who lack the very same abilities to love us that our primary caregivers did. What a strange phenomenon it is that we duplicate those very same destructive and hurtful dynamics that have already caused us such agony and sorrow.

Angela, a petite woman in her mid-thirties, was raised by a mother who spent most of her time in bed with undiagnosed depression. Although Angela believes that her mother loved her, she never felt loved by her. Rather, as a child, Angela felt like a burden and an obligation. She consequently learned to make few demands. Angela has been waiting all her life for her Prince Charming to sweep her off her feet and dedicate himself passionately to making her happy. For years she has longed for someone to give her all the love that was missing in her childhood.

Recently Angela met a man whom she likes very much and is hoping to have a relationship with. He, however, had an intrusive and demanding mother who expected him to "be the man of the house" at a very early age, due to an absent father. Therefore, he relates to the idea of being Angela's boyfriend as though he will again be placed into the position of being overly responsible for a woman, and be burdened by her excessive needs and demands. It is a big deal for Angela to assert herself by telling this man what she needs from him. How awful, then, for him to respond as though her needs were a burden and an obligation. It's her mother all over again—her worst nightmare come true.

It's not that our needs are wrong. It's that we've been going about trying to get them met in the wrong way. Even when someone else wishes that he or she could provide what was missing for us in our childhood, unless the original wounding has been sufficiently dealt with, it's like water through a sieve. Until we are healed, it doesn't matter how much someone loves us. The heart will soon be empty again, demanding to be fed with a ferocious hunger that refuses to be abated. An endless supply of ardor can do nothing to alter the deprivation of heart when one is emotionally anchored in the past. If you are "needy," this is your indication that you are operating out of old trauma and not functioning emotionally in present time.

Is it a trauma for a child to not be cared for properly? Not to feel loved and tended to with consistency, kindness, and adoration? Absolutely. Can the ravenous ache created by such a wounding ever truly be healed? Absolutely. But you must first be willing to give to yourself that which you did not get from your caregivers. You have to give up looking for others to give it to you. They can't. You cannot get what was missing in your childhood from another person, *until you are actively engaged in doing all that you can to give it to yourself.* It's what we call "re-parenting" yourself.

It's sad to realize that what we didn't get from our initial caregivers—attention, support, protection, and love, is water under the bridge. The understanding that you can never go back and undo that loss can feel tragic. As with any loss it must be grieved, with the ultimate goal of acceptance. For it is our lack of acceptance that causes us to tenaciously cling to the fantasy that someone, somewhere will come and make it all up to us. Holding on to this fantasy creates chaos in our love lives. We aren't going into our romantic relationships as adults, but rather as children posing in adult bodies. It's like giving a four-year-old the keys to the car: You can pretty much count on a wreck. Giving up the fantasy that our Prince Charming is coming to rescue us from our misery is a true initiation, and a necessary passage to becoming an adult who is ready to give and receive love.

It's time to identify what was missing for us so that we can begin providing it for ourselves. We must turn our attention toward giving to ourselves the things that were missing in our past to heal our hearts of their inner poverty and deprivation. Then we will no longer be drawn to those who wound us in the same way as our original caregivers. Then we will begin attracting potential partners who are healthy and whole enough to

The void Papa's death left in me became a kind of cavity … My connections with men are all about trying to reach my father, about trying to fill a childhood void, about believing that such a man exists and getting angry at poor innocent men for not being that man.

—Liv Ullmann

We all come to our
relationships like
hungry beggars
saying, if not
out loud, then in
an unconscious
whisper,
"What are you
going to do for me?"
—Daphne Rose Kingma

love us the way we want to be loved. Only after we've decided that we are worth loving and have actively begun to do so ourselves can we allow true love to take root in our lives.

Ideally our fathers provide loving protection, financial well-being, and instruction on how to navigate the external world. Our mothers provide unconditional love, nurturing, maternal protection, loving touch, and supportive encouragement that helps to launch us in the world. As these qualities of parental love are consistently demonstrated over and over, we internalize them. They become our inner landscape—that which we refer to as our "inner resources." It is the lack of inner resources that have been hurting our hearts so, and causing our lives to be so confused and unsatisfying. It's not really that no one "out there" is providing these qualities for us as much as it is that *we ourselves have been negligent in providing them for ourselves*. As adults, however, we can begin re-parenting ourselves by learning to incorporate that which has eluded us for so long.

I often see women who wish to find a husband but cannot seem to keep away from the bad boys—the ones who sexually use them, and then never call, or keep coming back without giving much of themselves. I call these boys "love thieves," deliberately not referring to them as men no matter what their age, as men come into their manhood by taking on the role of protector and provider. They come to take love, and offer little in return. Usually, if I inquire into the fathering these women received, I discover that they had an absent father, or one who was neglectful or indifferent toward them. What was missing for them was being protected and cherished by a man. For the most part, women who were cherished and protected by their fathers do not wind up in these situations. Their task, therefore, is to learn to cherish and protect *themselves,* activating their own male energy within themselves, as though they were their own fathers.

Another example is a woman whose mother was not a nurturing person. She, in turn, has difficulties self-soothing when she gets upset or afraid. This may even escalate to problems with addictive behaviors, since ritualistic conduct is often a substitute for the ability to self-soothe. The task for her, therefore, is to learn to nurture and soothe herself.

Recently I was talking with a friend who, before her current happy marriage, had two that ended in divorce. "It's as though," she began, "in my first marriage, I married my father and in my second, my stepfather. This time, however, I seem to have finally married the man who's right for me, and not just a re-creation of what was hurtful in my relationships to one or both of my fathers." As we considered this, she added, "You, however, seem to have bypassed that whole process and just married the right man for you, although it did take you an awfully long time to find him" (referring to the fact that I was forty-two when I married). "Well, in my case," I replied, "my non-marriage was actually the equivalent of your first marriages. Since my biological father was absent, and my stepfather neglectful and rejecting, I just re-created the lack of love and support in my life."

It's time to cut our losses. It's time to begin giving to yourself that which you've been waiting for someone else to give to you. Those things that your parents could not or would not provide for you actually become an opportunity to practice loving-kindness and generosity toward yourself, as well as toward them. It's an affirmation of the value of our lives to decide to love in the face of all that is not love. Perhaps your parents were doing the best they could. Perhaps they were not. What matters, however, is whether or not you find your way home to your own wholeness.

> What lies behind us and what lies before us are tiny matters compared to what lies within us.
> —Ralph Waldo Emerson

PRACTICE

Take out your journal, and write for several minutes on each of the following:

Describe your father's best, most supportive, and loving qualities.

When did you feel safe with him?

How often did he keep his word to you and others?

In what ways did he let you down?

Describe your mother's best, most supportive, and loving qualities.

To what degree did you feel connected to her?

When did you trust her to be fair and kind?

When did you not?

In what ways did she let you down?

Now write a list of what was missing for you in your childhood. Use the following list as a guide to help you identify what was missing:

Nurturing (soothing you when you were disappointed, loving physical touch on a regular basis, loving-kindness for no particular reason)

Basic Hygienic Care (washing of body, doing laundry, caring for your teeth)

Basic Life Skills (managing a checkbook, paying the bills, upkeep of the car and home)

Consistency and Dependability (kept their word, you knew what you could count on, life had a predictable rhythm, were able to earn a living)

Attention (spending time with you for no particular reason, noticing and responding to your moods, listening to you, understanding things from your perspective)

Encouragement of Your Talents (recognizing them, validating them, supporting them to grow)

Protection (from the hostile behaviors of: abusive siblings, the outside world, one another)

Being Cherished (delighting in and appreciating you, taking joy in your presence in the world)

Respect of Boundaries (honoring your privacy, protecting your right to say no)

Unconditional Love (loving you without needing you to "perform" in return, loving you without imposing their unfulfilled needs onto you)

When you have written your list, write or say out loud the following regarding *each* quality that was missing for you.

I, _____ release and forgive _____ for failing to _____. I give up failing to _____ myself. I promise to do my absolute best to begin _____ myself from this day forward, and I claim _____ as mine fully and completely.

BONUS: PRACTICE IN ACTION

Take at least one action today that provides for yourself that which was missing in your childhood (for example: If you had an un-nurturing mother, take special care to prepare your favorite meal tonight; if you were never taught how to balance a checkbook, ask a friend who is good with money to schedule a date to come over and teach you how they do it; if you were always expected to say yes to the demands of others, try saying no in response to a request).

LESSON 19
Reclaiming the Disowned Self

*Loving oneself is no easy matter just because it
means loving all of oneself, including the shadow where
one is inferior and socially so unacceptable.
The care one gives this humiliating part is also the cure.*

—James Hillman

The Sufi sage Nasrudin tells the story of two men. One man asks the other why it is that he has never married. The other man sighs deeply and confesses that he had looked for years to find the perfect woman. "Is it that you never found her, then?" asks the first man. "Oh, no," the second man replies sadly, "I did find her. It seems, however, that she was looking for the perfect man."

There is a certain grandiosity in thinking that we have to find the perfect person before we will open our hearts to love. The residue of childhood's magical thinking, coupled with the idealism of adolescence, keep us seeking perfection in ourselves and others—rejecting our human frailties and flaws as inferior and unworthy of love. But seeking perfection is actually the antithesis of love. For love, by definition, happens when it is safe to be flawed in the presence of another. Think of those whom you've met in life who seem perfect to you. While we may admire or even envy these people, we rarely love them. It is never our perfections that make us lovable, but rather our shortcomings and our perfectly imperfect imperfections.

Who you are right now, with all of your flaws and foibles, is quite enough for true love to take root in your life. You may have habits and patterns that thwart the development of love, but love *never* eludes us because we are not good enough. Love actually feeds on imperfections. It eludes us only because we push it away or destroy the seeds of its expression.

Intimacy requires us to offer, and receive, authenticity and truth. Therefore, the ability to be in full possession of all aspects of ourselves— our "good" as well as our "bad," our attractive as well as our unattractive qualities, our lightness as well as our darkness—is absolutely imperative for love. The capacity to be fully oneself is a necessity when it comes to creating love.

"This thing of darkness I acknowledge mine," wrote Shakespeare. Most of us, however, were taught to reject and disown much of who and what we are as we moved through childhood. We were not supported to own the dark sides of our nature—our petty selfishness, our desire to dominate, our envy, or our passion for retaliation. We were not assisted in accepting any aspect of our anger, nor were we encouraged to express and explore much of our sexuality. And so, somewhere along the way we split off from our feelings, and fragmented whole parts of ourselves in response to the subtle, and not so subtle, messages we received. The majority of this denunciation of our authenticity even came under the guise of "good" parenting: "You're not very *pretty* when you cry, dear." "Oh, come now, son, you can't *really* be mad at your sister." "You couldn't *possibly* want to play basketball. Girls try out for cheerleading, dear, not basketball!"

We didn't just forfeit our shadow qualities, either. We also obscured and diminished our light and our genius. We gave up our talents ("My brother was the musical one, so I tried instead to be the smart one"); our vibrant enthusiasm ("My mother was so depressed, I didn't want to make her feel bad by being too happy"); our brilliance ("My teacher thought I was just trying to get attention, so I stopped raising my hand in class"); and our passion ("It wasn't cool to be in the drama club, so I quit"). For a myriad of reasons, we systematically shut down whole parts of ourselves in order to convince ourselves, and others, that we were lovable and that we belonged.

Penny, a much-loved actress in her late twenties, complains of a constant anxiety that others won't like her. Although she is exceptionally beautiful and talented and has a large circle of dedicated friends, Penny often diminishes herself by talking about how neurotic she is, how stupid she can be, or how she drives everyone nuts. After several therapy sessions, Penny shared with me that her adolescence was marked by a constant

> That I feed the hungry, forgive an insult, and love my enemy—these are great virtues. But what if I should discover that the poorest of beggars and most impudent of offenders are all within me, and that I stand in need of all the alms of my own kindness; that I myself am the enemy who must be loved— what then?
>
> —Carl G. Jung

rejection by the other girls in her class. Her mother explained to her that the girls were envious of her. In response, Penny began a practice of diminishing herself in the hope that the other girls would stop feeling so threatened by her, and accept her into their group. It worked. Little by little, the girls accepted Penny. However, what worked then was not working now. Not only was Penny still anxious that others would not like her, regardless of much evidence to the contrary (which was really based on the fact that she was creating all these "friendships" built on a somewhat false persona of who she was), but she was also feeling bad about herself. Her constant chatter of self-diminishment was taking its toll. Penny had to take the risk of giving it up. She had to own her beauty and her exceptional talents. She had to stand in the center of what it was to have all of that talent, all that charisma, all that beauty, and all that personal power. It was a lot to own.

I thought it amusing that one of Penny's complaints was that she wasn't meeting any "powerful" men in her life. I had to remind her that she was the one who was disowning *her* power. It wasn't that there were "no powerful men out there." It was that she was attracting men who were mirroring back to her her own skewed relationship to power. I suggested that perhaps when she righted her own relationship to power, she would begin meeting others who had done the same. I recently ran into Penny. She shared with me that soon after making the decision to allow herself to be *all* that she is, she met a handsome, talented, and powerful man. A year into their relationship they are deeply in love and seriously considering marriage.

When we disown qualities that we have within us, we are often attracted to people who are expressing those very same qualities. Gerry kept dating musician-songwriters until she finally admitted her secret, lifelong dream of being one herself. She then gave herself permission to start playing the piano again, after many years of ignoring her early musical training. Kathy was constantly drawn to men who made a lot of money until she finally figured out that it was the money, and not the men, that she wanted. She promptly took the risk of changing her career so she had the capacity to earn more money herself. Sometimes it's not so much that we want that person, as much as we want to *be* that person.

During a recent workshop, Zan, a single woman in her early thirties, admitted to deep feelings of hostility that she secretly harbored toward men. "I'm so angry at my father for not being there for me when I was growing up. I've been completely frustrated with every guy I've been with because they all end up being just as unavailable and dismissive as my dad was." In response to this constant rejection, Zan learned to be tough and self-reliant. She became protective of herself in a way that caused others to say she had a lot of "male energy."

Zan shared that she knew she had to "forgive men," and to allow herself to soften into a more feminine, receptive way of being, in order to attract in an available, good man. During a meditation, she was surprised to receive guidance that, in addition to embracing her feminine side, she also had to embrace her "masculine side." Rather than feel ashamed by how "male" she is, she saw that she needed to love and accept this aspect of herself—even "thanking it" for helping her cope with all of the disappointment she has endured. She needed to appreciate what a great "father" she was to herself. It was not until Zan was able to do this, that her feelings of hostility toward men disappeared. Several months later Zan called to tell me that she was deeply in love and planning on being married to a kind and loving man.

Zan shared her observation that, as a culture, we value male energy, yet punish women for having too much of it. I added that we also value feminine energy (although not quite as much), yet punish men for having too much of it. And so the women reject their masculine energy, and the men reject their feminine energy. We are polarized in our inability to value and appreciate all parts of ourselves.

Our sense of belonging is one of our most primal needs. However, in order to remain connected to others—a part of a particular tribe, most of us have disowned entire portions of who and what we are—we desperately need to retrieve these abandoned parts of ourselves, and many of us need to do this before our ideal partners can come to us. These aspects of ourselves represent our gifts to others, our talents, and our unique flair for genius. They are the very qualities that will help our beloved recognize us when he meets us, for only when we are fully ourselves, will he see what we have to offer in a relationship. In the Gnostic Gospel of Thomas, Jesus said:

> Everyone carries a shadow, and the less it is embodied in the individual's conscious life, the blacker and denser it is. At all counts, it forms an unconscious snag, thwarting our most well-meant intentions.
> —Carl G. Jung

If you bring forth what is within you, what you bring forth will save you. If you do not bring forth what is within you, what you do not bring forth will destroy you.

PRACTICE

Take out your art supplies.

Draw a simple picture or representation of yourself in the center of a large piece of paper. It need not actually look like you. Allow yourself to be as a child, drawing more for fun than the need to do it "right."

One by one add the following qualities:

My power

My beauty

My talent

My greatness

My ugliness

My passion

My light

My sexuality

My anger

My love

When you are finished, take out your journal and answer the following questions:

What have I been hiding completely about myself?

Another problem with the idea of self-improvement is that it implies there is something wrong with who we are. Everyone wants to be someone else, but getting to know and love yourself means accepting who you are, complete with your inadequacies and irrationalities.

—Thomas Moore

If you admire greatness in another human being, it is your own greatness you are seeing.

—Debbie Ford

What have I been reluctant to express fully?

What parts of myself do I own and am actively expressing fully?

What parts of myself do I _want_ to own and express more fully?

What parts of myself do I want to continue to hide and why?

We have to be careful
that in throwing out
the devil, we don't
throw out the best
part of ourselves.
—Friedrich Nietzsche

BONUS: PRACTICE IN ACTION

Do at least one thing today that represents a willingness to risk expressing more of your authentic self (e.g., share an opinion when you normally would keep quiet; purchase a risqué article of clothing that expresses a previously hidden aspect of yourself; sign up for dance lessons to recapture a childhood fantasy, etc.).

LESSON 20
Individuation and the Ties That Bind

> Take your life in your own hands and what happens?
> A terrible thing: no one to blame.
>
> —Erica Jong

For the entire six months that Taryn has been dating Tom, she has complained about his flirtatiousness with other women. She's insecure enough, she says, without having to watch her back all the time. Sighing deeply, she shakes her head sadly, noticing that she's acting just like her mother did when her father was cheating on her. "I feel like she's inside me. I'm thinking her thoughts, feeling her feelings, and taking her actions. It's like I breathed her in or something."

It's uncanny how, without even trying, it seems that we are experts on creating situations and dynamics that all too well replicate the incompletions and struggles of our parents' lives. It's almost as though we are compelled to repeat the mistakes and poor choices they made. Perhaps we clandestinely believe that the only way to continue to be close to our parents is to mirror their misery. Perhaps we are trying to work through what we believe they could not, or would not, work through themselves. Or perhaps we are simply partaking in rituals that reinforce our sense of belonging to the tribe that we were born to. For a variety of reasons, we often create relationships that demonstrate limitations and disturbances similar to the ones our parents had. Our role models for love, our parents, became the ones we emulated no matter how screwy or unfulfilling their version of love was.

Megan's mother was mad at her husband's family from the very beginning of their marriage. They excluded her, insulted her, gossiped about her, and generally made their disdain of her known from the start. Her mother's main complaint, however, was not about how awful they were.

Rather, her biggest hurt was that her husband, Megan's father, never stood up to them on her behalf. Megan grew up with her mother's covert disdain and anger toward her father just below the surface at all times.

Megan and her mother had a lot to talk about, then, when Megan grew up and married a man with a family who hated Megan just about as much as Megan's mother's in-laws hated her. The two of them spent hours on the phone comforting each other by talking negatively about their respective in-laws, and even more about the men, their husbands, who were letting them down. Megan took a kind of covert pride in being able to bring such comfort to her mother, who was now vindicated in her disdain toward men. Although her mother would occasionally sigh, suggesting that perhaps Megan shouldn't be so much like her, she would soon begin colluding with her daughter again about how awful it was that they were treated so poorly.

"Nothing has a stronger influence psychologically on . . . their children than the unlived life of the parents," said analyst Carl G. Jung. The inability of Megan's mother to solve her problems with her in-laws successfully had a profound influence upon Megan and the decisions she made in her life. The incompletions of our parents' lives can place a huge burden upon our own, as we often feel bound to them through a kind of stealthy baton that has been handed to us. We haul around the disappointments, rejections, and unfulfilled goals of their lives like a ball and chain. The risks they never took, the communications they never delivered, the resentments they never forgave can weigh heavily upon our lives. As a result, our own dreams and goals become compromised as we attempt to fulfill tasks that were never ours to begin with.

Throughout history custom has dictated that various rituals be performed at puberty signifying the passage from childhood to adulthood. These rites of passage symbolically and publicly released the ties that one had to their parents. And while certain rituals are still in use today (bar mitzvahs, bas mitzvahs, high school graduation ceremonies, etc.), for the most part they lack the ability to truly initiate and launch a child into adulthood.

Adolescence, as we know it, is a fairly recent social construct. Before now (and in some remote parts of our world today), young people were

> All happy families resemble one another, but each unhappy family is unhappy in its own way.
> —Leo Tolstoy

In life, "changing" is
like being in a ship
on the sea: you must
build a new boat
with material from
the old one you're
traveling in; you can't
go on shore to
destroy the old one
first and then build a
new one—
but you have
to reconstruct
while sailing.
—Otto Neurath

often encouraged to begin their adult lives by joining the workforce, marrying and bearing children by the time they were thirteen or fourteen years old. By extending childhood to the age of eighteen (and beyond), we have created a sort of suspension of time between puberty and early adulthood. While this suspension is appropriate to the society that we live in, we have, for the most part, abandoned the rituals that mark the transition from being a dependent person, to being an independent one. We have no customs that celebrate the shift from being one who is taken care of, to being one who takes care of others; from being one whose identity is defined by their parents, to being someone who is defined solely by their own character, and standing upon their own merit and accomplishments.

These ceremonial passages that, for thousands of years, were performed at puberty served to feed power to those entering adulthood. In their absence, adolescence became a time of rebellion and revolt for many of us. Our natural instinct to separate and forge our way in the world occurred as a sort of mutiny against our elders. However, when separation occurs as an act of rebellion, rather than as a supported act of initiation, we may have trouble completing this passage successfully. Our attempts at forming new families (i.e., finding "The One" and entering into a committed union) are consequently handicapped by the incompletions we have with our parents and/or our parent substitutes.

Alan, a professional man in his mid-thirties, says he is actively looking for a woman to marry and raise a family with. Yet, he admits, he seems to be having a difficult time surrendering himself to a relationship. Alan describes his mother as "overbearing, demanding, and intrusive." Since his father was working much of the time as he was growing up, his mother relied heavily upon Alan, her only child, for company and companionship. She made it difficult for him to participate in anything outside of their home, or in any activities where she could not also be involved. Consequently when Alan left for college he felt both relieved to be free of the burden of her constant presence, yet terribly guilty for "abandoning" her. When his mother became depressed, it only further confirmed his assessment that he was letting her down by leaving home.

Alan gets lonely sometimes, being single. So he goes onto an Internet dating site and begins looking for a "nice woman" who is ready to settle down. But as soon as any relationship progresses beyond the initial dating period, Alan begins experiencing a panicky feeling in his stomach. In response, he vacillates between being overly attentive toward, and completely neglectful of, the woman he is dating, in an attempt to get past this feeling. She, in response to this lack of stability, begins making requests of him. She wants him to stop giving her mixed messages. She wants him to declare his feelings for her, and choose whether or not he wants to be with her. Alan reacts to *these* requests as though they are, again, his mother's unreasonable demands. He freezes up emotionally and finds himself thinking up various ways to escape the situation. He ends up feeling justified and relieved when he finally breaks off the relationship.

There are two pitfalls for those of us who do not successfully individuate from the families of our childhood. The first is that we may become fixated in a rebellious adolescent stance, unable to surrender ourselves fully to forming a new family. The second is that we may continue to be far too dependent upon one or both of our parents, which then makes it difficult for us to risk formulating our own identity fully.

David's parents, Holocaust survivors, migrated to the United States years ago, penniless and without any surviving family members to assist them. Together the couple built a real-estate empire worth millions of dollars, which David, their only son, manages for them. In appreciation of his efforts, his parents gave David a portion of their property each year until he himself was a wealthy man at age thirty. When David was ready to marry, he chose a woman his mother did not approve of. His mother tried desperately to convince him to sign a prenuptial agreement that she and David's father had prepared. It stated that his new bride would not own anything that David owned, although they would be husband and wife. Because David's fiancée was not marrying him for his money, she agreed to sign it. However, something changed in their relationship from that day forward. At first glance, it seemed as though it was the agreement that came between them. However, upon further reflection, we discovered that it was that David had placed his mother's needs and desires before those of his fiancée. He had superseded his own feeling that there was no need for a prenup, to allow himself to placate his mother's belief

You become mature when you become the authority in your own life.
—Joseph Campbell

Children begin by
loving their parents;
after a time they
judge them; rarely,
if ever, do they
forgive them.
—Oscar Wilde

that there was. David and his bride began engaging in a power struggle, which had to do with David's attachment to satisfying his mother's demands at all cost. David justified his need to please his mother by saying over and over again how horrible her life had been when she was a young girl. Since she had so tragically lost her other family members, he simply could not and would not also "leave" her.

For those who cut off communication (e.g., severing all connection, running away, or moving thousands of miles to avoid contact) as a substitute to authentic individuation, the ties to the original family can become even *more* binding. Betsy, who was in her early fifties, moved across the country when she was thirty-five to get away from her raging, alcoholic mother. She dutifully visits her mother once a year with very little contact in between visits. Yet Betsy is tormented by a continual internal diatribe of self-criticism that mimics her mother's voice. The voice tells her she's getting too fat, that she's going to run out of money, that she should be married by now, that she's going to end up homeless and alone, and on and on. When she is with her mother, Betsy tries desperately to become invisible, making as few waves as possible to avoid her criticism and her wrath. Yet here she is, encountering her internalized critical and raging mother day after day after day, in spite of her best efforts to rid herself of her mother's presence.

The ties we have to our parents and/or parent substitutes ideally serve as a platform from which to launch our lives. However, there are many ways that this launching can be sabotaged, leaving us crippled, as though trying to fly a plane with only one wing, or suffering under the weight of additional, burdensome cargo. When this happens, it is as though we are hauling around parts of our parents' psyches that desperately need to be released, before we are able to take on any new passengers, such as a spouse and/or children.

As long as we continue to define ourselves in reaction to our parents' needs and expectations, then our judgment will be colored. Too many of us had first or second marriages that were really an attempt to fulfill the fantasies of one or both of our parents. These were the expected or the hoped-for unions, the ones that validated the sacrifices our parents made on our behalf. But any conscious path will quickly shine a light on the flaws of such ill-advised unions. Often, when one or both partners begin to grow, such marriages will be revealed as far too superficial to last.

Even those of us with the best of parenting situations need to undergo a transformation from child to adult in relationship to our original families in order to prepare ourselves for love. Those who had multiple parenting situations (adoptive parents, foster parents, stepparents, etc.), will need to emancipate themselves from their proxy parents in addition to their birth parents. Those who are not yet married, particularly single women, often have a more difficult time experiencing this transformation as, traditionally, marriage is the one ritual that we all agree upon as the final emancipation from childhood. This is a tremendous disadvantage for members of the gay community, as same-sex unions are often denied this important, socially sanctified ritual of becoming an adult.

In the absence of appropriate rituals, therefore, we create our own. Our rite of passage includes honoring our connective roots while embracing our autonomy, and appreciating our past as the induction to our present. It includes releasing burdens that no longer belong to us, and letting go of inappropriate goals that we no longer need to fulfill. It includes surrendering the beliefs of imperfect people who made more mistakes than they cared to admit, and purging ourselves of relational dynamics that serve only to perpetuate the worst in ourselves and others.

Bhagwan Shree Rajneesh once said, "Don't try to force anything. Let life be a deep let-go. See God opening millions of flowers every day without forcing the buds." Individuation is such a letting go, such a shedding of our former childhood selves, in the spirit of celebration of the mature, autonomous, and ever-developing selves we are becoming.

> To find yourself, think for yourself.
>
> —Socrates

PRACTICE

Take out your journal. Answer the following questions for each of your parents and/or substitute parents (i.e., if you were adopted by a couple, that means your biological mother, your biological father, your adoptive mother, and your adoptive father; if your parents were divorced and one parent remarried while you were still a dependent child, that means your mother, your father and, your stepparent, etc.). Answer each of the following eight questions before proceeding to the next parent, using your imagination when necessary.

Who has _____ not fully forgiven and for what?

What have I not forgiven _____ for?

What did _____ always want that he/she did not get?

What did _____ believe was wrong about his or her life that could not be changed?

In what ways, if any, did _____ overtly or covertly pressure me to right what he/she thought was wrong about his or her own life?

What was romantic love like for _____?

In what ways, if any, have I been carrying on the burden of _____'s unfinished business?

What, if anything, could I now give up that did not belong to me in the first place?

BONUS: PRACTICE IN ACTION

It is not so much that we need to sever the ties we have to our parents, as it is that we need to re-create them from a more adult place.

Some time today, find a quiet half hour where you can do the following meditative ritual in private. Make sure that you have with you the journal entry that you worked on this morning.

The following is an adaptation from Phyllis Krystal's book *Cutting the Ties That Bind*. Read the meditation once or twice through and then do it to the best of your ability from memory. If necessary, you may open your eyes during the meditation to refer to the journal pages that you wrote this morning. You may wish to light a candle as a way to create a sacred space before going into meditation.

Thoroughly relax your body and focus solely on your breath, making sure that you breathe fully and deeply into your belly for several minutes before proceeding. One at a time, invite each of your parents to come sit before you in your meditation. Starting at your feet, begin weaving a vibrant blue light that runs in the shape of a figure eight between the two of you, placing each of you inside one of the loops. Once you have a sense of the blue light moving between you as a figure eight, expand it upward so that it surrounds your entire body from your feet to the top of your head. Notice that this light is always in motion, connecting you yet allowing each of you to sit in your own separate space.

Ask each parent as he/she sits before you:

1. to forgive you for any weaknesses and/or failures they believe you had;

2. to forgive you for your inability to fix that which they believe(d) broken about their own lives; and

3. to release you from any further obligations and/or expectations they have been holding that you are not 100 percent aligned with.

Tell each parent that you:

1. forgive them for any weaknesses and/or failures you believe he or she displayed as a parent;

2. forgive them for their inability to fix that which you believe(d) was broken about your life; and

3. release them from any further obligation and/or expectations you have been holding.

Some of you may find one of your parents trying to enter into your own separate loop, particularly if that person has a history of being intrusive. Do not allow that to happen. Instead, gently move them back into their own separate space and reclaim your space as your own. For still others of you, a parent might have been so toxic and/or dangerous, that it is better to imagine a picture of the person or a symbol of some kind rather than the actual person.

If, during the meditation, you discover you've been carrying something that you wish to let go of but don't necessarily want to return to your parent(s) (e.g., a depression, an errant belief, or an unresolved rage), you may offer it up to God with a prayer for release and freedom for yourself and your family.

When you are finished, thank them each for coming and release them, with a blessing, to go their separate ways.

LESSON 21
Release Ceremony

Maturity is a process of subtraction, not addition.

—M. Chadbourne

One of the pitfalls of being such a therapeutically savvy culture is that, often we can see where our problems come from, but then use that knowledge as an excuse to avoid moving forward in life; e.g. "I don't do commitment well, because my father left when I was four." While self-awareness is a vital facet of transformation, insight alone does not guarantee change. How many people do you know who appear to fully understand the nature of their problems, without seeming to be able to *do* anything to alter them? The essence of any true transformation lies in the letting go.

There is a time for everything, and not all of our challenges are meant to disappear just because we want them to, or think that they should. Some problems must simply be lived with, and some simply lived through. Many, however, have outstayed their welcome and are long overdue for release. We continue to entertain them, however, because we've discovered that some of our troubles actually have their advantages. In spite of our protestations to the contrary, we perpetuate many of our dramas because we've found that they leverage sympathy, help us avoid taking responsibility for our lives, and give us viable reasons for avoiding risk in life without much chance of being challenged. And so, we've grown attached to the very things we complain about the most. So attached, in fact, that we've even come to identify with them. We have been buried under the mountain of false beliefs, arduous expectations, and unresolved resentments that we've been carting around. Rather than see ourselves as innately capable of giving and receiving love, we have been frustrated by all sorts of burdensome attachments that have thwarted the expression of

Spiritual life is about surrender, not understanding. Whenever that part of you that wants to figure it out, or know why, or know what for kicks in, kick it out.
—Swami Chetanananda

love in our lives. In order to experience love, therefore, we will need to release all that is not love from our lives, so that the possibility of deep relatedness, our natural birthright, can begin to manifest itself fluidly and effortlessly in our lives.

"How important is it to you to find love?" I asked the group of women who had gathered together for a workshop. "Very important!" came their collective reply, as one after another they each chimed in and nodded their heads in agreement. "What, then, would you be willing to give up in order to have it?" I asked, slowly scanning the faces in the room. "Would you be willing to give up your rigid criteria of what 'The One' is supposed to look like? How about your need to be right? Could you let go of your pessimistic attitudes and beliefs about men? Because letting go absolutely of whatever it is that is standing between you and love is what is necessary to create an opening for love."

We have such noble ideas of what we would do to find love. Many of us would profess to lose it all—give up our social status and our precious possessions, forsake our family and friends, and move halfway around the world, if need be. Yet, ask us to give up our defenses, our habitual thought patterns, or our way of perceiving ourselves and others and suddenly we are full of excuses and all sorts of reasons why we must stay the same.

The truth is, we simply cannot continue to invest our energies in our neuroses, our dramas, our resentments, and our fears and think that we are a space for love. We aren't. Our cup is either full or it's empty. You can't have water and air in the same space at the same time. In order for there to be an opening for love, we must first surrender those things that are blocking it in our lives. And it is here that we are confronted with our profound attachment to those very things that we whine about the most.

We are standing at the crossroads, and we must make a choice. We can either hold on to the old ways, or we can jump off the cliff by letting go of that which is familiar. We are required to surrender those things within ourselves that do not resemble love—not so that we can get something in return, but simply because it is the better choice. And because it is the better choice, it leads to a better life, not necessarily an easier one or one that will deliver what we want on demand.

We have to give up those things that frustrate love *before* we have any evidence that taking that action will produce the results that we are after. We can't give something up with an attachment to a particular outcome. The Universe just won't bargain with us on those terms. Rather, our surrender must be absolute and unconditional: I must give up a relationship that doesn't serve me any more, even though I risk being alone for the rest of my life. I must give up the comfort of a destructive addiction even though I have no idea, at this point, how I'm going to manage the feelings that doing so might unleash. I must let go of manipulating others, even though I risk losing the only leverage I believe I have to get what I want. I must give up punishing myself, even though my circumstances have not changed, and may never do so.

Some people tell me that they would rather die than continue living without love in their lives. Yet trying to get them to shake up their routine, forgive someone who has clearly wronged them, or let go of old, outdated ideas about who they are and what is possible in their lives and . . . it's . . . like . . . pulling . . . teeth . . . !

Having the willingness to let go absolutely is *the one crucial key* to transforming our lives. Hence the stereotype of "bottoming out" before one is willing to change, which implies that most of us are not willing to let go of our way of doing things until we've completely bankrupted ourselves. Ask yourself, am I so stubborn that I must lose everything, and everybody who comes into my life, before I become willing to change? Am I so set in my ways that I would rather let loveless days, turn into loveless weeks, turn into loveless months, turn into loveless *years,* before I become flexible enough to try something new?

You must challenge yourself by asking, how willing am I to be inconvenienced? To be uncomfortable? To be wrong? How willing am I to surrender control? To follow directions? To take real risks where I might actually fail at something? Wherever you've answered with a resounding negative, or even hesitated just the slightest bit, is probably the exact place that you will need to go in order to expand your opportunities for love.

When we talk about "letting go" of our challenges, we are not talking about "getting rid" of them. Trying to get rid of a problem is like the compulsive overeater who goes on a crash diet rather than deal with the underlying grief and fear that is driving the addiction. That approach,

Growth is a detox process, as our weakest, darkest places are sucked up to the surface in order to be released . . . often, it is not a change in partners but rather a change in perception that delivers us to the love we seek.
—Marianne Williamson

however, is us trying to deal with the problem at the level of symptom, rather than at the level of cause. We must, instead, root out our false beliefs, and the underlying fears that motivate our behaviors. So while it's great to resolve that you are going to "give up drinking," for example, I encourage you to go deeper by adding, "I'm giving up destroying myself in order to try to control the feelings that I've been afraid to feel. I am now willing to feel what I feel and trust that I will be OK." Rather than stating, "I'm finally going to break it off with Gary," try going deeper by adding, "I'm giving up being run by fear that if I let go of Gary, I'll forever be alone and lonely. I'm willing to trust that I will find a better, more satisfying relationship, and that *even if I don't, I will be OK* as long as I am living with integrity."

If you feel desperate for the fulfillment of love, remember that letting go of everything in its way is the appropriate way to channel desperation. Be desperate enough to release all that is fear-based, all that is limiting, all that is predictable, and all that is "safe." Be desperate enough to embrace the courage it requires to surrender completely, remembering that growth is not so much a process of accumulation, as it is a process of release.

PRACTICE

The work you have done in the past two weeks culminates today, as we prepare ourselves for a release ritual designed to help you let go of all that has been blocking love in your life. This morning, we are going to do some preparation work for the ritual that you are invited to do later today. You will need your journal, extra paper, a pen, and a highlighter.

Go back through your journal and review your writings. Highlight those things that you see as standing between you and your availability to love. Some of these things you will feel completely ready to release today. Others, you will see as needing more work and exploration on your part as they are perhaps more pervasive and deeply rooted. Place a star (★) next to those things you feel ready to completely surrender today, and a heart (♥) next to those things you believe you need to "work on." Do this now.

Next, take some extra paper (not journal paper, as you will need to cut it up later in the day for the actual ritual). At the top of the pieces of paper, write on the lefthand side, "I Release:" and, on the righthand side, "I Embrace:"

Underneath the "I Release" heading, write a list of those things you are willing to completely surrender today (resentment toward a former lover, your mother's expectation that you be married with children by a certain age, your belief that nothing ever works out for you, etc.). These are the things that you placed a ★ next to. Make this list now.

Next, continue creating your list by including those things that you placed a ♥ next to. This part of the list represents those things that you are going to actively begin to explore further, perhaps with the assistance of a therapist or a trusted spiritual adviser (patterns of push-pull dynamics in all of your intimate relationships, any self-destructive behaviors, severe and chronic outbursts of temper, etc.).

If you have an altar, or a space in your home that is dedicated to sacred activities, put your list in this place, in preparation for doing your ritual later today. Carve out some uninterrupted time, no less than a half hour, for the ritual.

> What has been full must empty; what has increased must decrease. This is the way of Heaven and Earth. To surrender is to display courage and wisdom.
> —Ralph Blum

BONUS: PRACTICE IN ACTION

NOTE: If you are doing the course with others, you may wish to do the following ritual together. If you are doing the course alone, you may wish to invite a trusted friend to be with you to serve as your witness. You will need your journal, the list you wrote, a pencil or pen, scissors, a lighter or matches, and a place to safely burn papers (metal bowl, bathtub, large sink, burning pit at a beach, etc.).

There are many, many ways to perform a release ritual. If, for some reason, the following ritual is not appropriate for you (you are uncomfortable with fire, or you have no place to safely set a fire, etc.), please feel free to modify this ritual to suit your particular circumstances. For example, you can rip up the papers and throw them in the garbage, or put the papers, one by one on the ground, stomping on them, kicking them around, while verbally claiming your freedom. Feel free to be creative. There are about as many ways to perform a ritual as there are people on the planet.

RITUAL

Create a sacred atmosphere appropriate to performing a ritual. (Light a candle, burn incense, or put on background music that you love.)

Take out the list of things you want to release. Now, on the right side of the paper, underneath the heading "I Embrace:" write down what you would need to embrace to let each thing go. Write the "counter-thoughts" opposite the things you want to release.

Example:

I RELEASE:	I EMBRACE:
Blaming my parents for my problems	Forgiveness for both of my parents
Sexual shame	Celebrating the beauty of my sexuality
A desire for revenge toward my ex	Full responsibility for my part in what happened between us that caused our breakup and appreciation for all I learned

Before moving into the next part of the ritual, take out your journal and write down the things you are embracing, so that you document your healing.

Now, using your scissors, cut the list across the page so that there is only one issue (with an "I Release:" and an "I Embrace:") on each piece of paper. Bring your papers to a place where it is safe to burn them. Speak each thing that you are letting go of and each thing that you are embracing out loud and then burn it (e.g., "I release the sorrow of my mother's life and I embrace the freedom to be happy myself.").

For those things that you placed a ♥ next to that you are going to explore further, you can ask for the willingness to help you to overcome these difficulties (e.g., "I ask for the willingness to fully release my fear of intimacy and to embrace the courage I would need to risk being vulnerable with others.").

When you are finished, take out your journal again. Write a list of actions that you are going to take, and by when, to support what you've just released (e.g., I'm going to write a letter to my mom letting her know that I've forgiven her by Sunday; I'm going to give myself a beautiful home by going out and purchasing a bedroom set for myself this weekend; I'm going to work on releasing compulsive overeating by going to the Overeaters Anonymous meeting near my house next Tuesday night, etc.).

1. What did you notice, if anything, between the care you received as a young child and your ability (or inability) to trust others now?

2. What beliefs have you been holding on to about yourself and the world? In what ways and to what extent have these beliefs affected your love life?

3. What was missing in your childhood, and how are you, or are you not, engaged in giving that to yourself now?

4. What about yourself have you been hiding and why? What, if anything, did you do this week to begin expressing these disowned parts of self?

5. Share about your ability to release your parents or parent substitutes. Who were you able to forgive and who were you not? Who could forgive you and who could not?

6. Share your experience of doing the Release Ceremony, or actually plan a ceremony that you can all do together.

SETTING YOUR COURSE

*Life is a creation, not a discovery. You do not live each day
to discover what it holds for you, but to create it.*

—Neale Donald Walsch, *Conversations with God, Book 1*

Congratulations. Having released those things that have thwarted the realization of love in your life, we are now at the place where we can begin creating the very real possibility of love fulfilled.

This week:

* We begin by grounding ourselves in a vision of love abundantly realized

* We then create a strong and powerful intention to manifest love in our lives

* We clarify what we are seeking in a partner by becoming clear about our sense of purpose in life

* We learn about utilizing our intuition, enabling us to make good and wise decisions when it comes to creating healthy relationships

* We take a good look at how, when it comes to preparing ourselves for love, establishing personal integrity is one of the most essential things we can do

LESSON 22
Visioning

The vision process is always self-examination. It's never, "God,
I want this. Make this happen." It's always, "What do I have to
become to live the vision, to manifest it, to reveal it?" The visioning
process, then, is a process of transformation of the individual.

—Reverend Michael Beckwith

Recently I was flipping through some old journals when I came across an
entry dated February 22, 1999. It read:

Good Morning God:
What a golden morning—waking up at 5 A.M. to the rushing wind.
Thank you, dear God, for weather in L.A. This morning I am going to
write down my dreams and visions, to clarify and support them. My
dream is to be a writer of significance—to write that which exalts and
edifies the human spirit. I see a book . . . out in bookstores around the
country . . . having a life of its own. Also, by my birthday, I see a beautiful
engagement ring on my finger. It is reflecting a deep, rooted love between
my husband-to-be and myself. He is my perfect mate. I like myself when I
am with him. I feel supported and nurtured by our relationship. He is
open to having children. I feel protected by him—loved, respected, held
up—I love and am loved deeply and completely. I see this. I also see being
pregnant with my husband's baby. We are thrilled. My breasts and belly
are swollen. I waddle into the kitchen. He kisses my bare belly in bed. We
are happy to bring this baby into the world. Thank You, God—Thank
You, God—Thank You, God.

When I read this I did a double take. I checked out the date at least three times before I finally believed that I'd written it a full six weeks before I met Mark for that magical third time. It sounded so much like my real life, that I was stunned. At the time I wrote it I had no prospects for a husband, I was forty-one and childless, and I'd never had a book deal or even come close to getting one. That's the power of standing inside a vision.

Years ago Shakti Gawain, author of *Creative Visualization*, introduced many of us to visualization, a process that uses the power of imagination to help us manifest what we want in our lives. When we visualize, we create a mental picture of what it is that we want and then allow our hearts to feel the feelings that would accompany the having of it. It is both a mental and an emotional process. There is a slight variation to this process, however, called "visioning," and it is this that I wish to talk about today.

Christian mystic Florence Scovel Shinn distinguished between the two in her book *The Game of Life*, published in 1925. She wrote, "Visualizing is a mental process governed by the reasoning or conscious mind; visioning is a spiritual process, governed by intuition, or the superconscious mind." Whereas visualization can be limited by those things that can block one's ability to see where it is that you'd ideally like to go, such as low self-esteem or a lack of role modeling, visioning is a process that can more easily bypass our "issues," and go straight to a whole new set of possibilities for our lives. For the impressions and inspirations we receive when we engage in the visioning process usually live outside and beyond how we currently think of ourselves.

The writing I was doing that February morning was to reinforce and support a vision I'd had of myself previously while sitting in a meditation. Since, for many years, I'd thought of myself as a struggling artist (i.e., no money, hip, creative, and counter-culture) who was basically alone in life (i.e., single and strong enough to be just fine without a man, thank you very much), I was really stretching. The scenarios I was imagining had little to do with what my life looked like, or what was even logical, given my current circumstances. It wasn't so much that I was trying to wrestle God into giving me some fantasy of what I thought I wanted, as it was

> Hope is a waking dream.
> —Aristotle

that I was seeking to alter my consciousness to receive the possibilities that I'd glimpsed previously. Emotionally, I was trying this "possible" life on for size.

In order to manifest this vision, I realized that I was going to have to change who I knew myself to be. By repetitious writing, I was trying to break it to myself gently. Just to clue you in on what a major shift being successful and loved was for me, I'll tell you that the first time that Mark and I tried to go shopping for an engagement ring together, I stood outside the store crying. I absolutely could not tolerate going into that store. I had been a poor artist and a struggling student for so many years that I simply couldn't conceive of the fact that this man was going to plop down several thousand dollars on a ring for me. It was just more than I could bear. We did not go into the store that day and, in fact, it took us over four months to finally get the ring. (Lest you pity me too much, I'll admit that I have absolutely no problem spending my husband's money or, for that matter, my own at all anymore.)

Holding a vision always requires us to adjust ourselves in some way to accommodate that vision. It's a discipline to practice living our lives inside of a vision. We are used to defining who we are according to our past experiences and by what is happening to us right now. Yet when you aren't living your life out of a clear and powerful vision, you'll be driven. And when you're driven, you're grounded in a belief that you'll never have whatever it is you want. To begin relating to our lives according to the future that we are creating is something new entirely and takes some getting used to. When we are able to do it, however, we find that the need for suffering in our lives is greatly diminished. There's a saying that I frequently quote, although I have no idea who said it first, "Pain pushes until vision pulls." Once we master living inside of a vision, we are no longer confined to suffering as our main vehicle for personal growth. Rather than needing pain to push us, we grow because we are inspired by a possibility—a possibility of who we could become if only we'd release this block and embrace that quality. It's an ongoing process that we enthusiastically engage in because we see our own potential and believe that attaining it is possible.

Writing this book has recently called me to transform myself again. Not long ago, I was suffering from a terribly debilitating shyness that often prevented me from offering an opinion. On a recent New Year's Eve, sitting with a group of friends, we went around the circle and said what it was that we were letting go of. Although I didn't yet have a literary agent, let alone a book deal, the vision of this book compelled me to say that I was giving up shyness. I knew that I could no longer afford to withhold my voice if I was going to fulfill the vision I had. For the next few months, every time I went to speak up, I'd have to acknowledge to myself that shyness was present and let it go. These days shyness is much less of an issue for me. As a matter of fact, I frequently talk too much and have the opposite problem of thinking too highly of my opinions. Now, I'm challenged to give up arrogance. However, because I'm committed to living a life of deep relatedness and service to others, I'm willing to do whatever I need to in order to live consistent with that vision.

When you start living your life from your vision, you begin behaving in ways that might be foreign to you. That is because we usually make choices about who we are and how we behave from our past. In other words, we see who we are as a combination of our prior experiences. And because we do this, we tend to repeat past behaviors in the present because that is how we define who we are. Consider for a moment the possibility that it is our *future,* and not our past, that determines the kinds of choices that we make. A person who is committed to creating a loving, spiritual partnership in the near future behaves differently from a person who is still dealing with a series of failed relationships and identifies him or herself as being a person who has difficulty in intimate relationships.

Through the process of visioning, we are placed in the seemingly paradoxical position of letting go of our preconceived notions of what "The One" looks like while, at the same time, cultivating a sense of what it feels like to have him or her in our lives. But this cultivation is not so much about fanning out the specifics of what he or she will look like. It is more about glimpsing a possibility for your life and emotionally opening your heart to receive it. It is about being engaged in releasing that which is inconsistent with the fulfillment of the vision and embracing who we will need to be in order to manifest it.

Ultimately, we don't really have a vision as much as a vision has us. There is a vision that is just outside our conscious awareness—we need

> The only successful manifestation is one which brings about a change or growth in consciousness; that is, it has manifested God, or revealed him more fully, as well as having manifested a form.
>
> —David Spangler

only listen long enough to allow it to reveal itself. Once we glimpse the possibility, we simply say yes. Rather than forcing our will upon the Universe, we yield ourselves and become open and available to that which is birthing itself through us. We surrender completely and allow the vision to take us over.

PRACTICE

We are going to do a visioning this morning. Find a quiet and comfortable place where you will not be interrupted. Make sure that your journal and a pen are nearby. I invite you to read through the instructions once or twice and then do them from memory as best you can. You can peek if you need to.

Close your eyes and take a few deep, relaxing breaths meant to center and focus you. When you feel centered and quieted, ask the question either silently or out loud:

What does the fulfillment of love look like in my life?

Sit quietly in the question. If prayer is talking to God, then meditation is *listening* to God. Sit listening for the answer. Simply wait to hear the response to the question. You may be inspired by a refrain from a song, a poem you remember, or a metaphor of some sort that trickles through your mind. You may feel the emotional tone of peace course through your heart. You may see an image or a symbol. Simply listen without judging or assessing what comes to you.

After a few minutes, open your eyes and write down in your journal the images, feelings, and thoughts that came to you. When you are finished, move on to the second question.

What would I have to give up or release in order to manifest this vision?

Again, sit quietly in the question and repeat the previous instructions. After a few minutes, write down the images, feelings, and thoughts that came to you in response to the question. When you are finished, move on to the third and final question:

**What is it that I would have to embody or become
in order to manifest this vision?**

Once more, repeat the previous instructions.

BONUS: PRACTICE IN ACTION

This morning, you were given information on what it is that you would have to give up or embody in order to manifest the vision of love fulfilled in your life.

Do at least one thing today that anchors what came to you this morning in response to the second question you asked, "What would I have to give up or release in order to manifest this vision?" (For example, "I'd have to give up drinking and get into recovery" means that you might decide to attend an AA meeting; or "I'd have to forgive the person who abused me as a child" means that you might schedule an appointment with a therapist who can help you to heal from that experience.)

Do at least one thing today that anchors the response you received to the third question that you asked this morning, "What is it that I would have to embody or become in order to manifest this vision?" (For example, "I'd have to open up to the love that other people have for me" means that you might allow someone to do you a favor without immediately repaying it; or "I'd have to become vulnerable" means that you might try being more open and emotionally accessible to someone you've been defensive with.)

LESSON 23
Setting an Intention

It was through self-examination that I found the root cause
of disappointment: not stating your true intentions very clearly at
the outset of any endeavor. When you fail to do that, and when you
fail to let everyone involved know exactly what it is you want,
chances are you will be disappointed.

—Iyanla Vanzant, *In the Meantime*

There are four steps to setting an intention. We'll start with the first three.

The first step: to have a thought and/or a belief in a particular possibility. In this case, you must know and believe in your heart that you will find love. This is what Albert Einstein meant when he said, "Consciousness precedes all matter." We must believe in the possibility of a particular intention before it can come to us.

The second step: to speak your intention out loud. "And God said, 'Let there be Light: and there was light.'" (Genesis 1:3) As we are "made in the image and likeness of God," so we too, create through the power of our word. Most of us use language as though it were simply a descriptive, rather than a creative, tool. However, language is a powerful creative force that we would do well to harness.

And the third step: to take actions that support the manifestation of your intention, and abstain from those that sabotage it. Understanding alone transforms nothing: "Faith without works is dead." (James 2:20) Actually, faith without action is not faith at all, but merely an idea of faith that holds little power to effect change. We must ground our insights and understandings into the concrete world by taking actions that support what it is that we are committed to.

Our greatest chance for success in manifesting our heart's desire lies in the engagement of all three steps—believing in the possibility, speaking what it is that we are committed to creating, and taking actions consistent with that future. In other words, I believe that finding love is possible for me, and I tell those people who are capable of seeing that possibility as well (and probably even those I'm dating) that I'm committed to finding "The One." Then I do that which is consistent with that intention as well as refraining from doing that which is not. That's the climate in which love can "miraculously manifest."

Andrea, an artist in her early forties, told me how she felt when two of her friends became engaged within a short period of time. She'd been visioning to find "The One" herself, and had a true feeling in her heart that finding love was both possible and probable for her. Because of this, she was overjoyed at the good fortune of her friends, seeing their success as evidence that she, too, would soon find love. In the past, she confides, she would secretly have felt envious and threatened by their happiness. Within just a few short months, I was not surprised when Andrea herself met the man she would eventually marry.

Faith is a vitally important part of this journey. Recently I saw a single woman in my office. In her early thirties, Rochelle is sure that the opportunity to find Mr. Right has passed her by. She is furious with herself for not being more focused when she was in her mid-twenties when she was "at her peak," believing it's all downhill from here. In the meantime, she's seeing a man who appears to have a drinking problem and is emotionally unavailable. Instead of ending it, she keeps him hanging on while she sees other men behind his back. She desperately wants to get married so that her life "can begin" and thinks that, if nothing else works out, maybe she'll marry him. I ask her to choose between her goal of getting married and her goal of finding love. She thinks they are one and the same. I assure her that they are not. I assess her problem as not believing in her heart that love is possible for her. Because of this, she is engaged in building a relationship that is not about love at all, but rather about manipulation and selfishness. I assert that, while she does not trust that she will marry, I am fairly certain that she will. The question remains for me, however, which marriage she will choose to create—a lesser marriage created upon a foundation of fear and desperation or one that is based

> Success depends on where intention is.
> —Gita Bellin

If you are to
advance, all fixed
ideas must go.
—Joseph Campbell

upon the qualities of love. The latter would require that she rise to the occasion of cultivating the characteristics of love with the man she is currently with, so that she would actually be capable of creating a loving union.

Setting an intention, such as the intention to cultivate the characteristics of love, is a proactive, rather than a passive, process. Forty-year-old Kara, a dynamic and attractive corporate trainer, stands up in front of the room at a recent workshop. She publicly proclaims her intention to clear any blocks to having love in her life. One of the main blocks she acknowledges is her picture of what she thinks "The One" should look like. She surrenders her inflexible criteria and declares herself open to love, regardless of what it might look like. Many months later Kara calls to thank me. It seems that several weeks after the workshop, she met the man who she now considers to be the love of her life, and they are planning on being married soon. She laughs when she tells me that, before the workshop, she would never in a million years have been open to him. He's not at all what she thought she was looking for. Ten years older than she is, with two grown children, Bob lives in a city hundreds of miles away from her home in Los Angeles. As if that weren't enough, she says with a sense of irony, she discovered rather quickly that he had only recently separated from his wife of twenty-something years. "Do you think that I would have put *'married'* on my list?" she asked incredulously. Yet it's right—not only for her and for Bob, but for everyone involved, including Bob's adult children and his ex-wife, who has since moved on to better circumstances as well. "It's funny," Kara said. "There's a lot of conventional wisdom out there regarding finding 'The One,' but then there's the mystery of what enfolds when you are simply standing inside of the intention that you set."

It is an ancient spiritual axiom that our words have the power to create reality. In her book *Soulmates,* Dr. Carolyn Miller tells a story about actress Sophia Loren. As a child, Sophia was ruthlessly teased for being illegitimate, ugly, skinny, and poor. With such a disadvantaged beginning, Sophia attributes her success in life largely to her maternal grandmother. As a baby, Sophia's grandmother made up a song that contained words confirming that when she grew up, she would be happy, rich, beautiful, and adored. All of her dreams and aspirations would magically come true.

Over and over throughout her childhood, Sophia's grandmother sang this song to her. By her early twenties, in spite of having a difficult and destitute start in life, every word of that song had come to pass.

The words we say actually serve as a sort of instruction manual to the Universe. Recently, we had a visiting minister speak at our church who put it this way: "The whole Universe is genuflecting to you constantly," she said. "Yes, Master, whatever you say, Master. Be clear about the instructions you are giving." If you complain that "all the good ones are taken," then you'll probably meet only married or engaged people that you are attracted to. If you believe in your heart that you'll never find true love, then my guess is that you'll probably be right. "I thought you would never get here," [she] said. "I know, and that's what took me so long . . ." writes Marianne Williamson.

When we speak a new possibility for ourselves such as "I'm committed to having an extraordinary relationship," then all kinds of amazing coincidences, unforeseen opportunities, and unpredictable synchronicities are put into motion. That is why it is so important to have integrity with our word. It "trains" the Universe to take us seriously. If someone is inconsistent with their word, it is like a child who lies continually. You stop taking her seriously. She could tell you that the house is burning down, and you'd take your sweet time getting out. But if someone with a history of speaking the truth told you the very same thing, you would have quite a different response.

When I called my friend Naomi in December to tell her that I would be engaged by my birthday in August, I did so because I'd been successfully setting intentions in other areas in my life. Like an athlete who gets stronger the more she practices, I too was gaining strength in my ability to create with my word. I was getting better at it because I was getting better at being responsible for what it was that I had said. I had developed a certain level of consistency between what I said and the actions I took. It's like exercising a muscle. You get better at it the more you do it, and it's best to build yourself up slowly but steadily. For those who run marathons, taking a ten-mile jog is not that big a deal. For me, you'd end up scraping me off the pavement after the third or fourth mile. Most of our abilities have to be cultivated and developed one day at a time.

> We usually get what we anticipate.
> —Claude M. Bristol

By the time I made that statement, I had earned some trust in my ability to align my actions with my intention. By sharing my intention with Naomi, I invited her to support me in this. I could no longer flirt with unavailable men or date people who were not interested in getting married without Naomi asking me if I was being consistent with the intention I'd set. I will admit to you that, at times, I was completely irritated with her for doing this. At other times I was enormously grateful. I'm sure that supporting me during those months required a certain rigorous compassion on her part. She completely earned being the matron of honor at my wedding, and I really can't thank her enough.

Setting that intention out loud to another person obliged me to transform myself into the kind of woman who would actually be available to love another human being. Because I knew that, I didn't stop with Naomi but actually began telling most people in my life, including the men that I was dating, that I was committed to getting married. I tried to tell them in a way that didn't freak them out or seem like I meant that *they* had to be the one to marry me. However, since I didn't feel needy in my quest for a mate, choosing instead to stand in the commitment of what I was up to, they tended to relax a bit and even explore the possibility that I might actually be "The One" for them. And although, through all of my many love affairs over the years, I'd not been proposed to since my high-school sweetheart, I actually had another proposal right before Mark asked me to marry him. When you're ready, you're ready.

Inherent in this process of setting an intention is a certain paradox, and that is the fourth, and equally important, step. Without understanding this phenomenon, our ability to effect change in our lives will be drastically diminished. *We must remain completely unattached to the outcomes that we are committed to creating.* In other words, *we must do our best to live 100 percent committed to whatever intentions we set, without being attached to the results that we are getting.* We simply cannot get caught up in trying to force the river of life to go in one particular direction. Rather, setting an intention compels our own healing and transformation. It's not so much that we force the hand of God, as we become willing to be who we need to be order to manifest the intention. We speak the word and then we let go—trusting that, as we do our best to live congruently with the intention that we set, whatever happens is perfect. Anthropologist and author Ralph Blum says it this way: "Practice the art of doing without doing: Aim yourself truly and then maintain your aim without manipulative effort."

PRACTICE

Take out your journal. Keeping in mind that there are four steps to setting an intention, consider the intention you wish to set in relationship to doing this course. (Examples: "My intention is to release anything that blocks the fulfillment of love in my life," "My intention is to date only available people from now on," or "My intention is to meet my life partner by the end of the year.")

NOTE: Using a specific date adds a certain urgency that helps mobilize us to immediate action. However, if you feel too overwhelmed by doing so, I suggest you set an intention that you can completely own and align with, adding a "by when" time frame later on, if and when you feel ready.

Complete this sentence:

My intention is:

Notice if there is any part of you that doubts your ability to manifest your intention and list your concerns in your journal. Do this now.

Which of these doubts would I be willing to suspend or release entirely?

What more balancing and empowering statements could I make regarding my ability to manifest my intention? (Examples: "I am a strong and capable person who is worthy of love," or "I know and believe that my life partner is on his way now.")

Write these statements ten or more times each in your journal. As you write, feel it to be so in your heart.

BONUS: PRACTICE IN ACTION

Call at least one close friend or confidant today who can stand with you in the vision of your intention fulfilled. Share with this person the intention that you set for yourself this morning. Give that person permission to provide coaching and to "lovingly confront" you if and when you are making choices inconsistent with your intention. If you are doing this course with a supportive circle of friends, share your intention with everyone in the group the next time you are together.

Take at least one action today that is consistent with your intention. (Examples: Cut loose a tie to an ex-love that has been binding you to the past; tell the person you have been dating what you are up to in your life; accept an invitation that holds the promise of meeting new people, etc.)

LESSON 24
Clarifying Your Soul's Purpose

When love...[is] the context of your life, what details
cannot be reconciled? When one knows north,
all other directions are implied.

—Mark Austin Thomas

Most of us know at least one couple who appears to have it all—the money, the house, the kids—yet seem to lack certain inexplicable qualities like grace, joy, and enchantment. Both partners appear to be moderately content. Yet when we observe such unions, we know in our heart of hearts that what they have is not what we ourselves are looking for. The trappings of what society might call a "successful" marriage do not necessarily capture the level of soul connection that many of us are longing for.

Often, I find myself reminding those who come to me for counsel that they could probably walk out the door and get married within six months if that was all they wanted. The truth is, we've come to expect more from our unions than economic advancement and social compatibility. We've come to expect our unions on the material plane to also reflect unity at the level of heart, spirit, and soul. It's a tall order, and one that our parents did not necessarily accomplish.

Each one of us enters this world called to fulfill a particular destiny. For many of us, this calling lies just beyond our conscious awareness, and often beckons us with a sense of restlessness and dissatisfaction. In the past, those of us who were curious and concerned about this mysterious calling of ours, holed up in monasteries to ask questions such as "Who am I?," "What am I here for?," and "What is the meaning of my life?" However, these significant questions are more and more being asked and answered in relationship to one another.

Relationships that are able to transition graciously from the sexual-

An essential
part of becoming
marriageable
is to be a maker,
a person who
cultivates a life
of beauty,
rich texture, and
creative work.
If we understand
marriage only as
the commitment
of two individuals
to each other,
then we overlook
its soul, but if
we see that it also
has to do with family,
neighborhood,
and the greater
community,
and with our own
work and personal
cultivation,
then we begin to
glimpse the *mystery*
that is marriage.
—Thomas Moore

attraction/falling-in-love stage (which lasts anywhere from one to three years) into the attachment stage (which can last a lifetime) are often deeply rooted and organized around this idea of the fulfillment of destiny. The very best long-term relationships are usually founded upon a shared sense of purpose.

Monica came to me after being married for a relatively short period of time. Although she is a deeply spiritual person, Monica married a man who is a professed agnostic. He lovingly supports her to pursue her spiritual practice while, at the same time, eschews any particular path himself. While that was fine for her when they were courting, she is now questioning her decision to marry him, particularly since she is considering going back to school to become a minister.

Monica is in crisis. If she pursues her faith more fully, she risks alienating herself further from a husband who does not share her religious beliefs. However, if she does not pursue her spiritual goals, she risks sabotaging the fulfillment of what she believes might be her true destiny. The dilemma is an agonizing one.

I invite Monica to explore with her husband not only what he does *not* believe in, but what he actually *does* believe in, such as the ultimate need to help others in some meaningful way. I am hopeful that they are able to locate a shared sense of purpose that goes beyond doctrine and didactic religious beliefs. That way, they can stand united in a shared vision. Unless they can locate something outside of themselves on which to join, they are going to have a much more difficult time forging a thriving union. For many of us, finding our spiritual partner opens the gateway that leads to the fulfillment of our soul's destiny. That's why we are in such agony in his or her absence. However, the path to prepare oneself to receive such a love can sometimes take years. I believe that's one reason that many of us are waiting until we are so much older than our parents were before committing to marriage.

As with any journey, we must always begin it from where we are. In this case, we start with the self. While we may yearn to find "The One" who will inspire us to understand the value of our lives at a much more profound level, the way we draw such a love toward us is by already being actively engaged in seeking and expressing our highest destiny. Instead, many of us will settle for dramas and crises that serve to distract and divert our attention, rather than challenge ourselves to engage in this more meaningful pursuit. Hence, our love life reflects this penchant for drama, as opposed to a true sense of purpose and meaning in life.

Eileen Caddy, co-founder of the Findhorn community, once said, "A soul without a high aim is like a ship without a rudder." Just as knowing your sexual proclivity promises to bring clarity to your love life, so too does knowing your soul's purpose. Everything comes into focus. Connecting with this "high aim" becomes your reference point—a primary directive from which all other decisions are made, particularly the decision about who to create an intimate, loving relationship with.

It's not to say that Monica married the "wrong person." But she would have been wise to explore the larger context that both she and her husband were living in before taking the significant step of marriage. Now she has to backpedal and try to find a framework on which they can join, so that she will not feel compelled to live a diminished and contracted life in order to stay bonded to him. In the old paradigm of marriage, it was common for people to live compromised lives that were ultimately less than what was possible. In the new paradigm of marriage, we look to form unions that have enough vision and expansion to support us to midwife ourselves into being all that we are capable of being.

Many of us confuse our jobs and our roles in life with our purpose. We look to our ambitions in our attempt to define our soul's reasons for being. Yet Carol Adrienne, author of *The Purpose of Your Life,* tells us, "Our purpose . . . is not a thing, place, occupation, title, or even a talent. Our purpose is to be. Our purpose is *how* we live life, not what role we live. Our purpose is found each moment as we make choices to be who we really are."

Our soul's purpose is always concerned with who we are in relationship to other people. Its expression is always in who we are *being* much more than what we are *doing.* Doingness is simply the vehicle. My soul's purpose is equally expressed in playing a silly game with my daughter, as it is in writing this book. Both are demonstrations of love toward another.

Discovering our soul's purpose is rarely an event, although epiphanies

> Joy can be real only if people look upon their lives as a service and have a definite object in life outside themselves and their personal happiness.
> —Leo Tolstoy

do happen. More often than not, it's a process that requires patience and perseverance. In order to discover it, you'll want to pay attention to what stirs your passions, lights you up, and just comes naturally. When you are living inside of your soul's purpose, you are often in flow. You lose track of time. You're not that concerned about how much money you are, or are not, making. You feel alive, useful, of service, and a part of all that is.

The oft-quoted writing of George Bernard Shaw is worth repeating here:

This is the true joy in life, the being used for a purpose recognized by yourself as a mighty one; being a force of nature instead of a feverish, selfish little clod of ailments and grievances, complaining that the world will not devote itself to making you happy. I am of the opinion that my life belongs to the whole community, and as long as I live, it is my privilege to do for it whatever I can. I want to be thoroughly used up when I die, for the harder I work, the more I live. I rejoice in life for its own sake. Life is no brief candle to me. It is a sort of splendid torch which I have got hold of for the moment, and I want to make it burn as brightly as possible before handing it on to future generations.

Our soul's raison d'être is usually quite simple. We are here to help people. We are here to learn and to grow in wisdom. We are here to heal ourselves and others. We are here to help birth peace in the world. We are here to love and be loved. We are here to radiate kindness . . . or hope . . . or happiness. As you look to draw toward you the love of your life, remember to first recess deeply into yourself, to examine and explore the overall meaning and aim of this journey we call your life. For once you've located north for yourself, all of your other decisions will be that much easier to make, particularly the task of choosing your mate.

PRACTICE

Take out your journal. Write on each of the following questions:

What do I love to do?

What comes naturally to me?

What do I feel passionate about?

Now, complete these sentence stems with as many answers as you can think of:

The times I've been happiest in life have been when:

People have always told me that I'm good at:

When I was a child, I always wanted to:

The purpose of my life is:

Fill in the blank:

I am here to bring _____ to the world.

BONUS: PRACTICE IN ACTION

Do at least one thing today that expresses what you believe, at this point, to be your soul's purpose in the world. Make this action a demonstration of your intention to begin organizing your life more and more around this sense of purpose. This will usually entail seeking out others with a similar purpose to yours (e.g., finding a church or spiritual group with similar val-

> The defining characteristic of soulmate relationships is shared purpose.
>
> —Carolyn G. Miller

ues and aspirations; taking on a volunteer commitment with an organization that moves and inspires you; or joining a club that shares a passion that you have).

NOTE: Don't worry about "not having enough time." When you are living congruent with those things that are most important to you, life has a way of becoming more efficient and less frenzied, thereby leaving you with more time than you thought you had.

LESSON 25
Receiving Inner Guidance

Intuition is the discriminative faculty that enables
you to decide which of two lines of reasoning is right.
Perfect intuition makes you a master of all.

—Paramahansa Yogananda

While we may be in the habit of asking our therapist, parents, friends, or coworkers for advice, it often does not even occur to us to seek our own counsel regarding our problems by going within to our own inner reserves. Often referred to as the "Higher Self" or the "God Within," this inner reserve is an ever-present source of wisdom that is always available for the asking. Expressed frequently as a "gut feeling" or a "hunch," this inner prompting whispers quietly in our hearts, and lies in wait, longing for us to consider actively requesting its assistance.

Seeking guidance from within ourselves allows us to access wisdom beyond that which we might believe we possess. Connecting with this inner resource—that part of ourselves that relies more on intuition than on logic, more on instinct than on specific knowledge—is a timeless form of knowingness that relies little on external proof or circumstances. Because of this, many of us consistently override its promptings. We doubt its validity and accuracy, and, as a result, suffer painful, yet preventable consequences.

When Chad met Janice, he fell for her immediately. She was beautiful, charismatic, and seemingly everything he had ever hoped for. Soon into the relationship, he began to feel uncomfortable with her relationship with her soon-to-be ex-husband, with whom she was in the middle of a long and grueling divorce. Although Janice insisted that the relationship was long over and told Chad repeatedly that she loved only him, he found himself feeling insecure and anxious whenever her ex-husband's name was mentioned. Chad's intuition told him to be cautious and to wait until he knew Janice better before surrendering himself completely. However, because Chad considers himself a "spiritual" man, he thinks that he *should* love with an open heart at all times. Therefore, he talked himself out of this feeling, assuming that he was wrong to feel mistrustful since, after all, "spiritual" people are *supposed* to trust others. Soon thereafter, Janice told Chad that she wanted to go into couples counseling with her ex-husband so that she could "work on that relationship."

How many times have we plowed straight ahead, overriding our inner knowing with logic and reason? Almost every time I've done this, I've ended up regretting my decisions. When the stock market fell at the end of 2000, I, like many people, lost thousands of dollars. My intuition had told me to sell all of my tech stocks right before they plunged in value. For days, I had a gnawing feeling that was absolutely nagging at me to sell the stock. However, because the stock had recently dropped in value by $500, I negated this inner prompting and decided to wait. I didn't think my inner guidance was accurate when it instructed me to sell my stock at a loss. Had I listened, I would have lost only $500 instead of thousands. It was an expensive lesson.

Whenever we do not listen to our inner guidance, our ability to discern between "two lines of reasoning" becomes more and more compromised. Our ability to trust ourselves devolves into an increasing dependence upon the attitudes and opinions of others. When Janice was assuring Chad against his better judgment, he became more and more consumed by an ever-increasing need for feedback and approval from his friends and family. He was paralyzed to take any actions to protect himself because everyone he asked had a different opinion about what he should do. For every person who thought he was being foolish to open his heart to a woman whose divorce was not yet finalized, there was another who thought he needed to take a risk on what could be an extraordinary love. Because he was so dismissive of his own intuition, he began behaving with an intense desperation to have others tell him what to do. In situations such as this, where there really is no clear-cut right or wrong, all we have is our intuition to guide and help us to make a good, sound decision. How terrible then for Chad to be so estranged from himself and so thoroughly cut off from his ability to trust himself.

One woman I worked with became so alienated from her ability to access her own inner guidance that she developed an overdependence upon her daily horoscope. She would not leave home in the morning without first consulting the newspaper. If her horoscope foretold of a good day, she would feel hopeful and optimistic. However, if it forecast doom and gloom, she would become so anxious that she could barely get herself out the door to face the day. Her ability to connect with her own inner wisdom became weaker and weaker, as her dependence upon this external source of direction increased. Even though she could see how foolish her addiction was, she had little power to release herself from her obsessive need for someone else to tell her what to do and how to live her life.

Inner guidance is rarely concerned with specific bits and pieces of information, like a newspaper horoscope is apt to be. While someone might call a psychic hotline to desperately ask, *"But when will he call?"* our inner guidance might lead us, instead, to release the panic and despair we feel over him not calling. It might invite us to let go of our attachment to him calling at all, thereby helping us to love and respect ourselves more. This, in turn, eventually attracts in more love and respect from others— but not necessarily from *him*. And that has to be OK. Surrender is the beginning of wisdom.

Asking for our inner guidance is asking for wisdom over knowledge. Whereas knowledge is generally concerned with separate and fragmented pieces of data, wisdom is apt to address the deeper integral meanings of our challenges. Its goals are not necessarily to get us what we think we want, as much as they are to cultivate and encourage our spiritual growth. When it comes to discerning which path is the "right" path to take, we let go of trying to control the answers that come to us. We don't try to force things to go the way we think they should. We give up trying to fit square pegs into round holes. Instead, we yield ourselves, trusting that, even if we do not like what we hear, we are safe to surrender to the larger context of our lives, trusting ultimately that all is well. Herein lies inner peace.

Wisdom is helpful in making the choice of who to open our hearts to

> You must begin to trust yourself. If you do not then you will forever be looking to others to prove your own merit to you, and you will never be satisfied. You will always be asking others what to do, and at the same time, resenting those from whom you seek such aid.
> —Jane Roberts

You know more than
you think you do.
—Dr. Benjamin Spock

and who to be cautious with. Wisdom helps us assess our own readiness to enter into an intimate relationship. Wisdom can instruct us on what needs to happen in order to realize love with another person. Wisdom empowers us with a sense of how to handle difficult and potentially precarious situations.

How, then, do we access our intuition? How do we distinguish the voice of inner guidance from the voice of imagination or, worse yet, the internalized voice of the critical parent? How do we know that we are not simply making up an inner dialogue where we are imagining what our parents might say if we were to speak with them? These are the concerns I frequently hear from those who have not yet made this simple practice a daily ritual.

When I first began cultivating my ability to use intuition to guide my life, I wrote letters to God every morning. I asked God about everything that concerned me. I'd write out all of the feelings I was having and then ask very specific questions about the situations I was in. No question was too small or insignificant. I asked about the relationships I was in, the work I was doing, the money I did or didn't have, and the plans I was making. I even asked questions about food I was eating. I would always end my letters with the words "Dear God, please write through my pen. Thank you very much." Then I wrote a "Dear Katherine" letter back to myself. Before putting the words on the paper, I'd adjust myself to listen for them from within. Sometimes the words came quickly, sometimes slowly, but always they came. A whole new outlook, often one I'd never considered before, began flowing effortlessly through my pen. A depth of wisdom that I had rarely displayed in my life before began to show up. More important, perhaps, is that I actually began to act upon this new guidance that I was receiving.

After writing letters to God as a daily practice for about a year and a half, I began to get the guidance as soon as I asked the question in my mind. Eventually, I gave up writing the letters on a daily basis because I no longer needed to. I could hear the guidance immediately simply by asking a question within myself, and then listening for the answer. For me, it has become a way of living that diminishes drama and disappointment and greatly enhances love and abundance.

In his book *Conversations with God, Book 1,* Neale Donald Walsch describes this process when he writes, as though God were speaking:

So go ahead now. Ask me anything. Anything. I will contrive to bring you the answer. The whole universe will I use to do this. So be on the lookout . . . The words to the next song you hear. The information in the next article you read. The story line of the next movie you watch. The chance utterance of the next person you meet. Or the whisper of the next river, the next ocean, the next breeze that caresses your ear— all these devices are Mine; all these avenues are open to Me. I will speak to you if you will listen. I will come to you if you will invite Me. I will show you then that I have always been there. All ways.

Recently, a group of women gathered for a weekend workshop. We had just finished an exercise where the women had been asked to write letters to God and then answer these letters by writing, as God, to themselves. It was a beautiful summer day and we were scattered on the lawn of a large Victorian house that serves as a Zen center in the heart of Los Angeles. Suddenly, two butterflies with magnificent bright yellow and black markings, landed on the grass before one of the women. Amazingly, the two insects were interlocked with each other as they proceeded to mate right in front of her. The woman was startled as she stared at the butterflies who seemed unconcerned with her presence. The rest of the women began to draw themselves in a circle around the two butterflies, staring in wonder as they continued on together, seemingly unperturbed by the voyeuristic activity surrounding them. For a full ten minutes, we stood silently in a circle surrounding the butterflies, watching in awe. Finally, we left them and gathered again inside to share the meaning of this experience with one another. One of the women reminded us that, in Native American teachings, butterflies represent transformation. We all agreed that the butterflies were a confirmation and a validation of the work that they had gathered to do that weekend and the experience was one of comfort and encouragement to all of us—like a kiss from God for all of our efforts.

Yoga teacher Erich Schiffman says, "The moment you know that you do not know is the moment you open yourself to true knowing." Seeking guidance begins with an admission that you may not know the best course of action to take or the wisest decision to make. We then turn our attention within, ask a question, and listen. Be watchful. Guidance comes in many forms: creative ideas, insights, hunches, intuitive knowingness, premonitions, understandings, and even synchronistic occurrences. When it comes to calling in "The One," I encourage you to begin relying more and more upon the inherent wealth of information that lies within you, just for the asking.

PRACTICE

Today, I invite you to access a higher level of your own awareness through writing your own letter to God, whoever God is for you. You may wish to address this letter "Dear God," "God Within," "Higher Power," or "Higher Self." If you prefer, you can simply write a "Dear Wisdom" letter.

In your letter, write about the situations in your life that are difficult and challenging for you. Start by sorting through some of the feelings you are having and then move into specific questions that you have.

End your letter with the following sentence: "Dear God, please write through my pen. Thank you very much." Then write a letter back to yourself from God.

NOTE: The point of the exercise is not to get caught up in a debate over whether or not God exists, what you call God or what your relationship is to a Higher Power. The point is to access a level of consciousness that is beyond our everyday, normal awareness. If the idea of writing a letter to God is difficult for you, try doing it simply as an exercise without getting too significant about it.

BONUS: PRACTICE IN ACTION

Throughout the day, practice going within and asking for guidance. Practice with the seemingly small decisions, such as what to wear or how to prioritize your tasks. This will allow you to get comfortable with the process so that when the big choices need to be made, such as who to open your heart to or who to begin a sexual relationship with, you are already familiar with how to ask, listen, and act upon inner urgings. You will be much more able to trust your intuition if you are in the practice of using it frequently.

As you move through your day, remember to turn your attention within and ask:

> **What is the best choice I can make in this moment**
> **for myself and all involved?**

Then trust what comes to you enough to act upon it. Do what you are guided to do, whether it is through a strong inner prompting, a creative idea, a sudden insight, or an actual external sign.

LESSON 26
Establishing Personal Integrity

A double-minded man is unstable in all his ways.

—James 1:8

When we think of people who espouse the value of cultivating personal integrity, we often think of morally superior, holier-than-thou promoters of a particular religious ideology or philosophy. Most of us have at least one horror story to tell of someone who has taken a kind of perverse pleasure in pointing out our inconsistencies and faults. So it's not hard to see why we don't usually like being asked to examine our integrity. We think that it has something to do with judging and assessing our conduct according to the rules and tenets of others. So I want to make it clear that, when we explore this topic, we are not talking about moral dictates, as much as we are about your own subjective standards, and to what degree you are (or are not) able to live them.

Roget's Thesaurus defines integrity as "the state of being entirely whole." Integrity is not as concerned with absolute truths (e.g., murder is wrong), as it is with relative truths (e.g., if I say I'm a loving person, then I'm responsible for behaving in loving ways). A lack of integrity does not imply that one is a "bad" person. A lack of integrity simply suggests that one is being an inconsistent person—and an inconsistent person is a disempowered person. Whenever there is a contradiction within the self—a lack of wholeness and congruence—there is fragmentation and its resulting sense of angst. And when this happens, all sorts of symptoms appear that one might not, at first glance, necessarily attribute to a lack of personal integrity.

I have a client named Manuel who has been telling me for two years now that he is going to write a book. He feels that writing this book is directly connected to his life purpose and that once he writes it, he will be given opportunities to speak and teach that he would not be given otherwise. After a successful course of therapy, Manuel leaves, telling me that he is going to travel and write his book.

I do not hear from Manuel for an entire year. One day he calls me and tells me that he is suffering from terrible anxiety and depression and that he must come to speak with me right away. It wasn't long before I discover that, although Manuel has done some traveling, he has not even begun to write his book yet. He thinks about this book every day and every night and yet he fills his days with busy work and doesn't seem to "have the time" to sit down and begin it. I point out to Manuel that he is out of integrity with himself. I remind him of the importance of writing this book in his life. We come up with a plan that has Manuel setting aside two hours every day to work on his book. Three days later, Manuel calls me to tell me that the anxiety and the depression lifted the moment he sat down to write. He has felt completely at peace for the past three days.

When you are not taking actions that you feel you need to be taking, or when you are taking actions that are in conflict with your values, there is often a tremendous drain on your sense of wholeness and well-being. Smoking is a good example of this for many people. Even though they may not even have said that they were going to quit, usually people are at odds with themselves for continuing to engage in an addiction that they know is doing them harm. There is an inconsistency in the self and therefore, one is in a weakened state.

Nadia, a thirty-one-year-old corporate middle-management executive, was longing to get married and start a family. She knew in her heart that the younger man she was having sex with each weekend was nowhere near ready for a commitment. That was fine with her, she told me, because he wasn't someone that she would consider committing herself to anyway. He was "too immature, too selfish, and not successful enough." She rationalized their affair by saying that she was "just having some fun." However, when he didn't call one weekend, she became distraught. Her despondence was made worse by the humiliation she felt over her attachment to someone who clearly was "not good enough" for her. Nadia had been lying to herself about her capacity to separate her heart from her sexual activities. She had to admit that, somewhere deep inside, she'd been

> Integrity is doing the right thing, even when you know that no one will ever find out.
> —Oprah Winfrey

holding on to a fantasy that he "would grow up and become the man she needed." Instead, he became another notch in the belt of her long list of failed and disappointing relationships. This, in turn, fed into her desperation and willingness to compromise herself.

When we lie to ourselves, we sever ourselves from the source of our power—our own inner truth. We become fragmented and discordant within. It's what we mean when we say that someone is "lost." They've lost the congruence of themselves from which to operate. This inharmonious relationship with the self is a breeding ground for addictions and all sorts of destructive, self-sabotaging behavior. That's why the restoration of personal integrity tops the list of things we must refurbish in order to prepare the way for a loving relationship to enter our lives.

In his book *The Varieties of Religious Experience,* philosopher William James writes, "In the spiritual realm there are . . . two ways, one gradual, the other sudden, in which inner unification may occur." Classic "sudden" conversion experiences include moments in time where we see a truth that is ours and then claim it for our lives. In Nadia's case, she owns a truth about herself—she yearns to have the experience of love in her life. While she sadly realizes that she cannot make someone else love her, she understands that she can always offer love herself. She owns love as her own ethic, not as something to get, but rather, as is consistent with what love is, something to give. She then gives love to herself by deciding to be rigorously honest with herself about her feelings, and to honor her sexuality as something that is sacred and not to be thrown about lightly. She then extends love to her younger lover by releasing him fully to go his way, and live the life he needs to live. In her heart, she blesses his life and sets him free. She is complete; her integrity, restored.

The "gradual" experiences that Dr. James refers to is the daily practice of taking personal inventory and making self-corrections—righting our wrongs, telling our truth, and bringing closure to that which is no longer appropriate. This daily practice of discovering and strengthening one's personal integrity encourages us to examine our cross-agendas and inconsistencies, like when we say we want love but behave in unloving ways toward ourselves and others, or claim to be ready for a mate while, at the same time, cling to self-protective and defensive ways of being. As a rudder steers a sailboat—never quite on target, but in a constant state of correction and adjustment—so we, too, continually engage the process of looking for where we are out of alignment with ourselves so that we can restore our inner congruence.

The most basic measure of integrity has to do with keeping one's word. This is because language is such a powerful creative force. When we say one thing and then do another, say things that we don't really mean, or consistently break our word to both ourselves and others, we profoundly diminish our capacity to create the lives that we are hoping to create. It's as though we give the Universe a mixed message. "Take me seriously, God, but not too seriously." "Give me what I want, God, but I'll make You be the One to work hard to figure out exactly what that is."

One of the main reasons we don't keep our word is that, on some level, we don't want to be responsible for how powerful we really are. It's often harder for us to admit our strengths and our efficacies than it is to admit our flaws and our failures. As a matter of fact, we often form our relationships by bonding over our mutual inadequacies. Many of us secretly believe that when we're weak and impotent, we're not responsible for our lives—and we're relieved to be off the hook. It's a high price to pay, but most of us live that way. It's like having one foot on the planet and one foot off. I'll be human but refuse to really own all that that implies. Or I'll define being human as a weakness, and as an excuse to avoid responsibility—as in, "But, gee, I'm only human."

We want to form relationships that build upon our strengths and enhance our assets. We want unions formed upon strong foundations of respect and reliability that can withstand the true challenges of life that might come our way. And that goal begins, again, with the self—by building inner congruencies that enable you to stand solidly within yourself no matter what disappointments you may face. We begin by rooting out our inner divisions as a means of establishing what Dr. James referred to as "inner unification."

It is the penalty of a liar, that should he even tell the truth, he is not listened to.
—The Talmud

And I know when I'm on track—that is, when everything is in a harmonious relationship to what I regard as the best I've got in me.
—Joseph Campbell

Few have the
strength
To be a real Hero.
That rare man
or woman
Who always keeps
their word.
Even an angel
needs rest.
Integrity creates a
body so vast
A thousand winged
ones will plead,
"May I lay my cheek
Against you?"
—Hafiz, translated by
Daniel Ladinsky

PRACTICE

Take out your journal and write on the following questions:

What agreements have I made that I have not kept?

**What do I need to communicate to someone
that I've been putting off?**

Who do I need to contact regarding money that I owe?

Who do I need to forgive?

Who do I need to apologize to?

Who do I need to thank?

What lies have I been telling myself?

What excuses have I been making?

Now go back and review your list. Circle those things that you intend to "clean up" in your life. Write a list of actions to take that would restore integrity to your life.

BONUS: PRACTICE IN ACTION

Take at least one action today that restores integrity to your life. As you move through the course, continue restoring your integrity until everything that you circled has been addressed. Remember to take personal inventory on a regular basis to keep yourself light and clear. When your baggage in life is light, there is more room for love.

LESSON 27
The Practice of Prayer and Meditation

If I do not go within, I go without.

—Neale Donald Walsch, *Conversations with God, Book 1*

Most of us have very specific expectations about our lives—we have ideas about the age by which we think we should be married, how much money we think we're supposed to be making by now, and that we expect to live long lives in relatively good health. We'll say prayers of thanks when things go our way, and prayers of petition for the things that we *want* to go our way. Usually, along with those prayers is a covert attachment to what we think the answers should be. Then, if and when life doesn't go the way we think it should—we're still single on our thirty-fifth birthday, we don't get the promotion we were counting on, we lose a chunk of change in the stock market, or go through the depressing experience of having a friend or loved one come down with cancer—we can get pretty cynical and resigned about life.

When I graduated from high school, rather than go to a regular university, I decided to attend Bible college instead. I very much wanted my life to be used as a force for healing and love in the world and, at the time, it made sense to me to become a missionary. I wanted to help and serve people more than anything. So, for many months, I spent several hours a day in prayer and meditative contemplation asking God to use me for this purpose. Not long after I began this practice, everything in my life began to fall apart. The boy I'd dated all through high school broke my heart by marrying someone else, my best friend turned her back on me and took most of our mutual friends with her, and my parents completely stopped talking to me because I refused to go to a "normal" college like everyone else. As a result, the eating disorder that started when I was fourteen turned into a full-blown, raging addiction that began consuming my life.

Anything you do
has a still point.
When you are in that
still point,
you can perform
maximally.
—Joseph Campbell

For the next two years, I was extremely isolated and alone in life. Everything and everyone I thought I could count on had simply disappeared. I was terribly lonely. I was making minimum wage working at a day care center and couldn't make ends meet. When I needed a root canal, I didn't have the $250 that the dentist charged, and so instead, I paid $30 for him to pull the tooth out just to be rid of the pain. I felt completely abandoned by God. Here I was, dedicating my life to serving Him, and everything that could go wrong did. I became so angry that I dropped out of Bible college and refused to pray at all for several years. I simply would not talk to a God who could betray me so completely.

A few years later, upon entering a twelve-step program to help me heal the eating disorder, I was encouraged to begin using prayer and meditation again as tools for recovery. As arrogant as it sounds, I had to actually "forgive" God before I was able to pick up these practices again. Little by little, I had to grapple with accepting the disappointments I had endured. In order to re-engage a discourse with God, which is basically what prayer is, I had to allow the tears to flow, and I had to be brutally honest. Of all the prayer books I had contemplated, and all the sermons I had sat through over the years, none had prepared me to pray the prayers that I desperately needed to pray. "God: I don't even want to talk to You. I am so angry and disgusted with You. How *dare* You do that to me? I hate You. No, better than that. I don't even believe in You anymore. Even if You *were* real, I wouldn't want to know You." It wasn't pretty and it certainly wasn't "nice." But it was authentic. And because it was authentic, it was healing. My heart began to thaw, eventually freeing it again to love and be loved. Even though I pined for love, until I told the truth to myself and to God, I really had no room within myself to experience it.

Sometimes life is filled with such profound disappointment that we steal ourselves against it, just to make it through the day. We resist going into stillness because we can't bear to be face to face with the screaming in our psyches and the sadness in our hearts. We dread the possibility of being swallowed up by grief, fearing that, once we allow ourselves to start crying, we may never stop. Sometimes life can be like this. In response, many of us simply stop praying. We go on strike. We won't talk to a God who can appear to be so cold and indifferent. We desperately try to divert our attention away from inside ourselves. We turn on the television the moment we get home, and surround ourselves with demands and dramas designed to keep us as far away from our feelings as possible. Yet, what hope do we have for a loving, intimate partnership when we go to such lengths to avoid being intimate with ourselves? What hope do we have to trust another human being when we allow ourselves to become so mistrustful of God, however one defines God?

I didn't fully comprehend the meaning of those years of heartache and loss until many years later, when I was in my mid-thirties. At the time, I was working as a therapist downtown on skid row with men and women who'd been homeless and out on the streets. Sitting with a group of about twenty people who were all in recovery from various addictions or self-destructive behaviors, facilitating a seminar that I had created that was designed to help people heal from the most devastating of circumstances, I suddenly had an epiphany. It wasn't that God had disregarded my prayers, as I so fervently believed for so many years. On the contrary, He had answered them. I hadn't been abandoned at all. I realized in that moment that by entering a period of profound darkness and heartbreak, I learned what I would never have discovered at Bible college—how to build life back up from the inside out after suffering devastating disappointments, how to let a broken heart catapult one into being a more kindhearted, compassionate person, and how to forgive others after they'd done desperately hurtful things. And now here I was, helping others do the same. I realized in that moment that it was precisely what I had asked God for all those years before, and I felt both deeply grateful and terribly ashamed that I had doubted so deeply.

Ralph Waldo Emerson once said that prayer was "the contemplation of life from the highest point of view." I have discovered that my clients who pray for help and guidance tend to make much better progress than those who don't. It seems to allow them to view themselves and their challenges inside of a larger context. They feel less overwhelmed by their problems and more hopeful about possible solutions. Even those who do not necessarily consider themselves to be religious or "spiritual" will advance much more quickly once they begin to pray. I don't pretend to fully understand this phenomenon and yet, truthfully, I don't really need

> To stay present in everyday life, it helps to be deeply rooted within yourself; otherwise, the mind, which has incredible momentum, will drag you along like a wild river.
>
> —Eckhart Tolle

Cease looking for
flowers!
There blooms a
garden in your own
home.
While you look for
trinkets
The treasure house
awaits you in your
own being.

—Rumi

to. There's graciousness in simply receiving the gifts when they come and remembering to say thank you.

I do have a theory, however, on just how and why prayer and meditation can have this profound effect upon our lives. Prayer and meditation connect us with what I'll call a "parallel reality" to the reality we are currently experiencing. It is as though we tune in to another frequency and can see what's happening in our lives from a completely different perspective. From our ordinary conscious mind, it might look like love is completely missing. Yet when we tune in to the situation in prayer and meditation, we suddenly see it as an opportunity to give love, or we remember a previously unnoticed act of kindness and compassion. So often, it isn't that love is missing in our lives as much as we missed it when it was there. Prayer and meditation plugs us into the source of love and, therefore, renders us much more conscious and aware of its constant presence.

Recently, I saw the film *Fierce Grace,* a documentary about Ram Dass's recovery from a stroke. In it, several people were interviewed about what it was like to be in the presence of Maharaji, Ram Dass's guru in India, during the 1960s. It struck me that each of them had a similar experience of feeling a profound sense of love for themselves and others when they were with him. Without taking any of the psychedelic drugs that they'd been using before they met Maharaji, they were able to access a state of absolute affinity with everyone and everything, simply by being in the same room with him. So, for them, the experience wasn't so much that the Maharaji was extraordinary, as it was that they themselves were extraordinary when in his presence.

This experience of absolute love and affinity is what we are ultimately seeking to connect with when we pray and meditate. When we seek to commune with God, we do so not simply to comply with the conventions of others, or to be obedient to the dictates of religious doctrine. Rather, we do so in the hope that we will be profoundly altered by the experience. We are looking to immerse ourselves so thoroughly in the principles of stillness, peace, surrender, and joy that they have an opportunity to heal and transform us. Such is the motivation to dedicate oneself to a daily spiritual practice.

While most of us know that we "should" make the time to pray and meditate, we may not see how it can help us achieve our goal of actualizing love, and so we don't make it a top priority. Yet, there is a tremendous similarity between what scientific evidence indicates a daily practice of prayer and meditation provides a person, and the emotional maturity that demonstrates a readiness to create and sustain a loving partnership. That is why noted psychologist Martin Seligman calls Buddhism the "great tradition [that] focuses on achieving a serene state of mind that arises from becoming mature."

The ability to remain somewhat centered and balanced in response to a perceived threat (as opposed to becoming reactive and/or explosive), or to maintain a certain degree of calm in the face of disappointment (rather than becoming dramatic and defensive), is the mark of a person who is prepared to create a healthy, sustainable loving relationship. Those who know how to avoid becoming combative in reaction to stress make better, more reliable partners than those who don't. It pays for us to actively cultivate these abilities, and there is no more reliable way to do this than through a daily practice of prayer and meditation. It's the direct route—the fast track to developing the emotional maturity one needs in order to ensure a more successful union.

So let's talk about the "how to." No one has the market cornered on the "right" way to pray or the "best" way to meditate. It's all about finding—and then consistently doing, what works for you. Praying—the act of talking to God—is as simple as that. Talk to God. Tell the truth. If you find it easier, write a letter to God. Sitting or kneeling, eyes opened or eyes closed, whatever helps you to focus on this discourse, just do it. Meditation, sometimes referred to as "centering," can be thought of as the listening component of this divine dialogue. We still ourselves enough to actually hear what God is trying to say. As such, meditation is really the act of becoming fully present—open and available.

When we cultivate mindful attentiveness to the present moment, our driven need to do, do, do, and assess the value of our lives according to the list of our accomplishments diminishes. When we allow ourselves the space just to *be* (as in human *beings* rather than human *doings)*, we reaf-

What to do when you first awaken or before drifting off to sleep? Quiet your mind, lift up your heart, muse, mull over, make discoveries. Consider, conceive, create, connect, concede that it all starts within. Pray, read the Scriptures, sacred poetry or a meditation from an inspirational book.

—Sarah Ban Breathnach

firm the unconditional value of our lives. We relax our racing minds, and slow down enough to become present and available to our hearts and our bodies. We decelerate the mental activity that so often usurps our intuition and our deeper feelings. We are less vulnerable to make our choices from the rantings and ravings of the "should" mind, and become more empowered to make choices from the totality of who and what we are.

When we talk of meditation, most of us think of the traditional methods of sitting still while observing and releasing our thoughts, and/or focusing on the breath in some way. However, there are many ways to come home to the center of ourselves. We can close our eyes and silently recite a mantra. We can rock ourselves gently to the rhythm of a Buddhist chant. We can take a mindful walk alone on the beach. We can put on some music and dance a plea to God, create a prayer in our journal, or speak sacred text out loud. We can paint love on a canvas, breathe in unison with a sleeping child, or sit quietly inside a great cathedral to soak in its beauty and holiness.

Spiritual teacher Eckhart Tolle reminds us that "you 'get' there by realizing that you *are* there already." We must remember that, on some level, we are already profoundly connected to the forces of love. The more we go within to tap in to this supply, the more equipped we are to come *from* there in our dealings. We can then actualize lives where love and affinity are as natural and commonplace to us as breathing.

PRACTICE

Today, I invite you to do a simple meditation. Read the instructions once through and then do the meditation from memory to the best of your ability.

Sit up straight with your legs and arms uncrossed and resting easily. Close your eyes and relax your entire body. Starting at the bottom of your feet and working your way up through the body—your toes, your ankles, calves, knees, thighs, etc. until you reach the top of your head, release any tension you find. Breath in and out normally, without any effort, with your mouth slightly open and at rest. Feel yourself breathing but do not try to regulate your breath in any way.

Now, think of an Essence Quality that you chose in Lesson 4, such as Unconditional Love or Fulfillment, and say this word silently to yourself on each inhale, drawing this quality deeply into the center of your heart. On the exhale, release anything that is in the way of being completely immersed in this Essence Quality. Stay with this meditation for at least three minutes, or until you feel a deep sense of peace wash over you.

BONUS: PRACTICE IN ACTION

The apostle Paul admonished us to "pray without ceasing," indicating that none of our concerns are too foolish or insignificant to bring before God in prayer.

Today, we're going to practice bringing our concerns to a Higher Power by making a "God Box." A God Box is any container—a shoe box, glass jar, wooden container, metal can, or a paper bag—anything that you can decorate and put slips of paper in and take them out. Sometime today, find and decorate a container that you can use as your God Box.

Make a list of those things that you are worried or anxious about today—your relationship to a particular person, your money, your health, your livelihood, etc. You may want to put "finding my life partner" on your list. Take a piece of paper and cut or rip it into smaller pieces. Write down each concern you have on its own slip of paper.

One at a time, place each concern into your God Box while saying a prayer, surrendering that concern to God. Your prayer might sound something like this:

Dear God, I am giving this concern to You for Your keeping.
Please resolve this issue in the best possible way for all involved.

Once you've given your concern to God, you no longer have to worry about it. It's now God's concern. If you decide that you want to start worrying about that concern again, you literally have to go to the God Box, take out the slip of paper with that particular worry on it, and hold it in your own hands. When you are finished worrying, surrender your concern again to God by placing the slip of paper back into the God Box and repeating the prayer.

LESSON 28
Making Wise Choices

Choice is your greatest power. It is an even greater power than love,
because you must first choose to be a loving person.

—Caroline Myss, *Sacred Contracts*

Ever since the 1960s, when many of our conventions and social constructs were rendered wide open for critique and review, we've had fewer and fewer communal absolutes from which to live our lives. Discovering what's right for us, as opposed to what's right, period, has never been a project of such ambiguous proportions. This is largely because, in the history of humankind, we have never before dealt with as many moral and ethical uncertainties as we do today.

Contrary to the way human beings have been living for tens of thousands of years, we of the twenty-first century now make choices regarding just about every aspect of our lives that, just a mere hundred years ago, would have been inconceivable. We assert the right to choose our sexuality (gay, straight, bi and/or even trans), our religion (the one we were raised in, alternative, traditional, or none at all), our profession (women as CEOs and firefighters, men as homemakers and nurses), where to settle down and build a home (a lovely villa in the south of France, or a man-made igloo on the Arctic shore), what kind of diet we wish to eat (high protein/low carb, vegetarian, fruitarian, or junk food), whether or not to have children (birth control, vasectomies, or abortions), and—of course—who, and even if, we wish to marry (as opposed to, of course you will marry, of course it will be to someone of the opposite sex, and, as a matter of fact, that person has already been chosen for you). Freedom is an awesome responsibility. So, if you're feeling overwhelmed and confused about the enormous amount of choice you now face on a daily basis, welcome to the club. We all are. But nowhere is our anxiety more acute than regarding what appears to be the absolute chaos and total lack of predictability of our modern-day mating rituals. We respond to this free-for-all with a profound need for someone who can tell us "the rules." We wish that somebody would just explain to us how all of this is supposed to work. We want an expert—some book, talk show, or religious teaching—to provide us with some concrete structure to this madness called dating, courtship, and getting engaged in the twenty-first century.

But one of the realities of our time is that no such scaffolding exists as an absolute, agreed upon collective truth in modern-day America. Whereas once upon a time, everyone in the community could agree on how courtship was supposed to go, that simply is no longer the case. And so, unless we are part of some smaller community or culture where the rules of the game are clearly upheld, we are pretty much left to our own devices. We must find our own way amid the rubble of our failed courtships, our dashed expectations, and our ever-present ticking clocks. (And, yes, men have them, too.) There may be dating trends and statistical probabilities, but there are few absolutes anymore when it comes to the mating game. And that means that it is essential—*now more than at any other time in the history of humanity*—that we master the art of making good, healthy, and wise choices, based strongly upon an inherent esteem of ourselves and of others. As society is no longer making our choices for us, we recognize that our destiny is now in our own hands. It is both a wonderful and a terrifying charge. When we are in poverty, there is little to choose from. When we are in abundance, life is a constant series of choices. Therefore, one of the goals we aspire to in life is to actually increase the number of choices we are faced with, and to become better and better at fielding them.

On the most fundamental level, keeping your life free of the messes and entanglements that unwise choices create is actually one of the best things you can do to prepare yourself for love. Melissa, a twenty-something actress, is a natural beauty. She came to me for counseling after a series of failed relationships. Melissa's pattern was to attract people (women, in her case) who were unavailable for a long-term commitment. She was getting sick and tired of being sick and tired. She worked hard for many months to uncover some core beliefs that had kept her unconsciously choosing women who were not available to love and be loved. She found two underlying beliefs that she had been dancing with for years. The first was a covert belief that she was unlovable, an interpretation she made as a four-year-old when her father walked out on her and her mother, without looking back. And the second was a fear that, if she surrendered herself to someone, that person would somehow begin to control and abuse her. This was also a belief that was formed in response to her father, whom she remembered as being excessively dominating and bossy with both her and her mother. Armed with having made that which was unconscious now conscious, Melissa was hopeful that she would finally have access to creating a loving relationship.

As is often the case, the first several opportunities that Melissa encountered for romantic liaisons, were again with people who were unavailable. One was an actress who was on her way out of town to do a play in another city, with an anticipated long run. The next was a smart and savvy bisexual woman who, it turned out, was still living with her ex-husband. The third, Alison, was the "woman of Melissa's dreams." She was everything that Melissa had hoped for—charismatic, bright, funny, spiritual, beautiful, and extremely accomplished. Unfortunately, Alison also happened to be in a long-term relationship with another woman, and together they were co-parenting a child. He was only five, and Alison made it clear that they were committed to living as a family unit until he graduated from high school. Talk about a no-win situation. I wish I could tell you that Melissa wasn't tempted, but she was. It was agony for her to turn Alison down. But, after a few topsy-turvy weeks, turn her down she did. She made the difficult decision to avoid an avoidable drama, even if that meant that she would be alone in life. Two weeks after making this decision, Melissa met her partner, whom she considers to be the love of her life and her soul mate. Looking back, she now shudders to think how close she came to missing the opportunity to be with her mate, for what would surely have been another heartache and disappointment.

Our fantasy is that, once we see our pattern clearly and make a definite decision to do things differently, our external world will begin to change immediately. In lieu of meeting yet another unavailable person, we will suddenly begin meeting only available people who are ready to

> We have to work to be good people... Goodness always involves the choice to be good.
> —Liv Ullmann

make a commitment. Instead of meeting more mean and abusive people, we will suddenly begin attracting kind and gentle souls who offer nothing but love and encouragement. This is rarely the case. What is more likely to happen is that, instead of immediately attracting a whole new kind of person into our lives, we find ourselves attracting exactly the same kind of person, or a person who at first appears to be different but isn't really. We are challenged with temptations that are similar to the ones we have faced in the past. Only this time we're wiser. This time we know exactly where a particular path will lead. We must make the more difficult choice by saying no to the enticement of doing the exact same thing while hoping for different results. We must choose to remain empty-handed rather than settle for repeating past mistakes. This temptation will generally happen not just once, not just twice, but usually several times. It's as though the Universe is testing us—are you truly finished replicating the familiar and known? Have you really given up the need to prove that you aren't worthy of love? Are you willing to stand in the void rather than compromise yourself again? These tests come our way whenever we declare to the Universe that we are ready to change. It is as though we are the protagonists of our own mythical tales, challenged to slay our internal dragons by making the right choices, based upon faith, and requiring immense courage. We are all searching for our own holy grail—the promise of falling into a sacred experience of eternal and transcendent love.

Most of us, however, can point to a series of failed tasks and unmet challenges. We suffer with regrets about our past choices, particularly given the severe consequences that some of these decisions have rendered. But we needn't beat ourselves up about the shoulda, woulda, couldas of our lives. Rather, we need to accept all of the decisions we've made to date, and come to terms with the lost opportunities and losses we've encountered. If we can see our lives as a series of challenges that provide us with opportunities for growth, with the goal of advancing ourselves in wisdom and compassion, then it is easier to accept our past failures and disappointments. When we value life from the perspective of what we've learned, then failure is redefined. As there is no greater teacher than a missed opportunity and no greater lesson than the lesson of love gone awry, then those of us who have failed the most might also be the wisest and most compassionate among us.

Contrary to pop culture, life is not so much about getting what we want when we want it, as it is about appreciating what we have when we have it. It's about learning to make choices that validate the value of the lives we have right now. Every decision we make, even the seemingly small and insignificant ones, have weight and authority in the Universe to either create a life that we love and cherish, or one that is filled with compromises and disappointments. Let's learn to value the making of the "right" choice not because it's the right choice for others, not because it's the expected choice, the easiest one, or the path of least resistance. No, let's instead, learn to value the making of the right choice because it is the right choice for us. Because it is the choice that is most true to who and what we are. Because we rise to the occasion of our lives and gather the courage required to fulfill our most sacred task of all—the task of loving ourselves absolutely and reflecting this love in all aspects of our lives.

> Like heroes in a mythic journey, we are meant to struggle to make the right choices.
> —Caroline Myss

PRACTICE

Take out your journal and write on the following questions:

What choices have I made in life that I regret most and why?

What lesson(s) did I learn as a result of making these choices?

What good came from each of these choices?

What choices have I made based upon the values of others (parents, friends, advisers, teachers, etc.) rather than upon my values?

What were the consequences of those choices?

What choices do I feel most proud of and why?

What lesson(s) did I learn as a result of making these choices?

What good came from each of these choices?

What choices am I facing today and in what ways could
I respond that would reflect a deep honoring and respect for
myself and all involved?

BONUS: PRACTICE IN ACTION

As you move through your day, notice what you do each time you are faced
with a choice. Do you look to others to try and second-guess what choice
would please them, automatically responding the way you think you are
"expected" to, or rise to the occasion of asserting what truly is best for you
and others in any given situation? Wherever you find yourself automatically trying to please others at your own expense, or making a poor choice
simply out of habit, try making a different choice than the one you feel
compelled to make (for example, if your boss always expects you to work
late at the last minute, try telling her that you aren't available to do so
tonight; or if you are shy and normally avoid the limelight, try taking a risk
to share your feelings with a group of people, etc.).

Before bed, take out your journal and write down the different choice(s)
that you made today and what it was like for you to make them. Write also
about any insights you had regarding your relationship to making wise
choices.

SUGGESTED STUDY GUIDE
FOR GROUP DISCUSSION

1. Share your vision of love fulfilled in your life. What would you have to give up or embody to manifest this vision?

2. Share the intention you created this week. What actions have you taken, if any, to support your intention?

3. Share about your sense of purpose. What are you passionate about and what outlets do you have to express your passion in the world?

4. What is your experience of going within for guidance? What guidance, if any, did you receive this week?

5. Where has your integrity been out of balance and what have you done recently to clean it up?

6. What choice did you make in the past that you regret and what valuable lesson came from that experience? What similar choice(s) are you facing today and how are you considering responding?

FIRST THINGS FIRST

The truth about intimate relationships is that they can never be any better than our relationship with ourselves.

—James Hollis, *The Middle Passage*

We've all heard it said countless times. "You have to love yourself before you can love another." But what does it mean to love ourselves? And how exactly do we set about to do it?

This week:

✳ We begin by addressing the need to make a fundamental commitment to ourselves before we are ready to commit to another

✳ We challenge our notions that all selfishness is bad, elevating our ability to give ourselves what we need as the foundation for giving to others

✳ We examine our ability to receive the love that others are moved to give us

✳ We take a look at our relationship to our bodies and our sexual selves

✳ We consider ways we might become more emotionally intimate with ourselves, thereby enhancing our ability to be intimate with someone else

LESSON 29
On Making Commitments

Real love is a prayer and a deathless promise.... Emotions and desires can come and go as they please, and circumstances can change in startling ways, but real love never wavers.

—Karla McLaren, *Emotional Genius*

Thirty-nine-year-old Donna had never been in a committed relationship. Although she complained that she always seemed to meet unavailable men, she eventually had to admit that it was she herself who was ultimately unavailable. Once she took responsibility for her reluctance to surrender herself fully to another person, Donna met Anthony, a forty-nine-year-old widower who appeared to be looking for his new life partner. After several months of dating and developing a friendship, Donna leaned in over dinner one night, took a deep breath, and asked Anthony if he would consider dating her exclusively, in the hope that their relationship might go to the next level. She admitted to him that she felt ready to commit to one person, and she was hoping that person would be him. Anthony paused for a long while before confessing that he didn't see a future for them. While he had grown to care about her very much and hoped that they would always be friends, he just did not feel that she was the right person for him. For a few minutes Donna felt hurt and rejected. But then she looked up and smiled. "I've just had a breakthrough," she said. "That's the first time I've ever been willing to commit myself to anyone. I'm disappointed that you said no but I'm damned proud of myself for asking." They laughed together and toasted to a new Donna. Within the year, Donna was happily, joyfully engaged to another man, and Anthony remains a good friend to this day.

Many people have an almost paralyzing fear of making commitments. How would you know if you are one of these "commitment phobic" people? Well, if you find yourself always in relationship with unavailable people, as Donna did, then that's probably a pretty good clue. Commitments both entice and terrify us. We inherently know that in order to create deeper meaning in our lives, we must risk surrendering to someone or something beyond ourselves. Yet yielding ourselves in this way obliges us beyond our passing moods or situations, and calls us to be bigger than our current circumstances.

In the context of lifelong partnership, love is not an emotion. Love is a course, an utterly steadfast, stable path that deviates not in the face of hardship or challenge. It is an undeniably fixed and invariable promise that does not waver, even in the face of death. While we may look for a mate who shares our hobbies, is sexually attractive, makes us laugh, and helps us to feel good, these things are not the substance of love. All of our criteria for finding a mate—the person has to look this way, have that kind of job, dress like this, be hip, have this much money, etc., are all things that will disappear with time. None of them will last. All that will last is the love that was given and the love received. True love must transcend our limited views of love, for true love stands in its own category. As such, it is not dependent upon the endless ebb and flow of our emotions and on the ever-changing agendas of our current likes and dislikes.

We are usually so consumed by, and in reaction to, the emotions we are experiencing in any given moment that we often forget what it is to be committed to something this large, this grand, this universal. Many of us don't even know where we are standing in life, and are tossed to and fro and every which way according to the current tides, or ideas of the masses. One client of mine, a single man nearing forty, has a hard time making any commitments at all. Even arriving at our sessions on time has proven to be burdensome for him. He is completely engaged in whatever emotion he happens to be feeling at the moment, and any infringement on his ability to explore and express that emotion fully, disturbs him deeply. At a distance, his way of life seems somewhat admirable and romantic. In reality, he is the prisoner of his emotions and his prison is costing him relatedness and love. Underneath his adventurous spirit, he is lonely to the core. He very much lives with the sadness that comes from continually disappointing those who love him. And he is terribly con-

He who would go a hundred miles should consider ninety-nine as halfway.

—Japanese proverb

> We know what happens to people who stay in the middle of the road. They get run down.
>
> —Aneurin Bevan

fused much of the time because he has no center, no commitments from which to ground his life.

Our commitments are that which we orbit around. They are our sun, and they feed us the ability to organize our lives around that which is meaningful to us. Many of us resist making commitments, however, because we fear that we will be overcome by the vastness of the promises we make, as though we might disappear and lose ourselves completely. Rather than respond to this fear by developing a healthy ability to establish limits and set boundaries, we settle for the dramas and distractions inherent in a commitment-free life. Rather than learn how to remain a separate and whole individual, while honoring and relating deeply to others, we simply run as fast as we can. The very thought of surrendering ourselves to this extraordinary experience is enough to make us bolt. In vying to keep our options open, we land nowhere and belong to no one.

Without commitments, we stand isolated and alone in life. Our entire sense of interconnectedness and belonging is directly related to our willingness to commit to one another. If you don't yet have your mate in your life, then commit yourself to an idea, a path, a cause, or a community. Many single people are in tremendous amounts of pain because they have nothing to care about, nothing to surrender themselves to, nothing to love deeply. But there are millions of people in the world who need our love every day—millions of animals, children, and elderly who are withering and dying for lack of love and belonging. We can't be so selective, and still thrive in life. We can't say, "I'm just going to withhold all the love I have to give, until that one specific person that I deem worthy comes along," and think that life will feel as though it's worth living. That kind of stinginess dries up the soul and is an agony for the heart.

One of the reasons we're suffering from such severe loneliness and depression today is because we've come to value the pursuit of personal gain as superior to the pursuit of the collective good. The pursuit of personal gratification (and not necessarily the pursuit of happiness) has become synonymous with a constitutional right. As long as I can get away with it, I'll do as I please, when I please, and to whom I please, no matter if others get hurt. Oftentimes that way of thinking is even considered entrepreneurial and industrious. In truth, most of us have become so unrelated to those around us that we're blind to how our actions do and do not affect them. However, the less we are willing to be responsible for how our actions affect those around us, the lonelier and sadder we will ultimately be in life.

Our ability to commit to the well-being of others is, of course, predicated upon our ability to commit to our own well-being. Without this fundamental pledge to ourselves, we are limited in what we actually have to offer others. I remember distinctly the moment my entire life transformed itself. I was in my mid-twenties and living in a tiny studio apartment in the meatpacking district of New York City, long before that was a fashionable part of town. I was struggling terribly with an eating disorder I'd had since the age of fourteen, trying desperately to heal myself, but with little success. As I stood at the corner, waiting for the light to change (what a great metaphor), I was having a silent dialogue with myself. I was trying to figure out what was missing in my attempts to stop hurting myself by my addictive, compulsive behaviors. Tears began rolling down my cheeks as I realized that no one had ever fought for me in the way that I was being called to fight for myself. No one had ever gone to the wall to ensure my safety and well-being. No one had ever risen to heroic heights in order to make sure that I had a chance to thrive in life. In that moment, I made a commitment to take a stand for my life. I would fight for me. I would go to the wall for me. I would be my own heroine. And the light turned green.

I have seen it demonstrated time and time again, first in my own life and then in the lives of others—that everything of substance you will ever have to offer to anyone else in this lifetime begins with a commitment that you make to yourself. There is simply no skipping this step, particularly for those of us who had less than ideal parenting where the ability of our caregivers to commit to our happiness and well-being was somewhat limited or compromised.

Commitment is the matter from which miracles are made. Many of us want proof that something is going to work out the way we want it to before we make a commitment to it. We want to know that it's a sure bet, a good and solid place to invest our energies. While this is understandable, there is a certain synchronicity that reserves itself for when one

> The more one forgets himself—by giving himself to a cause to serve or another person to love— the more human he is and the more he actualizes himself.
> —Viktor E. Frankl

If I love myself
I love you.
If I love you
I love myself.

—Rumi

makes a wholehearted investment of oneself that simply cannot be foreseen. The most miraculous and unanticipated events can happen out of a stand taken by someone in a moment of truth and passion. Just as true, the most promising of possibilities can easily disappear and slip right through our fingers simply because we were too cautious or too fearful to surrender ourselves fully to the fulfillment of their potential. This phenomenon is what German poet Goethe, was addressing when he so accurately wrote:

> Concerning all acts of initiative (and creation), there is one elementary truth, the ignorance of which kills countless ideas and splendid plans: that the moment one definitely commits oneself, then Providence moves too. All sorts of things occur to help one that would never otherwise have occurred. A whole stream of events issues from the decision, raising in one's favor all manner of unforeseen incidents and meetings and material assistance, which no man could have dreamed would have come his way.

PRACTICE

Take out your journal and answer the following questions:

What are my commitments to myself?

What are my commitments to God (as I understand God)?

What are my commitments to others?

Which, if any, of my commitments have become obligatory and outdated, and should be either renegotiated and/or released?

What new commitments can I make to help expand my sense of connection and belonging in the world?

BONUS: PRACTICE IN ACTION

Take at least one action today that stretches you to go beyond business as usual that is born out of a commitment you've made to others (for instance, volunteer for your political party, make a financial pledge to a local charity). Tell at least one person all of the things that you are committed to in your life today (such as taking care of your physical well-being, finding "The One"). Tell this person of any commitments that you have decided to let go of (for example, the old, outdated relationship that no longer serves you, the volunteer commitment that leaves you feeling drained and uninspired).

LESSON 30
A Case for Selfishness

*If you are attached to being the lover or the giver—as opposed
to giving when giving is needed or loving when loving is
needed—then you are bound to be depleted. I must always
maintain my own core or I have nothing to give from.
Periodically, it is appropriate to take a break from giving.*

—Reverend Amy Wiggins

Andrea, an attractive, educated woman who owns her own home, came
to a recent workshop and told us all a story. While on a first date with a
man she'd met on the Internet, Andrea mentioned that one of her
specialties was homemade banana pudding. The man enthusiastically
expressed that he *loved* banana pudding, and so she promised to make
him some. He suggested that they have a picnic the following Sunday, and
Andrea agreed. She was so excited that she purchased all of the ingredients the following day. However, when he hadn't called her by Thursday
night, Andrea started getting anxious. When she hadn't heard from him
by Friday, she called him and left a message. He didn't call her back that
night. Nor did he call on Saturday. Nor did he call on Sunday. Instead of
letting it go, however, Andrea proceeded to make him the promised pudding because she "said she'd do it." She drove across town and knocked
on his door Sunday afternoon, with a smile on her face and a big bowl of
banana pudding in her hands. He answered the door, looking uncomfortable and unpleasantly surprised. Andrea could see that he had company—another woman who was glaring at her from across the room.
Andrea sheepishly gave him the pudding, mentioning that he and "his
guest" might enjoy it. Of course, she never heard from him again.

This over-attaching and giving away of ourselves to someone who has not yet displayed their intentions toward us is all too common among those of us who are more used to being the "giver" than the "receiver." Andrea thought she was being generous, and yet she ended up feeling completely humiliated and devalued by her behavior. Upon reflection, she saw that what initially appeared to be a charitable gesture on her part, was really a covert attempt to get something that she wanted. She wanted the man to like her. She wanted him to want her. She made that pudding because she was auditioning for the role of girlfriend. However, as she admitted, that's not really giving. That's manipulation. To her credit, she got the lesson. She is now much more conscious about overly attaching herself to someone she barely knows, who has not yet demonstrated a high regard for her.

Some of us give because we can't *not* give. It's our way of getting by in the world. At least if I give, the thinking goes, others will like me. Better yet, they may even come to need me. Then I won't be so alone in the world. Giving becomes a kind of barter to belong—a bid for love, rather than an expression of it. This kind of giving does not allow for selfishness of any kind, and yet it is excessively selfish. Anyone who has been in relationship with someone who has played the martyr role knows how selfish giving can be.

Buddhism encourages us to discover selflessness, while Christianity admonishes us to "die to self." Yet, not until we've developed a fundamental sense of self is it appropriate to surrender in this way. Not until we've experienced how delicious and enjoyable healthy selfishness can be, do we actually have something to present as an offering. Years ago, at one of her lectures here in Los Angeles, I remember Marianne Williamson saying, "You have to actually *have* an ego before you can give it up."

"Healthy selfishness" means you know your limits, and you set them. It means you prioritize self-care *over* caring for others. It insists that you communicate your feelings, even when your feelings are inconvenient to others. It includes the ability to rest when tired, and to ask for what you want and need, *when* you want and need it. It is the healthy expression of entitlement.

I have a doctor in my practice who can't say no to any of her patients. She ends up working too many hours (since she can't turn anyone away)

Don't ask yourself what the world needs. Ask yourself what makes you come alive. Then go and do that. Because what the world needs is people who have come alive.

—Harold Whitman

for too little money (since she undercharges those who can't, or simply don't want to, pay her prices). She is too exhausted to date, go out with friends, or do anything fun for herself. She resents going to work all the time and yet, even if a stranger calls to make an appointment, she'll instruct her assistant to schedule the person. She is always at the mercy of what others want from her. She is very lonely but she only has time to feel those feelings when she is not working. Recently, she has begun scheduling patients seven days a week.

As a girl, this doctor had an overpowering, dominating mother who never allowed her daughter to say no to her tyrannical demands. When parents are profoundly self-absorbed and needy (as in "narcissistic"), as this doctor's mother was, the children will often grow up to become "accommodators." With little awareness of their own needs, they have an exaggerated awareness of the needs of others. They become driven by an intense need to take care of those around them, but usually do so at their own expense. It took a while, but the doctor finally began to understand that she was assuming that her patients were just like her mother. She began setting limits little by little, and was stunned to discover that people were usually pleasant and agreeable when she needed to say no to them. It was an absolute revelation that changed her life.

People who have poor boundaries—those who don't set limits, prioritize self-care, or even *know* what they are feeling, let alone express their feelings to others, usually end up in relationships with people who suck energy, take more than they give, and have little real love to offer. You'd think that someone as "nice and giving" as my patient, the doctor, might attract in a "nice and giving" man. To the contrary, every man she has ever had a relationship with has been either excessively narcissistic, or an alcoholic whom she ended up financially supporting. When we don't honor ourselves, we attract in people who don't honor us either.

Many of us confuse intimacy with a collapse of boundaries. We idealize love as meaning that we have no secrets, and hold no thought for ourselves. But nothing could be farther from the truth. You must be a strong, separate self, before you can sustain love with another person. The idea that intimacy with another depends upon your ability to tolerate your own separateness, might, at first, appear paradoxical. Yet, until you have a strong sense of self, you will probably have a hard time enduring the pull toward fusion, which often passes for intimacy. The tendency toward merging yourself with another, more commonly referred to as "losing yourself" in relationship, happens when one or both people lack a fundamental connection with themselves as the foundation for connection with another.

In order to engage in a healthy, loving dynamic with another person, you must be actively engaged in the process of discovering who you are at all times. That means that you must be willing to explore and admit your thoughts, feelings, and behaviors to yourself and others, even if you think they are unacceptable. You must be willing to be honest with yourself and another person about both your strengths and your shortcomings. You must be willing to "tell on yourself" when you have less than loving motives, as we all do at times.

This doesn't mean that I'm an advocate for "no holds barred" communication that frequently passes for intimacy. I don't believe we need to tell those we love everything we think or feel about them. Communication for communication's sake is not the goal, because you have to ask yourself, what am I communicating here? Am I communicating hatred and anger, or am I communicating compassion and kindness? Because if we want happy and healthy relationships, we need to be adept at the art of communicating love. Therefore, I'm an advocate of the "bring your best, most mature and loving self to your relationship" type of communication. But again, the only way to do that is to truly know yourself, so that you can deal with those parts of you that are petty and small and will hurt the relationship if not dealt with authentically.

It's also very important to balance self-care and healthy selfishness with an awareness of the impact we have on others. I had a boyfriend once who had the maddening habit of withholding any and all expressions of love, both emotional and physical, for long periods of time whenever he was angry, which was often. He would hold me at a distance just enough to upset me, but without letting me go. After a while, I would get angry back and try to push him to either be in the relationship or to end it. He would reply that he was just "taking care of himself." He'd then tell me that he thought that I was an excessively angry person. "Do you think that the

Lift up the self
by the Self
And don't let the
self droop down,
For the Self is the
self's only friend
And the self is the
Self's only foe.
—Bhagavad Gita 6:5

Thou shalt not
give beyond thine
own capacity.
—Catherine Cardinal

way you are behaving has anything to do with how angry I am?" I'd ask. He'd reply, in an all too common misunderstanding of what it is to have good boundaries, "I'm not responsible for how you feel." I finally figured out that there was nothing to do but leave. He was just too unkind. I learned a good lesson, though. I now only allow people into my inner circle who are willing to be responsible for the impact that their behavior has on those around them.

It's important that we know our limits. It's important that we understand what we *don't* want, what we *won't* put up with, and what we absolutely *will not* tolerate. We must be clear about which opportunities presented to us are ones that we should pass on. This is actually one of the reasons why making "the list" is a good thing and why we will eventually get to it. Because, if "spiritual" is near the top of your list, then you probably don't want to spend your time getting to know someone who doesn't really value the spiritual path. If "financial security" is a main priority, then you probably shouldn't be seeing a struggling artist, because you'll only torture him for who he isn't, and undermine the talent that he is.

Saying no creates boundaries that serve as the container for love. When we are authentic with ourselves by setting our limits, honoring our feelings, prioritizing our own well-being, and clearly defining our wants and needs, we identify the path we are on, making it much easier for love to come to us. Because, as Henry Kissinger once said, "If you don't know where you are going, every road will get you nowhere."

PRACTICE

Take out your journal. Complete the following sentence stems with as many answers as you can think of:

I find it difficult to say "no" when . . .

When I do say "no," I feel . . .

I prioritize self-care by . . .

I compromise self-care when I . . .

What I really want in a romantic partner is . . .

What I absolutely need in an intimate relationship is . . .

What I absolutely will not settle for in an intimate
relationship is . . .

BONUS: PRACTICE IN ACTION

Challenge yourself by saying no at least once more than you ordinarily
would today (for example, when your coworker asks you to help him by
working through lunch, when your sister-in-law asks you to watch her
three kids next Saturday night, when your friend asks if you can lend her
the money she needs to purchase a coveted sweater). Notice how it feels to
do what is right for you, even when someone else is disappointed and
noticeably displeased.

Your second task is to do at least one thing today as an exercise in self-
care (e.g., schedule a massage for yourself, go for a walk when you "should"
be working, don't answer the phone when you need a break).

LESSON 31
The Art of Receiving

Someone who does not know how to receive love will, of course,
end up feeling unloved. We then grow bitter or cynical, making us
less and less attractive, keeping love at a distance, and bolstering
our belief that a loving universe isn't really that loving in *our* case.

—Marianne Williamson, *Enchanted Love*

I took a style and wardrobe class recently, and met a smart and attractive woman named Sally. A sixty-year-old, divorced redhead, Sally won everyone over immediately with her warmth and self-effacing humor. On the first night of the class, she confided in a few of us that men hit on her quite often but rarely wanted more than sex. I was enchanted, but not too surprised, that men would find Sally so irresistible and desirable. I confess, however, that I was a little baffled as to why they did not seem to want more from her than sex.

One night, the instructor took us all shopping. It was great fun picking out outfits for one another and trying them on to the enthusiasm of a collective thumbs-up, or to the groans and moans of a collective thumbs-down. The instructor picked out an outfit for Sally to try on that she absolutely balked at. It was in her colors and in her size, but the style was much softer and more feminine than she was used to. The shirt had ruffles cascading down the center and the skirt flared out with a beautiful ruffle on the bottom. She reluctantly put it on. Everyone absolutely cooed over her in this outfit. I looked her straight in the eye and said, "If you wear that, someone is going to ask you to marry him." She looked terribly uncomfortable as she shook her head, vehemently saying, "I'd feel way too vulnerable in this dress." She couldn't take the outfit off fast enough.

Receptive energy is soft, open, and vulnerable. When we are receptive, we are open to taking in the energy of others. Literally, we are available for penetration, on every level. What I discovered while shopping with Sally was that, while she was a lovely woman, she just wasn't that available. She had no intention of feeling too exposed and defenseless when it came to men. However, I've learned that if a man can't access your softness and your vulnerability, he'll settle for the sex instead. And you'd probably think that that was all he wanted.

Most of us are pretty good givers, especially when we're allowed to give on our own terms. We women have actually been brought up to put the needs of other people before our own, but a lot of men have learned a thing or two about self-effacing sacrifice and capitulation, as well. Most of us can caretake and borrow against ourselves with the best of them. Often, we've served as nursemaids, lay counselors, and unsalaried secretaries to those in our lives. The less common phenomenon is the woman who has learned how to *be supported,* in addition to knowing how to support others, and how to *be nurtured,* in addition to know how to nurture others.

When we look for our spiritual partner, we are looking for someone who gets our greatness, and not just someone whose greatness we see. Contrary to the marriages of the 1950s where the wife devoted her entire life to supporting the success and fulfillment of her husband's vision, current-day spiritual partnership is a two-way street. Love and vision flow in both directions. You want to know that the person you are choosing truly sees the highest vision of your life, and understands the possibilities of what it is to be you.

I dated a man once who told me that he thought I was too self-important in my desire to be a leader and a teacher. He thought it was arrogant of me to want to write a book. That was the last date we ever had. Not because he was a bad person. I just didn't want to have to convince someone of my greatness. It's just not a good use of my energy.

Many times, we choose to be with people who don't really get us and, therefore, can't really support us. We do this because (1) we don't quite believe in the possibility of our own greatness and (2) because we're not even aware of what it would be like to be supported. We're so used to going it alone that it doesn't even occur to us to look for someone who would love to put the gust in our sails and the wind beneath our wings. We're just not used to be given to in this way.

> The art of pleasing consists in being pleased.
> —William Hazlitt

After spending the weekend away locked in a hotel room so I could write this book, I was driving home on the freeway when I had a realization. The impact of it forced me to get off at the next exit. I parked by the side of the road, so I could just sit there and let myself cry. I'd just left my husband home alone with a two-year-old for three days so I could meet my publisher's deadline. He had not uttered one complaint about this difficult task, and actually was the one who encouraged me to go. After being on my own until well after the age of forty, with no one to pick up the slack, or cover for me when I needed help, I actually had someone in my life now who was *so* on my side, and *so* in my corner that he'd do just about anything to have me win in life. Not only did he have my back but, cliché as it sounds, in that moment I realized that he'd probably even take a bullet for me. That's really something to have. That's really something to *allow* yourself to have.

It's important that we let ourselves be receptive and available to the impulses that others have to give to us. Just as love that only comes *in* is off, love that only goes *out* is off, too. Love is fluid. At its best, giving and receiving are barely distinguishable from one another. Many of us think that it's somehow noble to thwart the attempts of others to give to us. We think it's gracious to keep our needs to ourselves. But when we refuse to allow others to be generous and extend themselves for our well-being, we don't allow them to express the best of who they are. We don't allow them the opportunity of coming into the fullness of their capacity to love. We actually stop the growth of love, putting up a roadblock in its development.

Terry feels very alone in life. Not only is she single, but she is also alienated from her family, through no fault of her own. Like many people whose families have disappointed and betrayed them, Terry has learned to not need other people too much. Her aloneness is very, very difficult for her, even more so now that she has been unemployed for nearly a year. With no one to back her up, her dwindling financial stash is a downright inadequate safety net. The man Terry has been dating for several months now recently offered to pay for all of their dates, given her current circumstances. She declined his offer, insisting that she pay for half of everything, just as she had done all along.

I tried to explain to Terry that by refusing his offer, she was averting the very thing she wanted the most—love—from taking root in their relationship. When a person freely offers to extend themselves on our behalf, they do so because, on some level, they know that it's good for them to do so. His impulse to begin providing Terry with the safety net that is missing from her life is his way of expressing his love for her. That she didn't expect him to pay for her is endearing, given the situation she's in. That she won't accept his offer to pay, however, is questionable. Terry tells me that she is afraid that she would be a burden to her boyfriend if she let him pay for their dates. I tell her that that would probably be so if he didn't actually love her. Yet, if he doesn't love her, then she probably shouldn't be with him.

That old saying "It is better to give than to receive" is telling only half of the story. We are all pining to love in such a way that we are inspired to give of ourselves. That's why we look for charities to give to, why we volunteer for organizations where people come to depend upon us, and why we birth children who we can love and sacrifice ourselves for. We are all looking for something or someone who will compel us to extend ourselves beyond our own little lives. We want to give in a way that creates meaning, fills us with a sense of purpose, and a feeling of usefulness. When someone decides that we fit that bill for them, when they are inspired to care for us, provide for us, and nurture us, to decline that love is like sending back a great and magnificent gift unopened. There is really nothing noble about it. It's frustrating and disappointing for all.

Love can't take hold in an atmosphere where people won't be vulnerable. It can't blossom when people want to play it safe by staying in the "giver" position. What Terry is really afraid of is being loved. What she is really afraid of is surrendering herself and letting go of control. She is so used to being autonomous and alone that, in spite of her chronic complaints about it, she doesn't even know who she'd be if she allowed herself to be loved and cared for. Allowing someone else to love her is actually an assault to her identity.

English poet Joseph Addison, once wrote, "The grand essentials to happiness in this life are something to do, something to love and something to hope for." Allowing yourself to receive the love that another

> What things soever ye desire, when ye pray, believe that ye receive them and ye shall have them.
> —Mark 11:24

Your love has
made me sure.

—Rumi

offers, is often the greatest gift that you can give to someone . . . and, of course, to yourself.

PRACTICE

There is a greeting that some at my church say regularly: "Love in, love out." This morning we are going to practice a simple "Love in, love out" meditation. Read the meditation through once or twice and then do it, as best you can, from memory.

Sit in an upright, relaxed position, connecting deeply with your breath and your heart center. Do a body scan, releasing any tension you may find. Breathe in deeply and slowly, expanding the energy around your heart, and saying to yourself as you breathe, "I receive love from everyone I meet today." On the exhale, repeat, "I give love to everyone I meet today." Repeat this breath for several minutes.

BONUS: PRACTICE IN ACTION

Practice the art of receiving all day. Be aware of each kindness and thoughtfulness shown to you, and consciously receive the love inherent in that gesture. With each greeting, and each question of concern such as "How are you?," repeat silently to yourself, "I receive love from everyone I meet today."

Based upon a commitment to expand your capacity to receive love, make one or more requests today. Making requests is essential in allowing other people to give to us. It is also essential in building self-esteem because it requires us to practice a sense of worthiness and deservability. The requests can be as simple as "Can you give me a ride to the meeting tonight?" or "Will you help me carry these books to the car?" Or they can be more complicated, such as asking your mother to come to therapy with you so that you can complete some issues from the past, or asking your boss for a raise because you truly believe that you've earned it. Stretch yourself. If fear comes up, simply breathe through it, and take the action any-way. The results you get are not as important as your willingness to take the initiative to ask for what you need and want. Regardless of whether or not this particular person says yes or no to your request, asking will open you up to receiving and help you to increase your healthy sense of entitle-ment.

NOTE: Make sure that you give the other person permission to say no to your request. That's what keeps it a request as opposed to a demand.

Before bed, take out your journal and write down the request(s) you made, the response(s) you got, and what each exchange meant to you.

LESSON 32
Body Acceptance and a Woman's Sense of Self-Esteem

> Being preoccupied with our self-image is like...
> coming upon a tree of singing birds while wearing earplugs.
>
> —Pema Chödrön, *When Things Fall Apart*

Sexual, romantic relationship is not just a union of heart, not just a union of soul, but also a union of the body. When we become lovers with someone, we offer up our body as a home and sacred resting place for them. As such, how we feel about our bodies has a huge impact on how open—or how closed—we are to forming such unions.

"It's odd," Samantha said, "but whenever I'm nervous about an upcoming date, my focus goes straight to the size of my thighs. Do I look too fat in these pants? Will he think my butt is too big? You'd think that, instead, I'd be more concerned with how I was feeling about going out with him or whether or not I thought I had anything interesting to talk about." The other women in the group nodded in recognition.

It's all too common for us to transfer any anxieties and insecurities we feel onto the roundness of our bellies or the number on the scale. Being "too fat" has become the catch-all for any feelings of self-doubt, shyness, or unworthiness that we might have.

Usually, when I ask a woman if she loves her body, she'll start telling me what she doesn't like about it. She's already so engaged in an inner dialogue that is constantly chronicling her physical imperfections and flaws, that it's near impossible for her to not respond with a list of things she'd like to improve. But imagine, if you will, calling up a dear friend ten, twenty, thirty times a day to tell her how fat and physically flawed she is. How long do you think she'd tolerate that? How long would you? How is it, then, that so many of us put up with this loathsome dialogue within ourselves day after day after day?

We want to be five pounds thinner, two inches taller, have bigger breasts and smaller hips. We want to firm up and pare down and we want to do it yesterday. Yet, it's very hard to change anything about ourselves while engaging in a diatribe of self-criticism, as most of us do. That would be like me trying to get my seventeen-year-old stepdaughter, Sarah, to change something about herself by telling her everything that's wrong with her, and all the things I don't like about her. Yeah, right. She'd likely respond by digging in her heels and doing absolutely everything in her power to stay exactly the same. Until Sarah knows that I love and accept her absolutely, 100 percent as she is, she is not going to be willing to comply with my demands that she be any different.

We're all like that. The more you tell yourself that your body is too this or too that, not enough this and not enough that, the more you'll likely stay the same, or become even more of whatever you're criticizing yourself for. That's why a lot of diets fail. Because we start them on the basis of how much we hate how we look, or because we'd just as soon die before we'd let anyone see us naked this way. Many diets are just another self-punishment—another way we get to hate ourselves. They're like being put on a strict budget after a naughty spending spree. Just take a look at the collective credit card debt in this country to see how well *that* one works. It's only when we alter our eating habits out of love and respect for ourselves that lasting change has any real chance to take root in our lives.

While most people will acknowledge the massive amounts of misogyny in our culture regarding women's beauty, the majority of us will go right on indulging our right to measure ourselves according to extreme and superficial standards. This form of self-abuse isn't a once-in-a-great-while phenomenon. Self-loathing is rampant. It's actually considered "normal" for us to dislike our bodies. It's "normal" for us to assess our self-worth according to our current dress size. It's "normal" for us to condemn and judge ourselves in punitive, harsh, and disparaging tones when it comes to our physical appearance.

I frequently remind women that, in some parts of Africa, female cir-

> Love built on beauty,
> soon as beauty, dies.
> —John Donne

cumcision—the cutting and mutilation of the clitoris—is also considered "normal." In many remote villages in India, bride burning remains a common and "normal" practice. In some areas of the Middle East, forbidding the education of women, with its resultant poverty for themselves and their children, is, once again, a "normal" phenomenon. Just because something is "normal" does not mean it is not also deeply destructive. Similar to how it is in many Third World countries, we women ourselves are often the ones to perpetuate the abuse of passing these "normal" practices down to our daughters. And on and on it goes, until people wake up from the trance and begin to consider another way.

From the age of nine, when Isabella entered the early stages of puberty, her weight-obsessed, obese mother began a constant commentary on Isabella's size. By the time she was a teenager, Isabella hated her body and loathed going shopping for clothes. Although she was only slightly overweight at the time, her image of herself as obese, like her mother, grew with each passing year.

I met Isabella when she was in her late forties. Although she was only slightly larger than the average woman, her image of herself remained fixed in adolescence. She believed that she was "too fat" and, therefore, unattractive. She blamed her weight for the many disappointing experiences she'd had with men, and felt angry and resentful toward her body for "betraying her." This antagonistic relationship with her body caused her to relate to herself as though she were a talking head, ignoring herself almost entirely from the neck down, which is actually what *I* suspected was more at the root of her difficulties with men. I mean, really, if Isabella is hell-bent on rejecting herself, what chance does anyone really stand with her?

When she came to me, Isabella was struggling with a multitude of health issues. Over the years, she had so tried so hard to un-inhabit her body, that I wasn't surprised she was having these problems. As a matter of fact, I was amazed that she'd been healthy for as long as she had, given that she'd been in a completely hostile and adverse relationship with her body for well over thirty years now. As a neglected child might begin getting into trouble in order to draw attention to herself, so too did Isabella's body begin demanding attention from her. Isabella was forced to begin tending to herself with gestures of loving-kindness and self-care. Little by little, her body began to respond to her attempts to heal, but only in direct proportion to Isabella's willingness to re-create her relationship to it.

It was difficult for Isabella to give up her malevolent attitude toward herself. She wants to lose weight as a precondition to accepting herself. I keep telling her that it's the other way around—that she has to accept herself exactly as she is, as the precondition for transformation. Sometimes we hold on to the very things that are causing us pain. As of this writing, Isabella is still struggling with her tenacious attachment to the idea that she's "too fat to love." She's hauling the burden of her mother's self-hatred around like a monkey on her back. It always amazes me how we'll fight tooth and nail to defend the right to hate ourselves and live compromised lives.

When our relationship to our own body is adversarial, we'll do things such as over, or under eat. We'll make poor food choices, abuse drugs and/or alcohol, and engage in promiscuous and/or high-risk sex. We'll smoke cigarettes, exercise compulsively, and deny ourselves water. We'll forget to rest. We'll relate to our bodies as a series of things that need to be improved upon and/or fixed. We'll fracture and fragment ourselves, objectifying our bodies as much as we complain that men objectify us. We'll reduce our value down to the number of calories consumed that day.

If you are operating under the assumption that who you are before the surgery, underneath the hair dye, and without the makeup is unacceptable, then you may find yourself driven to find a mate with all of the "perfect" criteria (e.g., someone with the "right job," the "right look," from the "right family"), as a way to compensate for what you consider to be your own inadequacies. You may find someone who has all of those external qualities and think, for a while anyway, that you have found love. But, sooner or later, these relationships tend to reveal themselves to be somewhat empty and soulless. The kind of love that we are looking for rarely comes from this way of seeking. There is no heart in it and soul connections are always revealed in the heart. That's why love doesn't always look the way you might think it should. Just like you, yourself, may not look the way you think you should.

> Does my body
> make me look fat?
> —*New Yorker* cartoon

Opening our hearts to ourselves with all of our quirky and irritating physical imperfections—breasts that are "too small," bellies that are "too big," thighs that are "too fat," and feet that are "too flat"—is the most wonderful preparation for love there is. For when we take a lover to our bed, it's all about opening ourselves totally and completely to the experience of being loved and adored for exactly who we are, and exactly who we are not, as well as being willing to extend this sweet state of grace to another.

The most important thing we can accomplish in this lifetime is true self-appreciation and self-acceptance whether or not we see the number that we want on the morning scale. Until we develop the capacity to love and appreciate ourselves *just as we are,* we will go through life with our noses pressed up against the glass. No matter what externals we manage to manifest, in spite of ourselves—right livelihood, the "perfect" mate, healthy children—we will always feel just a little on the wrong side of happiness.

Our bodies are the hosts of our great spirits and the home of our grand souls. They house the vastness of the life force that moves in and through us, and grant us the gift of life itself. To relate to them as anything less than this miracle is a distortion of who and what we are.

PRACTICE

We're going to do an open-eye meditation this morning. Please read through the instructions once or twice and then do it from memory as best you can.

Take off all your clothes and sit or stand comfortably in front of a mirror with your hands relaxed and resting by your sides. Take several deep breaths, relaxing your entire body as your lungs expand and release, expand and release. Do a full body check for any tension you may be holding, beginning at the top of your head and moving down through the bottom of your feet.

Now, start with the top of your head. Notice any judgments you have about your hair or the size and shape of your head. For each judgment you find, talk to the part of your body that you are judging. Take the following three steps with each and every judgment you find:

1. Ask that part of the body to please forgive you for being so harsh and unloving toward it

2. Tell that part of the body something that you can truly appreciate it for

3. Thank that part of the body for something

Here's an example.

Judgment: "I hate how frizzy my hair is." Step 1. "Please forgive me, hair, for telling you over and over how ugly you are." Step 2. "I really appreciate how curly you are. I also like your color and texture." Step 3. "Thank you, hair, for being so full and wild when it rains."

Go through your entire body, doing this process with each judgment you find. For those parts of the body you have no negative judgments about, simply do Steps 2 and 3.

NOTE: If you have a particularly critical and fractured relationship to your body, you might wish to do this meditation on a regular basis until all judgments are neutralized and appreciation is restored.

> The body is a sacred garment. It's your first and last garment; it is what you enter life with and what you depart life with, and it should be treated with honor.
> —Martha Graham

BONUS: PRACTICE IN ACTION

Watch the judgments that pass through your mind today about your physical appearance. Each time you notice that you've criticized yourself for any perceived physical flaw, take Steps 1 through 3 again silently to yourself as you move about your day.

LESSON 33
On Sexual Healing

> Your desire for a new beloved needs to be addressed to
> the spirit of love that resides in every human heart, and to be
> broadcast to the four corners of the earth, reaching out across
> time and space to the unknown partner who is waiting for you.
> Then all the possibilities are open and the magic can unfold
> in its own mysterious and unpredictable way.
>
> —Margo Anand, *The Art of Sexual Magic*

There was a time when I thought I had to go out and "get" myself a lover.
I looked for him as though I were shopping for a new coat. He had to be
the right size, the right color, and have the right kind of style. Most
important, he had to look great on me. I tried on more than a few good
men, but took them off just as fast. Without really meaning to, I created
a lot of hurt feelings. It wasn't intentional. I just didn't have much wisdom when it came to taking a lover.

We all have our stories to tell, although many of us would prefer not
to. Nowhere have we made more drama for ourselves and for others than
in the bedroom. We've misidentified lust as love, and chemistry as connection, more times than we'd care to admit. Decisions that seemed just
fine at midnight looked anything but by the morning's light. We've used
poor judgment, acted out of desperation, been confused, and made mistakes. Welcome to the twenty-first century, where the rules of sexual conduct seem to be to simply make up your own. In the process, most of us
have, at one time or another, been pretty badly burned by the flame of our
own passions.

Sexual energy is a vortex of power like none other. At its most exalted,
sex is nothing short of evidence of our God-like status. Entrusted with the

power to create life and blessed with the ability to breathe healing and vitality into the heart of our lover, we are bestowed with a beautiful and glorious gift. Our desire for sexual bonding illuminates our need to immerse ourselves fully in the forces of love, and merge ourselves with that which lies beyond our individual selves. The loss of separation entered into during sex—the tangling and twisting of legs and limbs, saliva and sweat, is reminiscent of the one time in our lives where our merging was absolute. It is about as close as we will ever come to returning to the oneness that existed for us while still in the womb. As such, sexual union can be likened to a return to source energy. It is the deepest affirmation of life there is.

Yet, as with all powers, sexual energy is also frequently abused and tragically misused, and many of us have suffered severe consequences because of it. At its most debased, sex is the assertion of dominance, a thief who steals power from its prey. Ask any survivor of rape, incest, or sexual abuse what it is like to have one's innocence and sense of personal safety ripped away in this most horrid manner. For many, it is an initiation into the underworld, where years can pass as one struggles through the maze, trying to find their way home again.

All of us wish our broken, crooked places could be made straight again. We want the sorrows and the shame of our sexual woundedness, whether they be self and/or other inflicted, to rise up and out of our bodies, leaving in their place only the lessons learned and the wisdom gained. We know, in our heart of hearts, that we need to reclaim our sexual wholeness. Yet, what we may not be aware of, is how desperately true that is. Sexual energy resides in the second chakra, which is the power base of creativity. As such, sexual energy is the fuel for our creative ventures, whether we are creating another human being, a project, or a loving relationship. When we are not in full possession of our sexual power, because we are holding shame, hurt, defendedness, or rage in this area of our bodies, we are operating at a profound deficit. It's like trying to talk with laryngitis. Our creative powers are blocked, and we are compromised in our ability to invent and initiate the lives we are striving for. It's as though we are working against ourselves. The heart wants love, and the mind thinks it's time to settle down, but the genitals would never even consider

Many a woman has a past, but I am told that she has at least a dozen and that they all fit.
—Oscar Wilde

Don't knock
masturbation.
It's sex with
someone I love.
—Woody Allen

surrendering and letting go completely. We are at odds within ourselves and we become deeply frustrated by this inner divide.

It's not just the most wounded of us who are so divided and disconnected from our sexual centers. Actually, most of us are. Culturally, we hold spirituality and sexuality as belonging in two entirely different camps and Western religions have done us no favor in splitting the two. We've generally come to perceive spirituality as an upper-chakra activity. When we pray and meditate, we contemplate God from the heart up through the top of our heads, as though S/He lived in the sky and only we lowly mortals, down here on earth. We rarely include our genitals and our bellies in our conversations with God.

At the other end of the spectrum, our sexuality is generally considered a lower-chakra phenomenon. Split off from the ethereal energies of the Holy Spirit, sexual energy is experienced from the heart down (if we are fortunate enough to have our hearts connected to our genitals, at all). Our wild sexual passions are widely considered to be a part of the intricate web of temptation and corrosion. Spiritual mystic Osho, once said, "Sex has been called original sin, but there is nothing original about it, nor is it sinful." Yet, for hundreds of years, we have been programmed to think that way.

In the past, being spiritual meant that we left the body. At this point in our spiritual evolution, however, we are called to bring the spirit fully into the body, thereby healing the inner divide. In this context, lovemaking is transformed from an activity of the "flesh," to an activity of the divine. However, we've not yet quite caught up. We're still segregated and confused within our own bodies. In fact, we are so fragmented and fractured regarding our sexual energies, that few of us really trust ourselves when it comes to making good, sound sexual decisions. We don't know our own sensibilities. "Is casual OK, or do I wait until he's committed?" "Should I ask what we need to know upfront (i.e., does this mean we're monogamous?, when was the last time you've been tested?, how do we feel about each other?), or simply cross my fingers and hope for the best?" Given that intuition and wisdom come to us through the sixth (the "third eye") and seventh (the "crown") chakras, and that sexual hunger lives mostly in the first (the "root") and second (the "creative center"), how do we know where to go within ourselves for the answers to our own questions? It's not just the guys who don't know which part of the body to think with any more. It's all of us.

Most of us harbor at least a small amount of shame for past sexual indiscretions—choices that we wish we'd made differently. Our transgressions stay with us somehow, soiling some secret part of our soul, as though something precious and irretrievable has been lost or, worse, stolen from us. We all need to forgive ourselves for some lack of judgment we displayed at one time or another. One man had been in therapy for a year before he dared confess an incestuous incident he'd had when he was ten with his little sister, who was seven at the time. Having finally confessed his horrible sin (for that was what it was for him), after carrying it in secretive shame for nearly twenty years, he was able to make amends with his sister. She was both touched by his grief and deeply healed by it. She assured him that she'd long ago dealt with it and had come to understand it as play between children who were simply curious and adventurous. Their relationship became stronger and he, free for the first time, felt as though a great burden were lifted from him. He had confessed to the part of him that was "perpetrator" and, in so doing, was free to denounce that role by committing himself to becoming "protector" and "provider" to his sister, and, consequently, to all of the women in his life. Not long after, he became engaged and is now very happily married. He attributes his availability to creating a loving relationship with his wife to having healed this sexual wound, which had been seriously eroding his regard of himself as a good and honorable man.

Not all violations are so easily erased. Statistics indicate that nearly one-quarter of us (one-fifth of all men and one-third of all women) were sexually assaulted in childhood. Sexual abuse in childhood can have severe consequences, made more acute because the perpetrations occur at a time when one's personal boundaries are only in the rudimentary stages of formulation. At least when we're adults, we know when we're being violated and we understand that our road of recovery must include reclaiming our sense of power and protection. Children, though, rarely understand what is happening to them. The very people they are supposed to trust suddenly turn on them, infecting them with dark and disturbing forces. They know intuitively that something is very, very bad, but they can't compre-

> Not having tasted
> a single cup of
> your wine
> I'm already drunk.
> —Rumi

Experience is the
name everyone gives
to their mistakes.
—Oscar Wilde

hend what it is in any substantial way. For those who have undergone such an ordeal, I don't have to tell you that surviving childhood sexual abuse is a spiritual path unto itself.

Severe sexual woundings don't just go away. I've met people who twenty, thirty years later, still find that mistrust is globalized to any situation that includes the possibility of closeness and love. Learning to trust another person fully, surrendering both emotionally and physically, is nothing short of a miracle. (So, thank God, we actually *believe* in miracles.) There are clear stages of recovery, and I know very few people, if any, who've been able to navigate that difficult terrain alone. I do know people who've shut down sexually, either through complete abstinence, or some form of dissociation (spacing out, drinking too much, compulsively overeating, bulimic behaviors, etc.), but generally at the cost of intimacy and love. If you've been abused and have not yet received treatment, do yourself a favor. Either make an appointment with a therapist or call a rape hotline, even if the incident happened a long time ago. At the very least, they'll be able to tell you where to go for help.

There is an argument to be made for abstinence during this period of focusing your energies to call in your life partner. However, there are some instances that exist outside of conventional thinking. Just as not all committed sexual encounters are healthy and empowering ones (I recall a client who had been repeatedly raped by her husband), not all noncommitted sexual encounters are "bad" ones, either. I suggest that you make a commitment to yourself that all of your sexual encounters will be honoring and empowering ones. Ask yourself what you need to know *before* taking your clothes off. Stay present and conscious to all parts of yourself when making your decisions. Give yourself permission to change your mind if you become uncomfortable. Make sure that you are safe and that your expectations are realistic. Many of us use sex as a way to try to slip relationship through the backdoor, and it usually winds up to be yet another disappointing experience. If you're going to have sex with someone without a clear commitment, please do yourself a favor and don't expect sex to solidify the deal. I believe that many of us have learned that lesson one too many times.

Culturally, we have reduced sexuality to its most primitive function—

that of a physical act between body parts. In doing so, we have omitted the subtleties of such a soulful encounter, and the inherent power dynamics involved. Much of our focus on sex has to do with how to have more of it, and for longer periods of time. Yet, sexuality extends far beyond penises and vaginas. True sexuality moves us into an almost hedonistic view of the many tactile pleasures and delights available to all of us on any given day. Sensual pleasures such as eating, listening to music, dancing, gardening, or creating art flourish in the lives of the celibate, and rightly so. Our sexuality always transcends whether we have a partner at this particular point in time, or not. Sexuality need not always be literal, and surrendering to passion is not always about orgasm.

My vibrantly creative and beautiful friend Lora, an actress and talk-radio host, has been holding the high watch for her man for well over a year. A highly sensual woman, Lora loves to dance. Every Sunday afternoon, she puts on her tights and her dancing shoes, and spends hours on the dance floor, dancing freestyle. Sometimes she dances alone, sometimes with a partner, sometimes with a group of people. She is in one moment soft and sensual, in another primitive and wild. At times she is light and playful, and then she'll suddenly become heavy and sad. Through all of her moods and emotions, she connects deeply with her body, and allows herself the luxury of self-expression and surrender. She feels the gazes of admiration and desire from the men around her and yet she knows that she is there for herself and herself alone. Contrary to many other areas of her life, Lora's dancing is one place where she doesn't have to perform. In essence, she is there to make love to herself.

Massages, rubbing scented oils into your skin, working with clay, kneading bread, lovingly primping and preening yourself are all ways to be sensual during this period in your life without actually going to bed with someone. We are not simply waiting for someone to show up before we allow ourselves to express the lover that we already are. What I finally learned through all my trial and error was this: that it is far more important in life to *be* a lover than to *get* a lover. In the words of Sufi poet Rumi:

Lovers don't finally meet somewhere.
They are in each other all along.

Hindsight is always twenty-twenty.
—Billy Wilder

You arouse me with your touch although I can't see your hands. You have kissed me with tenderness Although I haven't seen your lips. You are hidden from me.
—Rumi

I believe in the flesh
and the appetites,
Seeing, hearing,
feeling are miracles,
and each part of me
is a miracle.
Divine am I inside
and out, and
I make holy
whatever I touch or
am touched from,
The scent of these
arm-pits
aroma finer than
prayer, this head
more than churches,
bibles, and all
the creeds.
—Walt Whitman,
Song of Myself

PRACTICE

Take out your journal and pen. We are going to begin with a meditation. Read it at least twice, then do it as best you can from memory.

Sit comfortably, close your eyes and take a few moments to connect with your body and your breath. On each exhale, breathe out any energies of former lovers (or anyone with whom you've had a sexual encounter) that you've been holding on to. Release any shame, hurt, or anger that you've been holding in your second chakra (your genitals and lower belly). With each inhale, reclaim your wholeness and power, retrieving any portions of your heart and/or soul that you either gave away or was taken from you. Continue to breathe this way until you feel clear and free in your second chakra, or until you feel ready to proceed. Give yourself as much time as you need.

When you are ready, call the lover of your future into your meditation. Imagine him before you, lovingly gazing into your eyes. Feel your heart open in response to his love. Lovingly offer your body to him as a home and a sacred resting place. Feel him receive this offering as he, in turn, offers his body up to you with the same level of love and devotion. Begin to imagine what the touch of your beloved will feel like. Imagine what it feels like for him (or her) to stroke your hair and your face gently. Feel your beloved kiss your neck, your chest, your belly, your inner thighs. Now allow yourself to touch and kiss your beloved in the same way back. As you do this, feel the intense love and attraction that exists between you. Notice that you feel very safe with this person. There is a sense of complete trust and surrender that is both natural and joyful.

When you are ready, open your eyes and write about this sensual, loving relationship from the perspective of how it feels to actually *have* it.

BONUS: PRACTICE IN ACTION

Allow yourself to have a highly sensual day today—dress in sensual clothes, wear a sensual scent, move in sensual ways, eat sensual food, make sensual art, listen to sensual music, write sensual poetry, etc. All day, continue to express and enjoy your own sensual energy.

LESSON 34
On Developing Emotional Literacy

An inability to notice our true feelings leaves us at their mercy.
People with greater certainty about their feelings are better pilots
of their lives, having a surer sense…about personal decisions
from whom to marry to what job to take.

—Daniel Goleman, *Emotional Intelligence*

Rachel and Robert, both artists, have only been together for seven months now, although Rachel already sports a beautiful engagement ring on her finger. While all was bliss for the first few months, lately it seems that the relationship has been deteriorating fast. The couple has come to see me in the hope that they can find their way back to some sense of union and harmony or, in the very least, understand this recent turn of events between them.

The most glaring problem that I noticed almost immediately was Robert's very real struggle to articulate his feelings. To almost every question posed to him regarding his feelings, he would respond rather awkwardly, with a shrug of the shoulder and an "I don't know." The most he seemed to be able to say was that he felt "criticized" by Rachel. I tried to help Robert by explaining that, while I understood that he heard her questions and requests as criticisms, that "criticized" was not actually a feeling.

Robert was also unable to understand Rachel's feelings when she tried to share them with him. In response to her very real agony and loneliness, he would look up and reply that "love is a two-way street, you know." He seemed almost incapable of authentically empathizing with her emotional pain. Please don't think that Robert is a bear of a man. On the contrary, Robert is a soft-spoken, humble, polite, and very likable person. He simply lacks the ability to be connected to his feelings, and is therefore unable to empathize with others in any meaningful way. This handicap, however, is seriously impairing the possibility of love between them.

According to Daniel Goleman, author of *Emotional Intelligence,* divorce rates in America have recently soared to a whopping 67 percent among newly married couples. He acknowledges the erosion of social pressures to stay in bad marriages, as well as the lack of economic necessity to do so, as possible causes for this insanely high number. He asserts, therefore, that the emotional dynamic between a couple is that much more critical to the stability of the relationship. Emotional attunement and empathy are more acutely necessary now than ever before to ensure a successful union.

The ability to create an emotional attuned relationship necessitates that both partners share at least a moderate capacity for emotional literacy. Emotional literacy includes the ability to accurately read one's own feelings, to manage them by self-soothing or delaying impulsivity to some extent, and then to comprehend and respond appropriately to the feelings of others. We don't have to do these things perfectly, but solid relationships will require that we be able to do them at least reasonably well, as emotional literacy is the currency of all loving relationships.

Empathy, that crucial ingredient to a great relationship, is enhanced in direct proportion to one's ability to identify and be present with one's own emotions. Most of us collapse our emotions with our thoughts to one degree or another; e.g., "How do you feel?" "I feel that he's being a jerk!" rather than "I feel hurt, ashamed, embarrassed, humiliated, etc." In her book *Living with Feeling,* psychotherapist Lucia Capacchione helps the reader to identify their feelings by articulating for us nine "families of feelings." These "families" are as follows: **Happy:** Includes blissful, delighted, enthusiastic, excited, glad, gleeful, grateful, and joyful. **Sad:** Includes discouraged, disheartened, down, gloomy, grieving, hurt, lonely, and melancholy. **Angry:** Includes agitated, bitter, enraged, exasperated, furious, irritated, mad, and resentful. **Afraid:** Includes anxious, fearful, horrified, nervous, panicked, scared, shaky, and terrified. **Playful:** Includes adventurous, childlike, creative, free, lighthearted, lively, spontaneous, and whimsical. **Loving:** Includes affectionate, compassionate, friendly, kind, nurturing, tender, trusting, and warm. **Confused:** Includes ambivalent, bewildered, conflicted, hesitant, perplexed, torn, troubled, and uneasy. **Depressed:** Includes burned out, dejected, despondent, helpless, hopeless, listless, weary, and withdrawn. **Peaceful:** Includes calm, contented, relaxed, quiet, satisfied, serene, and tranquil.

Our ability to recognize what we are feeling when we are feeling it is what Daniel Goleman calls the "keystone to emotional intelligence." That doesn't mean that we have to know "why" we feel the way we do, or whether feeling that way is "good" or whether it's "bad." Both analysis and assessment are secondary when it comes to being emotionally literate. The most important thing is that we are able to identify how we feel in the moment that we are feeling it and be able to share that with another person in a constructive way.

Rather than simply honor our feelings this way, most of us, in contrast, negate, repress, ignore, or stuff them down. We shame ourselves for feeling the way we do ("I shouldn't feel this way"), deny that our feelings exist ("I don't really feel this way"), or try to talk ourselves out of our feelings ("I need to stop feeling this way"). It's not even personal. Our whole culture is addicted to all sorts of distractions and quick fixes to help us escape our unpleasant or difficult feelings, and few of us have any sense of mastery over simply being with our own emotions.

Many of us will try to distance ourselves from our feelings in an attempt to be "more spiritual." This is a common, but disastrous, mistake. Our "negative" emotions of anger, fear, guilt, and shame all have their very necessary place in our lives. When we cut ourselves off from the gift of their presence, it's like trying to function in life without our hands. People without hands manage, but life is much more difficult for them than for those of us who have our hands.

Energy healer Karla McLaren writes about the benefits of *all* of our emotions in her book, *Emotional Genius*. Anger, she assures us, is the keeper of boundaries, the emotion that helps us to maintain healthy separation from others. When anger is repressed or ignored, she asserts, we will have difficulty honoring ourselves appropriately by setting limits, protecting ourselves from abuse, and/or avoiding unhealthy entanglements. Fear, the emotion we resist the most, has its place in our lives, as well. The keeper of intuition and hyperfocused awareness, fear allows us

> Self-awareness...[is] ongoing attention to one's internal states.
> —Daniel Goleman

Be open to
your happiness
and sadness
as they arise.

—John and Lyn St. Clair
Thomas

to be fully present and alive in the moment. When fully honored and embraced, fear keeps us active, energized, and completely engaged in the world around us. The sister emotions of guilt and shame also serve a necessary function in our lives as the restorer of integrity when we've broken our own or someone else's boundaries. We need to learn to be fully present and available to all of our emotions in order to reap their benefits and learn from their wisdom.

When Barbara met Charles, she pretty much knew from the start that she wanted to be with him. Although Charles was much more ambivalent, he came around little by little. After a couple of years, when he moved from California to a beautiful home in the mountains of Colorado, he invited Barbara to come with him. She was joyful at first. But because he'd never really committed himself to the relationship, Charles continued to travel alone and for fun, almost as much as he did before he met her. Barbara was alone and isolated much of the time and she became desperately unhappy.

When we spoke, Barbara couldn't get out of bed, she was so depressed. However, she kept telling me why she thought she shouldn't be feeling the way she was feeling. He was a great catch, he'd never promised her more than this, she should be stronger, more self-sufficient somehow. The more she told me why she shouldn't be feeling sad and depressed, the more I pointed out that, regardless of what she thought she *should* feel or not feel, she actually *did* feel sad and depressed. I asked her what sadness and depression was trying to tell her. Eventually, she gave herself permission to simply be with whatever she was feeling without judging herself so severely. When she was able to honor her feelings in this way, they had an opportunity to heal her and guide her into a much more satisfying and happy life. She decided that she needed more from Charles and confronted him, being fully responsible for her part in creating her situation. When Charles was unwilling to give her more, she moved back to California and began a new life—one that honors her desire for stability and closeness with others on a whole new level. She now uses her emotions to help guide her choices and she is finding life more rewarding and rich than ever before. Not surprisingly, Charles actually followed her back to California and has recently asked her to marry him. It's not so much that she played the "unavailable" game. It's that in becoming fully present to and honoring of herself, there is now actually more of Barbara to love, and she began capturing his attention more than she had before.

When you know yourself, you don't need to defend against being known. We develop our capacity for intimacy by giving up our need to see ourselves a certain way. It's challenging to be authentic about some of our emotions, motivations, and weaknesses. Who among us does not wish to think of ourselves as good, strong, and loving people? Yet, truthfully, being human means that we have it *all* within us—the capacity to abuse as well as to nurture, to destroy as well as to create, to hate as well as to love. It is because we embody the whole spectrum of possibilities, that our choice to grow ourselves in our capacity to give and receive love is so extraordinary.

> When your emotions are allowed to take their proper place in your whole life, all healing is possible, because all energy is available.
> —Karla McLaren

PRACTICE

Today, we are going to practice working with the "Observer Self"—that part of us that simply notices and observes whatever we are experiencing in any given moment without doing anything to change it. When we are standing in Observer Self, we need not react to our feelings, fix them in any way, analyze, or judge them. We simply *identify* and *be* with them.

Sit quietly for several minutes, focusing on your breath in order to become deeply present with yourself. Become very aware of your body and be with any sensations you are experiencing fully. Move your awareness into any area that is particularly tense and notice what emotions, if any, are being held in that part of the body. As you release the tension you find, allow yourself to feel the emotion(s) fully.

Notice that you may have several emotions that you are feeling all at once. One at a time, identify the feelings you are experiencing (e.g., excitement, fear of disappointment, happiness, sadness). Take some time just to be with the feelings you notice are present with you. Welcome them, even the more difficult ones. Simply pay attention to the feelings you feel without resisting or judging them in any way, breathing deeply and just being with them.

Now, ask each of these feeling states if they have any information they wish to give you. (Examples: Excitement wants me to keep expanding myself beyond who I've known myself to be; fear of disappointment wants me to remember to not have falsely high expectations; happiness wants to celebrate the challenges I've overcome that have brought me to this place; sadness wants me to remember those in life I've lost who are not with me to share this special moment.)

Write in your journal about your experience of being fully present with your emotion(s), and any information that your emotions had for you.

BONUS: PRACTICE IN ACTION

Throughout your day, pause to simply be present with yourself, noticing and observing whatever you are feeling in any given moment. Do nothing to change how you are feeling. Instead, simply identify and acknowledge the feeling(s), breathe into it, and be with it. You may also ask if the feeling(s) has any information it would like to give you.

LESSON 35
Cultivating Solitude

When we are alone and quiet, we are afraid that
something will be whispered in our ear, and so we hate
the silence and drug ourselves with social life.

—Friedrich Nietzsche

American poet Marianne Moore once wrote, "The best cure for loneliness is solitude." Yet many of us who have come to know solitude have done so with great reluctance and resistance. Particularly now, in what is commonly called the Age of Distraction, when our TV sets fill our homes with visions of mass destruction one moment and images of the emotionally distraught pouring their hearts out to voyeuristic talk-show hosts the next. It takes a deliberate, intentional act of will to carve out any solitude at all in this society.

However, lest we think this a modern-day phenomenon, well over a hundred years ago, Ralph Waldo Emerson, in his essay "Self-Reliance," penned these words: "Society everywhere is in conspiracy against the manhood of every one of its members." He was, of course, referring to the constant pull to conform ourselves to common convention, usually at the risk of abandoning our inner quest to discover our own thoughts, feelings, opinions, and morals. Emerson continues, "It is easy in the world to live after the world's opinion; it is easy in solitude to live after one's own; but the great man is he who in the midst of the crowd keeps with perfect sweetness the independence of solitude."

It all sounds well and good. After all, we are aware that a certain amount of solitude should precede relationship, so that one has a solid enough sense of self to have something to offer. However, there is a monster at the mouth of the cave. For the first step in cultivating solitude is to face our own loneliness. There is no way around it. You cannot transform

Enter into the stillness inside your busy life. Become familiar with her ways. Grow to love her, feel *[her]* with all your heart and you will come to hear her silent music and become one with Love's silent song.

—Noel Davis

All sins are attempts to fill voids.

—Simone Weil

it intellectually—you've got to actually go right into the center of your lonely feelings so that you can soothe and comfort your frightened, despairing heart yourself.

I know. You suddenly want to earmark this page and turn to tomorrow's reading. Please don't. Please don't steal this brilliant healing from yourself. The years we've spent hiding from ourselves have cost us and we've grown weary and worn. We must find it within us to gather the courage we need to face the monster down and heal the terror of our aloneness.

At first, when we go within, we might discover an edginess, a sadness, a rage, or a despair. That's OK. We allow ourselves to simply be with what's so, enlarging our sphere of compassion for ourselves and for the rest of humanity who also suffer from this terrible feeling at one time or another.

Jungian analyst Dr. James Hollis describes solitude as "that psychic state wherein one is wholly present to oneself." We must remember that loneliness is not the real enemy—alienation from ourselves is. We are never lonely because we have lost contact with others. We are lonely because we have lost contact with ourselves.

I had an affair with a married man once. I did the classically cliché thing of thinking that he would leave his wife like he said he would. One night, when I needed him and he was not there, I paced the floors of my apartment, face to face with a loneliness that I'd avoided for years. I began to shout and dance its pain in my body. I cried its aching cry as I lay despondent and sobbing on the floor. It wasn't so much that I was crying over him as it was that I was crying over all the years that I'd felt abandoned, unsupported, and deserted by others. He was just my latest attempt to avoid feeling those feelings. Rather than helping me to run away from them, however, my relationship with him had caused me to run right smack into the center of them. I don't know how long I carried on that way but in the morning, when I woke up, I woke up at peace. I called my married friend and broke it off with him. It was the first time that I had enough of myself to be that strong. I had faced down the beast and I had come out whole.

How often have we sold ourselves short by becoming entangled with people we knew were wrong for us because we were too scared to be alone? How many times have we let fear keep us in relationships long after they have fulfilled their purpose? In what ways have we sacrificed ourselves to avoid the risk of sitting in our own silence? It's time to face our fears and transform our ultimate aloneness into a source of strength. The difference between a good relationship and a great relationship rests upon the solid ability to return home to one's own sense of self—to maintain "the sweetness of solitude in the midst of a crowd," as Emerson would say.

After that experience, I began to actively cultivate solitude as a practice. Each day, I made sure that I spent some time alone and in silence. I turned off the television, unplugged the telephone, and refrained from listening to music. I put down my books, my journal, the newspaper, and any creative project I was working on. I sat. Or I walked. Or I watched my breath. Sometimes I was bored. Sometimes I wasn't. But it did not matter. I did it anyway. For the longest time, there was a certain sadness present that I was alone. I stopped being afraid and made a companion of it. Invited it in for tea, so to speak.

These minutes of solitude became the foundation for what I would call my "down days." I would let those closest to me know that I was taking a whole day for silence, so they shouldn't panic when I didn't answer my phone. I allowed myself to read, write, and occasionally listen to soft instrumental music, but that was it. Otherwise, I rested, pet my cat, did yoga poses on the floor of my bedroom, and listened to the quiet. Sometimes I went for a walk to look at the trees. But all the time I watched my breath, and listened to my heart. We became good friends.

And then one day the sadness was gone. In its place was a sense of peace and stillness. I still wasn't thrilled to be single and alone, but ultimately, I was OK with it because I was OK with me. Today, with a husband, a toddler, and a full-time private practice, I truly miss that time in my life. What a luxury to have those long stretches of hours to just be. That's why it's important to appreciate where we are in life and what we have when we have it. I remember someone telling me once that I really could have it all—I just couldn't have it all at one time.

This is a special time in your life. Don't miss out on the opportunity that it presents by wishing you were somewhere else. The secret to being

Real action is in the silent moments.

—Ralph Waldo Emerson

Go placidly amid the noise and the haste, and remember what peace there is in silence.

—Max Ehrmann

The self must know stillness before it can discover its true song.
—Ralph Blum

happy in life is to choose what you have. What better time to cultivate solitude than when one is single. It's a gift. Don't throw it away.

PRACTICE

Spend anywhere from five to fifteen minutes this morning sitting in the stillness. No newspaper, no television, no journal, no book, no telephone calls, no Internet, no pager, no activity.

Begin now.

Then take out your journal and write about that experience.

Spend at least five minutes each day in stillness and solitude, if at all possible.

BONUS: PRACTICE IN ACTION

Schedule time in your busy life for a "down hour" or a "down morning" or a "down day" this week. Any amount of time you can commit to will be fine. Just make a date with yourself to go within and spend some time with your most intimate of companions—yourself.

SUGGESTED STUDY GUIDE
FOR GROUP DISCUSSION

1. What commitments have you made to yourself and others and how do these commitments help you to be the best you possible?

2. How is it for you to prioritize self-care over caring for others (e.g., to say no when you need to, set appropriate limits, disappoint someone, and so on)?

3. What do you notice about your ability (or inability) to receive from others?

4. Share about your body image and how it affects your love life.

5. How safe and/or free do you feel to express your sexuality?

6. What feelings have been the more difficult ones for you to feel and in what ways have you avoided them?

7. How is it for you to be alone with unstructured time on your hands?

A LIFE WORTH LIVING

You cannot have a happy ending to a miserable journey.

—Abraham Hicks

Truly loving relationships require a certain level of maturity and generosity of spirit—those same qualities that improve our overall satisfaction in life, with or without a partner.

This week:

✳ We will continue to expand our capacity to give and receive love by practicing generosity toward those we've been blaming and making wrong

✳ We will examine key elements that make up a happy life

✳ We will challenge old fears that have prevented love from taking root in our lives

✳ We will practice taking full responsibility for the quality of our relationships

✳ We will examine current communication patterns with the intent of improving our ability to create more meaningful connections with others

LESSON 36
Generosity—the Essential Ingredient

Marriage is no way of life for the weak, the selfish, or the insecure.

—Sidney Poitier, in *To Sir, With Love*

The Dalai Lama was once asked if he were ever lonely. "No," he answered simply. When asked what he attributed this to, he replied, "I think one factor is that I look at any human being from a more positive angle; I try to look for their positive aspects. This attitude immediately creates a feeling of affinity, a kind of connectedness." The Dalai Lama has what we might call a "generous listening" for others.

We tend to like those who are generous with us, allowing us to make mistakes and be imperfect without holding it against us. When people are generous, we feel like we can breathe around them. We feel like we can be more authentically who we are. Generosity is a spacious phenomenon.

Yet, most of us are pretty stingy. Rather than looking for people's positive traits, we assess them, instead, through the filter of who we think they should or shouldn't be, and how we think they should or should not be behaving. Instead of extending ourselves with open, unguarded hearts, we enter the majority of our encounters defended and closed. This withholding of ourselves is so common that we just think it's normal. And yet, this way of being is really a reaction to a culture where fear is so predominant and pervasive. It has little to do with who human beings really are and what human beings really need in order to feel right with the world.

I took a weekend seminar once that was about developing the capacity to love others more fully. Most of us in the room thought of ourselves as fairly evolved in this regard. After all, we had paid good money and given up an entire weekend to learn more about how to be a loving person. Who does that except someone who is pretty far along the path already? But the facilitator challenged our notions of ourselves by asking,

"How long do you think you could keep your heart open if, after confessing your deepest passion and adoration for someone, they made it clear to you that your love was not reciprocated? How long do you think that you could continue to be generous with your love in the face of such a rejection?" Most of us had to admit, not very long.

Yet, what better opportunity to give love than when one is not getting what they want? It's easy to be generous and loving toward those who are generous and loving toward us. However, to extend ourselves beyond what's easy—to give in a way that compels us to let go of something that we are attached to—that is where true generosity begins.

Our more frequent response of reflexive defensiveness creates for us an emotional vacuum. When we hold back our love and light from others for any reason, we end up feeling starved for love ourselves. In her book *Enchanted Love,* Marianne Williamson writes, "To the extent that love has dried up in my life, it was always because I became miserly with my expression of compassion. To the extent that love has blossomed in my life, it was always because I expanded my willingness to express the love that often cowers like a child in a corner of my heart." In our reluctance to extend ourselves in love, we create an intense hunger for love in our hearts. Our drive to find "The One" is intensified as a kind of compensation for the love that is missing in our lives. We are filled with a deep and enveloping longing to be loved. We pine for someone who will take care of us—maybe even heal us or give us that which we've never had.

In her book, *In the Meantime,* Iyanla Vanzant reminds us that "We go into relationship looking for love, not realizing that we must bring love with us." Rather than look for someone to get love from, we need to focus more on finding someone that we can give love to—someone who inspires us to expand beyond the limitations of our self-absorption and our narcissism. And this requires that we be adept in the practice of giving love, even when giving love is not the easy thing to do.

Generosity is an act of abundance, yet not all self-sacrifice is a kindhearted gesture. Sometimes our "generosity" comes with a covert agenda to manipulate another person into being who we want them to be. Yet we'll dress up our selfishness with altruistic words and sacrificial gestures, trying to pass ourselves off as something we are not. You know. You've

The most effective way to achieve right relations with any living thing is to look for the best in it, and then help that best into the fullest expression.
—J. Allen Boone

It always boils down to the same thing— not only receiving love but desperately needing to give it.
—Audrey Hepburn

probably dated that person. The one who gave to you in the hopes that he or she would get something in return. Even more to the point, you've probably *been* that person. The one who is sweet . . . and kind . . . and goes out of her way to be understanding. Until, that is, you start to get it that the person in front of you is *no way* going to be able to give you what you want. So often, when I was dating, I had to keep reminding myself that, even though the man I was dating was completely unable or unwilling to give me what I wanted, that didn't mean that he was wrong. It just meant that he was wrong for me.

There is a Native American custom that judges a person's wealth, not by what they have, but by what they give. In order to continue giving without an attachment to getting something specific back, one must be connected to an inner source of wellness and wealth. Buddhist nun Pema Chödrön says, "The journey of generosity is one of connecting with this wealth, cherishing it so profoundly that we are willing to begin to give away whatever blocks it. We give away our dark glasses, our long coats, our hoods, and our disguises. In short, we open ourselves and let ourselves be touched."

When we find ourselves wondering why we don't have more love in our lives, we would do well to consider more ways that we might begin to give it away. Love that can't get out has a hard time getting in as well. Blocks do not just happen one way because, on some level, giving and receiving are the same experience.

Although it can feel almost counterintuitive to look for ways to give love when one is feeling so deprived, to do so is as though we take a stand for our lives, demonstrating a commitment to have the experience of love in our lives. In *The Prophet,* Kahlil Gibran calls those who have little but give anyway, "the believers in life," assuring us that "their coffer is never empty." That's because life always has a way of balancing itself out. In his essay "Compensation," Ralph Waldo Emerson encouraged us to live with such profound generosity that the Universe Itself would be compelled to reward our efforts. Advising us to "love, and you shall be loved," he believed that "all love is mathematically just, as much as the two sides of an algebraic equation." Therefore, he admonished us to "put God in our debt."

It feels good to be a big person—the one to forgive, the one to apologize first, the one to give up saving face. There is always that initial "But I don't *want* to!" However, once you take a deep breath and give up the need to be right, to look good, to punish someone for hurting you, or to make someone wrong, then you are free to experience a profound love that becomes a way of life, and not just the goal of an exclusive experience with the one person who is missing from your life.

Being generous is a spiritual discipline. The more you practice it, the stronger you become. Being generous is more than a good idea—it is an essential ingredient to creating love. While developing your "generosity muscle" might appear to be optional for you at this point, your very future most likely rests upon your ability to practice the kind of self-control required to love another human being.

As divorce rates would indicate, we are having quite a difficult time finding and sustaining love at this time. This is happening because it takes such a profound bigheartedness to love someone for the long haul—beyond the initial attraction and courtship period—and we simply aren't used to stretching ourselves so. To give up *having* to be right, *having* to prove someone else wrong, *having* to have the last word, *having* to be understood—that is the mark of a person who is capable and truly ready to create a loving relationship that will last and flourish over time.

> Love is not love
> When it is mingled
> with regards
> that stand
> Aloof from the
> entire point.
> —William Shakespeare

PRACTICE

Take out your journal. Write on the following question:

Who in your life are you making wrong?

Now choose a person from your list and write on the following question:

What is _____ wrong about?
(person's name)

Now pretend that you *are* this person. Completely surrender yourself to his or her perspective. Complete the following sentence stems as though you actually *were* this person. Write for several minutes, exploring various reasons why, from this perspective, he or she may be right.

I am right because:

What _____ doesn't understand about me is:
(your name)

BONUS: PRACTICE IN ACTION

Take at least one generous action today. This could include, but does not have to, telling the person what you wrote about this morning, why and how they are right. Other generous actions might be apologizing to someone, forgiving someone, or giving up being right in the midst of a conversation. This giving up is not a begrudging resignation. It is a deliberate act of enlargement on your part. If you've truly been generous, you won't have a feeling of self-righteousness or superiority, but rather, you will feel as though your soul has expanded and grown larger. This is you being the biggest person you are capable of being. Go ahead and stretch yourself.

LESSON 37
On Being Happy

Most folks are about as happy as they make up their minds to be.

—Abraham Lincoln

Years ago, while attending Overeaters Anonymous meetings to help heal the eating disorder I'd had since adolescence, I became familiar with the abovementioned quote. It both annoyed and intrigued me at the same time. How, I wondered, am I supposed to be happy when I come home alone each night to an empty apartment? How can I love myself when I'm still so overweight and out of shape? How can I enjoy my life when I have so little money? I'd wanted to dismiss those words as irrelevant to my life, spoken by a man who understood nothing about the kinds of challenges most of us face today. However, the more I understood Abraham Lincoln as a man who experienced many caustic disappointments and even more bitter failures, the more I couldn't simply dismiss his words as some Pollyanna philosophy spoken by a person of privilege who knew nothing of how difficult life can be.

In my early thirties I was dealing with overwhelming feelings of disappointment and loss due to a failed singing career and the end of a three-and-a-half-year romantic relationship. At the time I was working as a temp secretary, something I loathed and was ill-suited for, to say the least. My friend and mentor Debu Ghosh, a small man from Bombay, used to smile and say, with his Indian accent and a gleam in his eyes, "The secret to being happy, Katherine, is to choose what you have." Once I got over being completely irritated with him for what seemed to be a total lack of sensitivity on his part, I began to consider his words.

Even though everything seemed to be utterly miserable in my life, I was tired of my defensive posturing on why I had a right to be unhappy. It seemed pretty pathetic to me to be defending my victim position in life

Can you tolerate happiness?
If we don't believe ourselves worthy of happiness, we won't allow love to take root in our lives. It's outside of our beliefs about our lives and we'll sabotage love.
—Nathaniel Branden

and I grew weary of hearing myself complain. I began thinking of myself as one of those "feverish little clod(s) of ailments and grievances, complaining that the world will not devote itself to making you happy" that George Bernard Shaw was talking about in his famous quote. I became curious about this idea that one could simply be happy by choosing to be. As a spiritual challenge, I decided to take on cultivating the quality of joy, thinking, "Well, if I can be happy now, under these conditions, then I can be happy anywhere, at any time." So, instead of trying to change my circumstances, I began accepting them and blessing them as they were. I began to consider the possibility that life could be cherished and accepted on its own terms. I began relating to disappointment and struggle as an opportunity to deepen and expand myself to include the totality of the human experience in my definition of what makes a worthwhile life.

The disappointment and deep sorrow that I felt didn't go away. Nor did the fact that I was a complete disaster at being a temp secretary. However, my overall sense of humor and well-being kicked in. And, lo and behold, I began enjoying my life, as lopsided and puzzling as it was. I gave up resisting the circumstances I was in and began instead surrendering to them. I did this by simply accepting all that was happening and, even more important, all that wasn't. I even began saying prayers of thanks for everything almost as an experiment, to see if I could alter my experience without altering my circumstances.

Although we tend to believe that happiness exists as some sort of side benefit to having successfully mastered all the particulars of our lives, nothing could be further from the truth. Call it the biggest lie of all time, which we've bought hook, line, and sinker. We're not unhappy because we don't have enough of what we think that we want. We are unhappy because we are resisting what is so in our lives and are frantically caught up in trying to fix something that we perceive to be broken. That's an awful lot of pressure.

When I went back to graduate school to become a psychotherapist, I was in my mid-thirties. Not having much money, I lived in a small one-bedroom apartment in a funky part of Venice, California. Being single and broke at the age of thirty-five was not exactly what my mom had in mind while raising me, and it was hard on her. She did her best to support me, being very careful to say all the right things, but I'd watch her eyes dart back and forth over my neighborhood when she visited. Even though she wouldn't say it, I knew how worried and disappointed she was.

When she flew out from New York to attend my graduation, I was grateful that she'd traveled three thousand miles to be with me. We were excited as we spent the day before the graduation ceremony preparing for a party we were having the next day. As we were going from store to store, she began discussing my future plans, which, as she saw it, now included getting out there and making some *money*. The frustration she'd felt all those years while I delayed marriage and family to pursue an unprofitable singing career, followed by more years as a starving student, coated each word she spoke. I began feeling really pushed and pressured by her dissatisfaction over my life. After a while, I lost it. Standing in the kitchen while cutting up vegetables, waving a knife around like a lunatic, I cracked. "Mom!" I shouted. "What if I never have a lot of money? What if I never have what you think I'm supposed to have? Maybe this ratty little apartment is as good as it gets! Maybe this moment is the absolute pinnacle of my life!" And I stormed off to the one room that I could actually slam the door shut, the bedroom.

My poor mom. Her feelings were pretty hurt. After all, she'd only come to support me and let me know how proud she was of me. And she was basically just doing that thing that moms do by wanting more for their daughters than a single life filled with financial struggle and hardship. Upon reflection, I realized that I was not reacting to *her*, as much as I was to the constant internalized pressure that *I* felt. I was the one who thought that: (1) something was very wrong with my life, i.e., I *should* have a husband and lots of money by now, and that (2) things had better change soon, because I was definitely not OK the way I was. What I was essentially declaring to my mom, but really to myself, was that I was no longer going to be on some treadmill trying to get my life to fit anyone's expectations of what it was supposed to look like, including my own. I was going to accept who I was and what I had as enough, even if it meant that I lived alone in that silly little apartment for the rest of my life. My relief was palpable and that incident became a defining moment in my life. I had finally stopped resisting my life.

> Everything has its wonders, even darkness and silence, and I learn, whatever state I may be in, therein to be content.
>
> —Helen Keller

We cause our own unhappiness by refusing to accept life on life's terms. And unhappy people tend to create unhappy relationships, or none at all. We've heard of the studies that indicate married people are happier than unmarried people, and seen this as evidence that being married makes you happier. However, we've also got to consider the possibility that happy people are more likely to attract love into their lives than unhappy people are. And creating happiness begins with accepting, and surrendering to, the life you have right now. As is. Lonely and all. Failed expectations and all. Complete with disappointments, struggles, and heartaches. All of it. As it is right now.

Often we become attached and driven to getting married because we are invalidating the lives we are living without a partner as inferior and second-rate. The desperation we can feel comes from an unwillingness to accept the possibility of being alone. It comes from the belief that you must marry in order to have your life be full and rich and worth living. Another lie that we collectively perpetuate.

What makes life worth living is being actively engaged in becoming the finest, most delicious human being you can possibly be in this lifetime. What makes life worth living is finding people and projects that you can love and stand by and give yourself to completely. Too many of us long for relationships where we can hide out. But that isn't a soul mate experience, that's a survival experience. Living your "best life," as Oprah calls it, is now, in this moment, under these circumstances, whether or not your experience includes intimate love at this point in time.

You must be able to create a life that lights you up whether or not you have a lover, a great career, a lot of money, a great house, a healthy child, or a hit song. Part of creating this magnificent life may include being actively engaged in the pursuit of such blessings. However, to place the burden of validation of your life upon the achievement of such things is a terrible encumbrance.

Joy is an unconditional experience that is not attached to circumstances. It is a choice one makes to cultivate a consciousness of unconditional acceptance of what is. You may not like what's happening right now, but you can be with it. In giving up the resistance to what is so in your life, you allow yourself to be with and attend to your more difficult and troubling emotions fully. In so doing, you free yourself also to feel contentment, happiness, and a deep joy. Joy is the by-product of being emotionally fluid in life. It comes from the simple appreciation of being alive—and *not* in response to getting what we want in life.

In my life I find that I usually get what I want but rarely when I'm feeling desperate to have it. That's how it works. That's why people say that you'll find your soul mate when you aren't looking. It's not the "not looking" part that allows your soul mate to come to you; it's the nonattachment part that does it. Usually those people who "aren't looking" will allow only loving and healthy people into their inner circle, because desperation isn't driving them to compromise themselves. If they have to be alone for the rest of their life, they'd rather do that than create destructive, dramatic entanglements. They don't lose years of their lives entwined with people who treat them poorly or don't love them. They set about making their lives worth living by pursuing things that capture their interest, good friends and meaningful activities. It's not necessarily that they weren't looking. It's that they were busy enjoying their lives, with or without a partner.

Several years ago I had a funny experience that taught me a great lesson about how things come to you when you are no longer desperate to have them. When I was ten years old, I had a friend named Cathy Swift. Each day after school Cathy and I used to meet at my house and put on Monkees records at top volume. We would then proceed to sing and dance our way through the house. We pretended that Davy, Micky, Peter, and Mike were singing to us. We were madly in love with each of them, changing off one for another each week. One week I loved Davy and she loved Peter. The next week I loved Peter and she loved Micky. I would have gladly given my right arm to meet any one of them.

Fast-forward twenty years. Having met a guy at an informal Saturday-afternoon gathering, we made a casual date to meet later that night to see a play together. Peter seemed nice enough, but he certainly didn't look like he had much going for him financially, although I believe he was kind enough to pay for my ticket. But he did talk a lot about being in show business in a way that confused me. He struck me more as a struggling actor, yet he spoke intimately about having a great deal of success. Right

> Men who are unhappy, like men who sleep badly, are always proud of the fact.
> —Bertrand Russell

Life has no other discipline to impose, if we would but realize it, than to accept life unquestioningly. Everything we shut our eyes to, everything we run away from, everything we deny, denigrate, or despise, serves... us in the end. What seems nasty, painful, evil, can become a source of beauty, joy, and strength, if faced with an open mind. Every moment is a golden one for him who has the vision to recognize it as such.

—Henry Miller

before the curtain went up I said, "I'm sorry, should I know you? Have you done something that I would know about?" He smiled rather shyly and said, "Well, if I told you, it would ruin our date." With that, the theater went black. Suddenly, I got it, and gasped. I was out on a date with Peter Tork! I nearly fell on the floor! My friends Leo and Bill teased me for weeks, calling my answering machine to sing, "Hey, hey, we're the Monkees!" while giggling hysterically. See, that's how God is. It's when you're no longer attached that all good things come to you.

PRACTICE

Take out your journal and write on the following question. Begin each sentence with "I must have . . . ":

What do I think I absolutely *must* have in order to be happy?

Now go back and circle those things you can see that you are attached to having. *(Hint:* Whatever makes you angry, depressed, or upset to think of *not* having is probably something that you are attached to having.)

One by one, go through each thing you've circled and say this prayer:

Dear God:
I believe that I must have _____ in order to be happy. However, I am willing to release this attachment now, knowing that my life is good and beautiful exactly as it is, with or without this blessing. I accept that it is possible for me to have a sense of joy, with or without _____, and I fully surrender myself to what is currently so in my life today. Amen.

Do this with everything on your list.

BONUS: PRACTICE IN ACTION

Practice unconditional acceptance of your life today just as it is, and make a conscious choice to be happy whenever possible. Every time you feel yourself frustrated, disappointed, and restless today, thank God for your life, exactly as it is and exactly as it is not. Affirm the goodness of your life whether or not you are getting what you want at any given moment.

LESSON 38
Overthrowing the Boogeyman

> Anxiety is love's greatest killer. It creates the failures.
> It makes others feel as though you might when a drowning
> man holds on to you. You want to save him, but you know
> he will strangle you with his panic.
>
> —Anaïs Nin

Going into an intimate situation is risky business for anyone. Yet for those of us who've suffered traumatic experiences that remain unhealed (such as childhood abuse or abandonment), a loving connection can feel like a lifeline in a nasty storm at sea. The desperation with which many of us cling to a lover is usually more than the relationship can bear. One of two things will inevitably happen. Either our lover will eventually flee for his life, in spite of his initial good intentions to rescue us, or he'll rise to the occasion, fight the good fight, and end up going under with us. Either way, our efforts to secure a safe, protective harbor will, once again, have failed. Instead, we'll have gathered yet more evidence that, in defiance of our constant efforts to the contrary, life, in our case, is anything but abundant. No matter what we do or how hard we try, it seems that we cannot shake the constant re-traumatizing of ourselves, repeating again and again the dreaded terrors of our past.

It's not just dogs and bears that sniff out our fears, and then prey upon them. Life itself seems to know our worst-case scenarios and finds a way to present them to us in various forms and disguises over and over again. Those paths that I am loathe to travel are suddenly the ones I notice I am on. Those situations I would do anything in my power to shirk are the ones I find myself engaged in. Those people whom I would go to great lengths to avoid are, unfortunately, the very ones I find knocking on my door. It is as though the fears hidden way deep down in my heart serve as an irresistible aphrodisiac, seducing in the shadow side of life. No matter how we cut it, we cannot get around the fact that we are going to have to deal with the very things that we have been trying for years to escape. In fact, the only way out is through. The one, lone solution to overcoming our fears is to stop running so madly from them, turn around, look them in the eye and face them fair and square.

Holly and Ken fight constantly. Having moved to L.A. several months before to make it as an actress, Holly is far from home. She is straining with the burden of few financial resources and even fewer friends. She is living hand to mouth and is terrified each month that she won't make her rent. Enter Ken, struggling artist and actor himself. They fall madly in love and soon after, Holly begins telling Ken that she believes he should be taking care of her. He should move her into his loft, help her pay her bills, and provide the stability that she is lacking in her life. Ken wants more than anything to do the knight in shining armor thing, but he can't seem to get it together. He says he'll do something but then he forgets. He assures her that he's going to give her some money but then he doesn't have any to spare. He supports her by going with her as she tries to find a job but then misses an important audition in the process. Now, they are both angry with him.

The life they are creating together is just as volatile and precarious as Holly's has been for as long as she can remember. As a child, Holly's mother was an unpredictable rage-aholic, flying off the handle with little provocation. Holly was constantly terrified. She spent her childhood grabbing at straws in an attempt to feel a sense of safety and belonging to no avail. Holly's desperate attempts to get Ken to provide her with much-needed stability have actually served to push him past his breaking point. His inability to meet her intense needs are weighing upon him and he finds himself behaving erratically, with less constancy than he ever has before. Intensely frustrated, he finds himself displaying frequent outbursts of temper. He has become Holly's worst nightmare all over again, as she is having difficulty distinguishing Ken's anger from the abusive anger of her mother. As for Ken, his worst fear in life is that he'll be a screw-up and

> Some of us don't have relationships. We just take hostages.
> —Anonymous

I sit on a man's back,
choking him and
making him carry
me, and yet assure
myself and others
that I am very sorry
for him and wish to
ease his lot by all
possible means—
except by getting
off his back.

—Leo Tolstoy

won't be able to do anything right—hence, his need to be a knight in shining armor in the first place.

This is a couple who have come together to help each other heal. But the healing for Holly won't come by Ken's providing a safe harbor for her nor will Ken's healing come from his ability to get it right by rescuing Holly. Their healings will come when each one turns their attention away from the other as the source of healing. Their healings will come as each one finally faces down the fears that they're so desperately trying to use one another to assuage. They must each learn to call their terror by name and speak words of wisdom and healing to their own wounded hearts, for they will only be free to the extent that they are able to master the fears that are driving them so hard, and dominating their lives so completely.

Most of us are not as overtly and intensely fearful as both Holly and Ken are. Yet, truthfully, almost all of us are used to living with an undercurrent of fear just beneath the surface as though we were running a continual low-grade fever. We are so used to it that we barely recognize it. We call it stress, nervousness, worry, irritation, and/or a sense of restlessness. By whatever name we call it, we are all pretty much fear junkies, feeding ourselves an endless supply of angst and dis-ease. This undercurrent of fright feasts upon the present circumstances of our lives yet is not dependent upon them. Solve one problem and another one will come along shortly. We are attached to the drama of thinking that our feelings of anxiety are all about the situations that we are currently in. In truth, it's just the opposite—our feelings of fear are attracting those very situations that match, and then justify, their existence.

Fear is free-floating resistance to the inevitable ebb and flow of life . . . and, perhaps more poignantly, of death. Rather than recognize it as such, we attach it to this problem and then that problem, this projection and then that projection, this imagining and then that imagining. Rarely do we experience fear that is actually validated in the present moment. The neurotic anxieties we experience most of the time are generally divorced from any real or immediate danger. If we looked up and saw a tree were falling down on us, fear, in that moment, would obviously be justified. However, we feel fear just looking at the tree, noticing how close it is to the house, to the utility poles, to the road. We imagine what might happen if a storm just happened to come, if the tree just happened to fall, if it just happened to knock out the phone lines so we couldn't call for help, if it just happened to fall across the road so we could not drive ourselves to safety. We get ourselves so worked up that we start thinking that maybe we need to cut down the tree. Maybe we should move to a safer neighborhood, one where there are no such dangerous things as trees and houses and utility poles and roads. This is how we run our lives. This is how we run our relationships. (Or, perhaps more accurately, this is how we run *from* our lives and run *from* our relationships.)

We've allowed the fear of not getting what we want—of being hurt, rejected, disappointed, or abandoned—to dictate our actions, to stop us from taking risks in life, and to control our most intimate relationships. We each have our own version of what fear looks like when it's in the driver's seat and running the show. But now is the time to pull back the curtain on the Wizard of Oz and overthrow the boogeyman by challenging him face to face. Now is the time to inventory the fears that have been paralyzing us and debilitating the possibility of love in our lives. We can no longer placate these fears by trying to create a false sense of security, for fear can never be "fixed." It can only be contested, deconstructed and, ultimately, dethroned. Carl Jung once said, "If there is a fear of falling, the only safety consists in deliberately jumping."

Most of us have endured a litany of failures and disappointments in our lives and (to paraphrase the song), we're still here. For some of the sorrows we've had to bear, there is no explanation sufficient, no words big enough, to contain comfort and hope. Often, there is nothing to do but allow ourselves to sink deeply into the sadness that we feel and simply be with what is so in that moment. Facing our fears means entering the emptiness of life. It means accepting the possibility and the probability of the inevitable ebb after the flow, the predictable loss after the gain.

Although I'm not much of a painter (yet), I once painted a series of three paintings. The first was of a beautiful, lush tree, flourishing and abundant with blooming leaves. The second was of the same tree after having been pruned. It looked scrawny and sad, void of its copious greenery. The third and final painting was of the same tree yet again. This time, its beautiful leaves were so abundant and full that they spread far beyond

In real love you want the other person's good. In romantic love, you want the other person.
—Margaret Anderson

We are all, every one of us, full of horror. If you are getting married to try to make yours go away, you will only succeed in marrying your horror to someone else's horror, your two horrors will have the marriage, you will bleed and call that love.

—Michael Ventura

the confines of the canvas, unable to be contained. I did this as a reminder to myself that I could trust loss, that life is in a constant state of flux and change, and that emptiness is as much a part of life as fullness is. I am still learning to trust this truth.

The state of anxiety is born from an attachment to getting what we are demanding that life give us. Our acceptance of life is conditional. We are in resistance to what is or is not occurring. The next time you find yourself feeling anxious, ask yourself, "What am I attached to here?" If you can discover what your attachment is and then let it go, you may find that the fear you feel is greatly diminished.

We are all under the hypnotic spell of fear to one degree or another. It pulls us in, enticing us with its endless chatter of negative projections and imaginings. We must learn to call these anxieties by their names. We must learn to observe them without reacting to them. We must learn to talk back to them, soothe ourselves in their midst, and center ourselves with realistic and empowering self-talk. In response, these looming monsters shrink in stature and become more or less impotent to control our lives. As this is accomplished, we become more available to the many ways in which others offer love to us each and every day. They may not be offering it in the ways that we are demanding it or even needing it in that moment, but they are offering it in the ways that they have it to give. There is a beauty in being available to receive that love graciously and deeply into our hearts, and allow it to touch and nurture us.

PRACTICE

Take out your journal. This morning, I invite you to name your most chronic and troublesome fears. The following partial list is provided to help you identify those fears that feel the most threatening and pervasive in your life. Write down those fears that resonate with you. Then choose the one fear that seems to be the most intimidating in your life. There may actually be two or three, but for the purposes of the exercise, choosing one fear will do.

Abandonment	Anger	Annihilation	Appearing Foolish
Appearing Needy	Appearing Selfish	Appearing Stupid	Being Alone
Being Bad	Being Criticized	Being Denied	Being Hurt
Being Invisible	Being Ordinary	Being Unloved	Being Wrong
Death	Disappointment	Embarrassment	Emptiness
Failure	Feelings of Grief	Financial Insecurity	Loneliness
Loss	Making Mistakes	Rejection	Responsibility
Ridicule	Ruin	Screwing Up	Success

> He who fights with monsters might take care lest he thereby become a monster. And if you gaze for long into the abyss, the abyss gazes also into you.
> —Friedrich Nietzsche

Now take the one fear that has the most "juice" for you, and allow that particular fear to write a letter to you, saying all of the things it says to scare you (Fear of Being Alone tells me: "You'll never be loved. Even if someone does love you, they will eventually leave. You will never have anyone who really cares about you, who you can count on."). Write this letter now.

NOTE: If you are having difficulty identifying those fears that are running rampant in your life, answer the following questions:

What have I been driven to prove is absolutely *not* true about me?

What worst-case scenarios do I anticipate for myself and/or others?

**What have I been trying to get from others that I don't believe
I have within?**

Now write a second letter. This time you are going to talk back to your number-one fear. Rather than argue with it, see if you can actually speak to it as though it were an errant child, giving it some firm, yet compassionate, correction. After all, most fears arise in reaction to something that has actually happened that requires healing and a deeper surrender to life. Tell this fear that it is no longer allowed to dominate your life, much like you would a three-year-old child who has been having a temper tantrum. Thank the fear for its attempt to warn and protect you from the possible worst-case scenario. Reassure the fear, speaking soothing words that reaffirm that all is well with you. (For example: "Dear Fear of Being Alone: I understand you've been hurt in the past but that was then and this is now.

Look around. There are people in my life who love me. I am a good friend to others and I will always have people in my life I can count on and who love me, so calm down and stop being so frightened. Everything is going to be OK.")

NOTE: If the fear you are feeling is a valid and appropriate one (such as a fear of death when a loved one is dying), do the exercise simply as an exercise in self-soothing. It's not that all of our fears are unreasonable. To the contrary, many are a normal response to what is occurring in our lives. Often, however, we lack the skills we need to restore ourselves to balance and continue bringing the best of ourselves to the table. Our goal is to increase our ability to self-soothe and not necessarily to "get rid of" all our fears.

BONUS: PRACTICE IN ACTION

Throughout the day, rather than simply accept all thoughts at face value, see if you can notice when fear is the one talking to you. When you are able to identify fear, try talking back to it in much the same way you did when you wrote your letter earlier today. Speak to fear as though you were speaking to a frightened child (e.g., When fear tells me that I will never be loved, I remind fear of the truth that I am lovable and that I am actively creating love each and every day of my life). If you find yourself paralyzed by fear, unable to effectively talk back to it, then I encourage you to ask God for help. The following prayer is a guideline:

Dear God: I am being tossed to and fro by this bully called fear, and I'm unable to withstand its constant chatter. Please help me overcome the tirade of negativity that so fiercely demands my attention. Bring comfort and reassurance to my frightened heart. Bring courage and strength to my spirit. Help me to heal the parts of myself that have been so wounded and terrified in life. Help me to remember that I am loved, that I am safe, that I very much matter in this beautiful, vast, and glorious world. Thank you very much. Amen.

> Eventually, you get to the place in life where you are moving toward what you want faster than you are away from what you fear.
> —Mark Austin Thomas

LESSON 39
Being at Cause

Many of us treat life as if it were a novel.
We pass from page to page passively, assuming the author
will tell us on the last page what it was all about.

—James Hollis, *The Middle Passage*

I knew a woman once who was about thirty pounds overweight. She complained about her weight all the time, blaming her chronic boredom and loneliness on her dress size. No matter how many diets she tried, she could never seem to rid herself of the extra pounds she was carrying. Finally, she confessed to me that she was afraid that if she lost the weight, men would find her attractive and she wouldn't be able to keep them away. "So, lose the weight but don't bathe," I suggested.

Most of us go through life as though we were a bunch of pinballs, bouncing off everything and everyone who tries to touch us. Tender beings that we are, we are constantly in reaction to someone or something. If we look at what we *do,* instead of what we *say,* we will see that, ultimately, most of us are more interested in protecting ourselves from the risks of love than in the actual experience of it. We go to extraordinary lengths to avoid the possibility of being hurt, regardless of the hunger in our hearts. We rarely own outright how often we sabotage love by admitting, "I am more interested in being safe than I am in being loved." Instead, most of us will pretend to be looking for love while covertly doing all that we can to kill off any possibility of it. We may yearn for deep and meaningful connection, but we'll react as though any gesture of advancement from another were potentially a full-on attack. Perhaps, on some level, it is.

Nicole and Nancy, a lesbian couple, came to see me recently. Although they have been together for only a few months, they are highly reactive

Thoughts crystallize
into habit and
habit solidifies into
circumstances.
—Brian Adams

and volatile with each other. Their pervasive communication style is to blame one another for the flaws and failures of their relationship. Rather than listen respectfully to each other's complaints in an attempt to increase love and affinity between them, they listen, instead, for leverage. Where can I make the other person wrong? What can I blame on my partner? How can I defend my position? Unfortunately, this narrow, contracted kind of relationship is what many of us call "being in love." But it is the shadow side of passion, the underbelly of ardor. If love were a beautiful picture, this form of it would be the negative. In this highly reactive environment, each person is preoccupied with the need to defend him or herself. All that is wonderful about love is cast aside and, ultimately, sacrificed.

In a recent article in *O* magazine, Dr. David Burns, associate professor of psychiatry at Stanford University School of Medicine, reported on an intensive study he conducted with 1,500 people. He and his staff wanted to differentiate between what was happening with partners who were in a thriving, contented intimate relationship from those who were in a disappointing, miserable one. He found that "Only one thing emerged as having a causal impact on long-term satisfaction: blaming your partner for the problems in your relationship." In other words, the *one* disparity between happy, flourishing partnerships and unhappy, failing ones was whether or not, and how intensely, they played the "blame and shame" game.

When we are having a hard time being responsible for ourselves as the cause of what is happening to us, it is generally because we have confused and collapsed "being responsible" for "being wrong." For some of us, owning our part in the creation of a situation is likened to admitting guilt and/or complete defeat. Nicole and Nancy both have the same core wound of being shamed by a highly critical parent. As children, each of them were frequently blamed and made wrong with little provocation. Therefore, admitting responsibility for what was happening in their relationship, on some level, equated admitting guilt and was accompanied by deep feelings of shame and self-reproach. They could not admit responsibility without also admitting that they were fundamentally bad people.

All relationships are handicapped to the extent that we are unable to be responsible for what we, ourselves, are creating in the relationship. This goes for relationships with friends, family, coworkers, and acquaintances, as well as with lovers. Whenever we blame others for the current circumstances for our lives, we abdicate responsibility for our choices and we reinforce our own impotence. We construct an "either/or" world—either I am right (and someone else is wrong), or I am wrong (and, therefore, deeply shamed). In this world, we are preoccupied with blaming ourselves or blaming others. In this world, we believe that in order to be deserving of the air that we breathe, we *have* to be right. So we end up alienating others by making them wrong. It may be a loveless world, but at least we come out on top.

In her book *When Things Fall Apart,* Buddhist nun Pema Chödrön, states, "Blame is a way which we solidify ourselves." She talks about our resistance to giving up our way of conceptualizing life as a right/wrong proposition by being willing to enter the "middle way" where we are "sitting on the razor's edge, not falling off to the right or the left." She continues:

> This middle way involves not hanging on to our version so tightly. It involves keeping our hearts and minds open long enough to entertain the idea that when we make things wrong, we do it out of a desire to obtain some kind of ground or security. Equally, when we make things right, we are still trying to obtain some kind of ground or security. Could our minds and our hearts be big enough just to hang out in that space where we're not entirely certain about who's right and who's wrong?

True love feels perfectly safe to explore and admit one's weaknesses, because doing so is not an admission that one is bad or inferior in any way. In an expanded relationship, we have the freedom to admit our shortcomings because we do not fear that we will be punished or pummeled in return. There is a great sense of relief in being able to freely admit our faults without the fear of being judged. Just as there is a great sense of relief in being able to grant another person the right to also be flawed without using their flaws against them. In this atmosphere, there

Happiness and true freedom come only when we assume full responsibility for who and what we are.
—Leo Buscaglia

I'd rather be
happy than right.
—Hugh Prather

is little talk of who is right and who is wrong. Both partners are constantly engaged in an inquiry of how they are each personally responsible for what is occurring at any given moment. In this atmosphere, hearts blossom and love thrives.

My friend and spiritual mentor Debu Ghosh admonished me always to stand in being 100 percent responsible for the quality of my relationships at all times. We like to think of good, solid relationships as being a 50–50 proposition. However, the best relationships are really 100–100. Because when I am only 50 percent responsible, then I am always at the effect of what the other person does or does not do with their 50 percent. Now I'm not suggesting that if someone is being disrespectful or even blatantly abusive toward you, you should hang out and tolerate it because you think that you have love enough for both of you. What I am suggesting is that you seriously ask yourself how it is that you gave someone else permission to disrespect and abuse you, because that's *your* issue. You can make someone wrong and go to all sorts of lengths to blame them and shame them and to ultimately get rid of them entirely, but until you take full responsibility for how you have been an invitation for abuse, you'll most likely attract in another abusive person in spite of your best efforts to avoid re-creating that situation.

Whenever you are
pointing your finger
at someone, notice
that there are always
three fingers
pointing back at you.
—Anonymous

The extent to which I am in full ownership of all that is occurring in my relationships is the extent that I am empowered to make improvements in those relationships. When I become spiritually lazy and buy in to the first thought that I have without examination, usually a "victim" thought (e.g., "So-and-so is inconsiderate" or "So-and-so is not doing what he *should* be doing"), then I have no power to effect change. Victim consciousness goes something like this: "It's not my job," "I couldn't help it," "It just happened," "It's your fault," and so on. When you find yourself justifying your poor behavior or when you notice that you are making excuses and blaming others for your choices, stop and ask yourself, "What is it that I am unwilling to be responsible for in this situation?"

Although at times, standing in being 100 percent for whatever is happening in any given moment may not seem "fair," doing so is a way of living your life that assumes that you are powerful, persuasive, and creative beyond measure. It is a commanding way to live, and one that the Universe richly rewards. When you know that it's you calling the shots, you can begin aiming yourself more clearly to begin hitting the bull's-eye.

PRACTICE

Take out your journal. Answer the following questions:

Who am I making wrong and for what?

What can I be responsible for in this situation?

What could I accept about this situation that would help me to give up blaming and shaming?

What can I appreciate about this situation?

What are the strengths that I bring to my relationships?

What are the weaknesses that I bring to my relationships?

What, if anything, have I been unwilling to admit to others?

BONUS: PRACTICE IN ACTION

Your task is to take the charge off "being wrong" today by admitting your culpability at least one time. You can do so without making it into a big deal. Just freely admit your responsibility in a situation to a family member, coworker, friend, or acquaintance. You may need to apologize, offer to do something to rectify the situation, or ask someone what they need from you to make the situation right. If so, offer to do this, but do *not* beat yourself up or allow yourself to be shamed in any way.

Practice being 100 percent responsible for everything that happens to

Let go of your
attachment to being
right, and suddenly
your mind is more
open. You're able to
benefit from the
unique viewpoints of
others, without
being crippled by
your own judgment.

—Ralph Marston

you today. Examine your role in all situations as intensely as you would ordinarily examine the role that others are playing.

Before bed tonight, write about what it was like for you to freely admit your mistakes and flaws to others and your experience of being 100 percent responsible for everything that happened to you today.

LESSON 40
Living the Questions

To arrive is to be in prison.

—Henri Matisse

I can appreciate people who seem to have most, if not all, of the answers. They make me feel safe as though someone, somewhere has it all under control. In a world where tragedies happen and uncertainty reigns, knowing the answers provides a certain sense of comfort and security. Having acknowledged that, I must admit my preference for "living the questions," as I have come to believe this provides a much more powerful platform from which to grow and expand.

Living the questions requires us to sit with the messiness of what it is to be human without the ability to tidy everything up immediately. Sometimes, that is what it is like when one is seeking wisdom. There's no way around it. I confess that I often find it uncomfortable and disconcerting to tolerate the anxiety of not knowing. After all, how many of us are very adept at going through our days practicing what the Buddhist's call "Beginner's Mind" or what Christ was referring to when he admonished us to "become as little children" in order to enter the kingdom of heaven? For most of us, giving up our addiction to information and certainty presents a profound challenge.

It's important to differentiate between questions that help one to gain insight and wisdom and those that are asked in the hope of receiving a quick-fix answer. A while back, I led a weekend workshop for women. On the first night, thirty-nine-year-old Pamela had a difficult time refraining from interrupting me to ask for specific instructions on how to get a man. She wanted to know when she should tell him that she wanted a serious relationship and exactly how she should tell him so he wouldn't be scared away. She wanted to know when she should sleep with him to ensure that

> If love is the answer, what is the question?
>
> —Uta West

(1) she wouldn't lose him by waiting too long, and (2) that he wouldn't dump her because she was "too easy." She wanted to know if she should hide how financially successful she was so that she wouldn't intimidate a man who might make less money than she did and, thereby, frighten him away. I couldn't answer these questions for her—not because I didn't have opinions about those things, but because they would not have been helpful to her. Because nowhere in those questions was Pamela addressing that she didn't believe that any man would actually ever love and take care of her. She wasn't addressing how difficult it was for her to simply be present and to listen to others. Nor was she addressing the fact that she didn't trust people enough to let them get close to her. How did I know that after knowing her for only a couple of hours? Because she didn't believe that I was going to love and take care of her that weekend. She wasn't listening to the answers that I *was* giving her and she wasn't trusting that if she just let me run my workshop, she would get what she needed. When I tried to tell her these things, she got a headache and left early.

Our lives require us to be deeply engaged in the "right" kind of inquiry—one that will reveal to us our own nature and the blocks we have to fulfilling our highest potential. Other than a natural and organic (yet largely unconscious) evolution, the deliberate pursuit of self-awareness is our only real access to change. I mean, life does have a way of teaching all of us—even those of us who are the most reluctant of students. Yet, when we actually desire to grow ourselves beyond who we currently are, and take that on as one of the most important—if not *the* most important task we are here to accomplish, then inquiry becomes our greatest ally. For the catalyst of most life-altering transformations is usually a really good question.

How do we know what distinguishes a "really good question?" These past few weeks, we have been in an inquiry concerning your life—your attitudes, beliefs, thoughts, and feelings—as a way to help you discover yourself as the source of what is (or is not) happening in your life. This has not been a matter of blame, but simply a matter of discovering your access to change and where you have the power to alter something. So, let's look for a moment at the questions you've been asking yourself. Largely, they are open-ended questions as opposed to questions that simply require you to answer yes or no. They are also questions about your-self as the cause of your experience rather than questions about other people or things that you have no authority to alter. While it's valuable to understand the impact that your environment is having on you, empow-ering inquiry will always see you as having the ability to make choices and facilitate change in your life. So, rather than ask yourself something like "Why do men treat women so badly?" I encourage you to ask more pro-ductive and powerful questions like "In what ways am I allowing men to treat me disrespectfully?" "Who am I keeping an agreement with by attracting abusive people?" "How does the poor treatment I am getting reflect the way that I feel about myself?"

I always advise people to try not to ask yourself "why" questions, such as: "Why am I still single?" "Why don't men seem to like me?" "Why can't I get a date for Saturday night?" Why questions tend to be shame-based and lead absolutely nowhere. Instead, ask more provocative and thought-ful questions of yourself such as, "What am I getting out of being single?" "What is it about men that I don't like?" "What is my belief about my ability to get what I really want?"

Sometimes we avoid asking really good questions of ourselves because we fear that we'll discover some frightening truth that we will not be able to fix. In our fast food culture, we tend to want easy answers and quick solutions. However, growing ourselves wiser and more loving is not so much an event as it is a process. And it is less about perfection than it is about slow and steady improvement. Psychotherapist/author Thomas Moore, in his book *Care of the Soul,* encourages us to "see through our self-destructiveness and depression, our flirtations with danger and our addictions, and ask what they might be accomplishing in our lives and what they are expressing." In other words, he is encouraging us to culti-vate curiosity as a way of being rather than always feeling so compelled to fix what we think is so wrong with us.

As a follow-up to *The Road Less Traveled,* psychotherapist and author M. Scott Peck wrote *The Different Drum.* In it, he explained his theory on the four stages of spiritual development. These stages were profoundly helpful to me in understanding the value of on-going inquiry as a way of life.

> Wisdom begins
> in wonder.
> —Socrates

It's what you learn
after you know it all
that counts.
—John Wooden

Stage One, the "chaotic, antisocial" stage, includes those of us who are underdeveloped in our ability to love others much beyond what they can do for us. People in this stage are unprincipled and governed exclusively by their own will which vacillates according to their current needs and desires. They have very little self-awareness and even less interest in cultivating it. The questions people in Stage One ask revolve around trying to figure out how to get what they want without having to give anything up.

Stage Two, the "formal, institutional" stage, is a leap in consciousness from Stage One's "no rules apply to me" to "everything is about the rules." In this stage, we are very concerned with right versus wrong and good versus evil. God is external from us and if we want to avoid being punished, we need to obey His dictates to the best of our abilities. The only real inquiry here has to do with studying and memorizing the rules. It is in this stage that we tend to have a rigid mindset and think we have all the answers.

Those of us in Stage Three, the "skeptic, individual" stage, Dr. Peck describes as "more spiritually developed" and yet, many times, not as religious. Often, we are introduced to this stage through disappointment or disillusionment. Many people in Stage Three will even describe themselves as atheists or agnostics. They are highly principled people who may be deeply involved in their communities and with social causes. Those who are advanced in Stage Three are usually seeking truth in some active way, which means that they are very involved in asking questions meant to promote growth and self-awareness. If they do so deeply enough, Dr. Peck believes that they enter into the final and most advanced stage, Stage Four, which he calls the "mystical, communal" stage.

Stage Four is characterized by mystery and a fascination with the interdependence of all things. People in this stage are not afraid to acknowledge the enormity of the unknown nor do they feel compelled to reduce the mysteries of the universe down to palatable, known quantities. Sometimes, people in Stage Four will dedicate themselves to a religious order, but more often than not, they will develop their spirituality in more unconventional and individual ways. In Stage Four, people are able to tolerate the emptiness that comes with not having the answers. Living the questions is their daily practice.

I think of my two-year-old daughter, who is swept up in the mystery of all that is. Her curiosity and sense of wonder lead her throughout the day. Everything is a question. Because of that, she is constantly learning. What might we learn if we approached each day as though it held infinite opportunities for growth and expansion? Considering that what we already know has brought us to where we are and that where we are going is beyond what we already know, it seems that curiosity and a sense of wonder might be in order for us as well.

Albert Einstein once said, "We cannot solve the world's problems at the same level at which they were created." I would say that the same is true on a personal level as well. We cannot solve our own problems at the same level of consciousness at which they were created. For the most part, we know what we know and we know what we don't know. But what about all those things that we don't know we don't know? If we are ever going to move beyond where we are right now, we will have to venture into this territory as well.

We must expand ourselves to the next level of awareness. The promise of our expansion in consciousness always lies in that which is right around the corner—the next conversation we have, the next page we turn, the next moment we sit in the silence to listen. When you seek to know all of the answers, your life then becomes limited by that which you already know. When you seek to ask deep and relevant questions, your life is only limited by the extent of your courage and willingness to learn and to try something new.

Michael, a client whom I'd not seen in a couple of years, called me recently to invite me to his wedding. I asked him what he thought was the most important thing that he learned in our work together that had opened the way for love to come into his life. He thought only briefly before he answered, "I learned to be comfortable with being uncomfortable—that it's OK to be in unfamiliar territory where you don't know who you are or what you are supposed to be doing. Because that's where the possibility of love is."

> I know nothing save the fact of my ignorance.
> —Socrates

The only Beloved
is the living
mystery itself.
—Kathleen Raine

PRACTICE

Think about a situation or two in your life that disturbs or baffles you in some way. I now invite you to take out your journal and write down three questions for each one of these situations. Write open-ended questions that will help you to deeply examine the issues that these problems represent (e.g., "In what ways does it work for me to be alone in life?" and "What can I learn from this experience that will help me to become a more loving person?").

After you've written your questions, take a few minutes to write on each of them.

BONUS: PRACTICE IN ACTION

Today I invite you to move through your day with a childlike sense of wonder and curiosity. To help facilitate this, try doing the following walking/moving meditation on and off throughout your day. Read the meditation through once or twice and then do it, as best you can from memory. You may want to write down the sentence and carry it with you.

Without altering whatever it is that you are doing, bring your attention inwards by focusing on breathing in and out. Notice if you are breathing quickly or slowly, deeply or shallowly. As you observe your breath, move it down deep into your belly and relax any areas of the body that are needlessly tense. Notice everything you see in your path, landing your eyes on one object after another, saying silently to yourself,

"I do not know the nature of this _____."

For example: "I do not know the nature of this rug. I do not know the nature of this chair. I do not know the nature of this computer. I do not know the nature of this food. I do not know the nature of this person."

Do this rhythmically and calmly for up to one minute each time you do it throughout the day.

LESSON 41
Listening with an Open Heart

How do I listen to others?
As if everyone were my Master
Speaking to me His
Cherished last words.

—Hafiz, translated by Daniel Ladinsky

When I was still in my twenties, I had a girlfriend who was given a substantial financial gift by her elderly aunt, who must have been well over ninety at the time. As the aunt handed my friend a very generous check, she paused a moment to look deeply into her eyes. "Remember, love," she said with a quiet intensity, "the greatest gift you can ever give anyone is your complete and undivided attention. Never underestimate the importance of simply listening to others."

At first, I dismissed her words as the frivolous sentiments of an old woman who was preparing for death. But as the weeks went by, I became more and more impressed with the transformation I saw in my friend who, in an effort to honor her aunt, began slowing down and being more present with others when they spoke to her. Suddenly, it seemed to me that she was becoming more and more sought after and valued by others, as well as calmer and happier within herself. When I began noticing how much I myself was benefiting from her newfound, kinder way of being, I became a hard-core convert. Thus began my study of the art of listening.

The late humorist Erma Bombeck once said, "It seems rather incongruous that in a society of super sophisticated communication, we often suffer from a shortage of listeners." There are many things going on in the world right now that are profoundly affecting our ability to give our total and absolute attention to others. It's important that we make an effort to understand those things that are influencing us, even though it can be a bit like a fish trying to figure out what water is.

This time in history has been called the Age of Distraction, the Age of Anxiety, and the Information Age. Regardless of the term we use, it's clear that we are being showered with more and more demands for our attention. In her book *The Zen of Listening,* Rebecca Shafir tells us that we were exposed to six times as many advertising messages in 1991 as we were in 1971. In a single day, most of us will take in more information than those who lived a hundred years ago did in the course of a decade. When you consider how often we are interrupted, how much we are expected to know, and how frequently we are pulled in different directions, it's understandable that we often turn off our listening abilities, disengaging from those around us.

We have to ask ourselves what happens to our sense of belonging and our overall experience of emotional well-being when we shut down and stop listening to one another? Each day, millions of us are taking doctor-prescribed pills meant to diminish feelings of loneliness, low self-esteem, and a lack of connection. While I've seen firsthand the helpful effects of medication, I can't help but wonder where all of this collective anxiety and sadness is coming from. I can't help but struggle with the deeper meaning of our communal suffering and fear. Perhaps our feelings are trying to tell us something about the way that we are living. Perhaps we need to listen to this tribal moan, as though it were feedback on how we are doing.

Since loneliness has been identified as the number-one social problem in America, it seems clear that our distracted and hurried ways of relating to one another are severely inadequate for the human heart. In our hasty attempt to push the river of our lives to get more, do more, and be more, we have profoundly underestimated our need for simple closeness and connection. In so doing, we have forgotten how delicious it is to slow down, look someone in the eye and savor a good story. We have denied ourselves the opportunity to unburden our hearts by sharing the God's-honest truth about who we really are, while sitting face-to-face with someone who actually cares and wants to know. This is the longing for a soul mate—that one person in the world who inspires you to slow down

> The greatest problem of communication is the illusion that it has been accomplished.
>
> —George Bernard Shaw

> Shallow brooks murmur most.
>
> —Philip Sidney

enough to experience this exchange. But what if, as author Thomas Moore suggests in his book *Soul Mates,* we each have many "soul partners," as he calls them? What if every person you came in contact with today—coworkers, family members, neighbors, even the strangers you pass on the street—carried the possibility of a profound gift for you, and your job was to give each of them enough of your attention so you could receive it?

In our sound-bite world of savvy marketing and relentless networking, we have forgotten to be open and curious in the exchanges we encounter. Instead, we come to each interaction with closed hearts and fixed agendas. Our communication has become self-serving, as we listen more and more to find out what someone can do for us rather than listening to discover who they are. We listen not with an authentic desire to understand but, rather, to see how we can manipulate a situation to our advantage. We listen not for what we can learn but rather for what we don't like about the person speaking. Not as an act of curiosity, but rather for the chance to give a clever response.

On average, we decide within the first fifteen seconds whether or not we think someone is worth the time and effort it takes to listen to him or her. So we walk around selectively closing ourselves off to most of the people we come in contact with. No wonder so many of us are lonely. No wonder that prescriptions for antidepressants that treat social anxiety is off the charts. Many of us are walking around feeling like we have to sell ourselves each time we want some simple human contact.

In order to live lives of soulful and meaningful connections, we have to consciously choose to slow down, give up our hidden agendas and develop the capacity to focus on others by making an effort to understand them. We need to cultivate curiosity about ways of thinking that are different from our own. We must open ourselves up to who others are and what they have to teach us. We need to learn to be in the process of listening rather than being preoccupied with the potential payoff.

Authentic listening is simply the giving of our undivided attention to another without imposing our personal agendas, something that might take a little practice. It is the generous act of giving someone the space to be exactly who they are and exactly who they are not. Once you have mas-

The greatest compliment that was ever paid to me was when someone asked me what I thought, and attended to my answer.
—Henry David Thoreau

Blessed is the man who, having nothing to say, abstains from giving us worthy evidence of the fact.
—George Eliot

tered the ability to authentically listen with your whole body, absorbing even the rich subtleties in the unspoken, you will have discovered the key to intimacy. For truly, listening is love in action.

PRACTICE

Today I invite you to consider the possibility that when others speak to you, you are bringing covert agendas to the way you listen. By doing this, you are drastically diminishing the quality of your relationships and preventing others from bringing profound gifts of love and service to you. Go through the list below and identify those things that you think might be going on for you when you are attempting to listen:

I'm judging the speaker.

I'm judging myself.

I'm thinking of how I should respond.

I'm trying to make a good impression.

I'm fixated on forcing a particular outcome.

I'm on the defense.

I'm making the speaker wrong.

I'm making myself wrong.

I'm gaining evidence for how I'm right.

I'm busy trying to protect myself.

I'm self-conscious about how I look.

I'm trying to control the conversation to go a certain way.

I'm trying to fix a perceived problem.

Using the above list as a reference point, write in your journal for several minutes on the following question:

What is going on within me when I am listening to others?

BONUS: PRACTICE IN ACTION

Today, have at least one conversation where you consciously choose to slow down and give your complete and undivided attention to another person. Notice if you have any covert, personal agendas when that person is speaking to you. If you discover a covert agenda, try letting it go and simply bring yourself back to being present with the person who is speaking.

Go out of your way today to connect with those around you and look to discover the gift of each interaction.

O Divine Master,
grant that I may not
so much seek to
be understood,
as to understand.
—St. Francis of Assisi

LESSON 42
On Speaking Up

Ask, and it shall be given you.

—Jesus

There is no possibility of true relatedness when we are inauthentic in our speaking. Communication skills are never the goal, but rather the means—the goal itself is communion. How we give and receive information is simply our vehicle for getting there.

Sara, a high-powered executive in the entertainment business, was nearing forty when she met and married her husband, Peter. For the first few months all was wonderful. Six months into their marriage, Peter lost his job. Instead of looking aggressively for a new one, as Sara hoped he might, Peter took his time, enjoyed his days off and allowed his wife's salary to cover the mortgage on their new home. Sara was upset over Peter's laid-back approach to finding work but she kept it to herself.

When Sara was a little girl, her mother, an immigrant from China, had a motto. "Be sweet, be pretty, be smart." Reflecting an old Chinese custom, Sara had learned to speak only when she had something nice and encouraging to say. Otherwise, she kept her mouth shut. She was never given permission to speak her truth in her family, nor had she seen her mother do so. This was becoming a rather severe handicap in her ability to create a loving relationship with her new husband, who was third-generation American and had no understanding of the subtleties of relationships with women raised with this old-world way of being.

Sara came to see me one day so that she could have a safe place to tell the truth. At that point Peter had been unemployed for well over a year, and Sara was secretly contemplating a divorce. All this time, she'd never said one word to him to indicate her unhappiness. He thought their marriage was in great shape and he frequently and good-naturedly bragged about the "low-maintenance" woman he had married. Little did he know.

Sara was operating out of an erroneous expectation she had of how a "good" wife might behave in the face of a challenge. Instead of becoming a good wife, however, she'd become a "should" wife who was covertly judging her husband and losing all respect for him, without offering him the possibility of doing anything differently. Her inauthenticity was threatening to destroy the very thing it was initially designed to protect. In the meantime, her love for him was waning. True empathy—the key ingredient to good communication—was present only in its most superficial form.

"You know, Sara," I began, "you really haven't created your marriage yet." She looked at me a little confused. After all, she and Peter had been married nearly two years by now. I continued, "Taking vows just provides the framework for a union, but that relationship does not automatically exist. You have to build it. All you have right now is a commitment to create a union but because you are withholding so much of yourself from your husband, you are failing to fulfill it." Sara got a tear in her eye and nodded her head, indicating that she understood what I was saying to her.

We had to work quickly to get her to begin expressing the authenticity of what she was feeling before she threw away the possibility of love. When she actually began to share bits and pieces of what she was feeling, she was surprised to find Peter quite responsive and attentive. To her great relief, in response to her concerns, Peter took on part-time work as a consultant while he more aggressively pursued his search for a full-time position.

When we speak our truth, we are standing in the very center of our personal power. Saying no when you mean no, asking directly for what you want without regard for what others might think of you, asserting an opinion you suspect others will disagree with or having the freedom to admit that you don't know something when you don't are all actions that cause us to be more authentically and fully who we are.

Many of us struggle with addictions to alcohol, food, cigarettes, or drugs precisely because truth was denied in our household when we were growing up. We had to numb out our knowingness somehow. We weren't

> If there is something to gain and nothing to lose by asking, by all means ask.
> —W. Clement Stone

allowed to speak of things directly and so we stuffed our feelings, hid our pain and tried to get with the program—all at the great cost of having an intact ability to know and assert our truth. The healing and recovery for all addictive behaviors includes learning to cultivate a discipline of telling the truth, first to oneself and then to others.

Everything we aspire to in life—success, fulfillment, and loving relationships—depends upon our ability to assert ourselves by asking directly for what we want and setting clear limits with others. It seems simple enough, but for many of us, it's not.

Consider Dominick, an intelligent, attractive, and successful actor in his mid-fifties who has never been married. Although Dominick came to therapy purporting to want a relationship, he in fact avoids them like the plague. Dominick is terrified to make requests or set boundaries with anyone—men or women—because he fears that others will not like him. Instead, he complies with the demands made of him, so as not to cause trouble. He concedes to others even though he often feels resentful and irritated. In order to do this, he has to dismiss his feelings as unimportant and rationalize his self-deprecating behavior. In the long run, it's just easier not to go out on too many dates.

There are several reasons why we do not assert ourselves in relationships, and most of them start with the "F" word—fear. There's the fear of rejection, the fear of abandonment, and the fear of being humiliated. There's the fear of being known and the fear of not being liked, even by perfect strangers. There is the fear of being vulnerable and defenseless, which of course reinforces itself, since you can never really know that it's safe to be flawed with another unless you actually take the risk of being vulnerable with them. Then there's the fear that we'll never have what we want anyway (so why bother trying) and the fear that if we do gather the courage to ask for what we want, we will surely do it wrong. And, of course, there is always the fear that if you take any risks at all in life, you will most certainly find out that your worst fantasies are actually true— that you really are inferior and destined to fail.

Although many of these fears could easily be laid to rest if only we would challenge them, many of us live our entire lives dancing around and interacting with them, without so much as questioning their validity.

When you begin to consider what this costs us in aliveness and love, it's staggering. Sara could easily have gotten to the point where she threw away a potentially loving marriage to a good man who absolutely adores her and who would do anything to please her, *if she would only tell him what that was.*

Until we risk telling the truth, we cannot have an authentic experience of love. We can have entanglements, we can be "involved," we can even be married, but we will not have the experience of love. For even if you *were* really loved by another person, how would you know if you didn't allow yourself to tell the raw, naked truth and risk the consequences of that? You would just believe that you were being loved for the false persona you were presenting. The gift of authentic communication, then, is a gift that you give to yourself.

Often, instead of asking for what we want, we'll stay stuck in a complaint. When we are complaining, we are in a state of resistance to what's so. Anytime we are resisting the current reality, we are limited in our ability to creatively solve the problem we are faced with. A couple recently came to see me to help them decide whether or not to break up. Although they loved each other very much, they seemed to be fighting more often than not. The man began telling me what he could not tolerate in his girlfriend. She sat there stunned as he complained for several minutes about her poor eating habits and his disappointment that she rarely cooked healthy and wholesome meals for the two of them. When he was finished, I turned to her and asked if he'd had ever made a request that she cook for him. Looking hurt and sad, she shook her head no. In their entire three years together, she had no idea that he wanted her to do this. Had he asked her, she assured us, she would have been happy to accommodate his request.

The man had been engaged in a fantasy that if his girlfriend really loved him, she would know what he wanted without his having to tell her. But operating under the illusion that others *should just know* is magical thinking. While magical thinking helped to develop the qualities of wonder and imagination when we are children, adults who relate in this way are simply cultivating the qualities of passivity and resentment in their relationships. Clearly, the time for magical thinking has passed.

When we allow fear to dictate the quality of our communication, we will

> Silence is the virtue of fools.
> —Francis Bacon

often engage in passive aggressive behavior. We'll do things like come late to a party that we didn't really want to attend, burn a meal when we secretly would have preferred being taken out for dinner, or "have a headache" when it's time for bed after our partner has failed to live up to our covert expectations that afternoon. Rather than simply ask for what we want, we'll often use fear, obligation, or guilt to manipulate others into giving it to us anyway. Whenever we don't get our way, we'll do things like withhold our love as a form of punishment, remind the other person just how many times we've sacrificed ourselves for them, or mope around the house for hours at a time.

The bottom line between making a clear, direct request instead of a manipulative demand simply masquerading as a request is that you genuinely have the space for someone to say no. And that requires a certain fundamental trust in the goodness of your life—a knowing that you will be OK if that person is unwilling or unable to give you what you want. There is great freedom in this form of non-attachment. Once you have mastered this, then you are at liberty to ask anyone for anything at any time.

Speaking authentically requires us to know our own truth. Before sharing our feelings, we must understand what they are. Therefore, speaking our truth demands of us a certain rigor with ourselves. When I was learning how to identify and express the feelings I was having, I spent a lot of time journaling and reading to try to sort through the many emotions, sensations, and responses that had, for so many years, remained unnamed within me. I had to own feelings and thoughts that were contrary to my image of myself as a "nice" person. I had to tell the truth on myself, even at the risk of looking bad. There's no way around it. You really can't be that invested in looking good if you want to know the experience of love.

A word of caution: Keep in mind that the goal of communication is communion. Before you "speak your truth," you would be wise to first make a concerted effort to understand the perspective of the other person and to clear yourself of the need to be right, make someone wrong, blame, punish, strategize, or get your way. Remember, we are listening and speaking in the service of creating loving, harmonious relationships. I have learned, sometimes through the suffering of hurting another person, that before we speak our minds, we would do well to ask ourselves what exactly it is that we are trying to create.

PRACTICE

Take out your journal and write on the following questions. Don't censor yourself. Just write whatever comes to mind when you read the question.

> The cruelest lies are often told in silence.
>
> —Robert Louis Stevenson

What upsets have I been holding inside myself and who am I upset with?

What is this costing me?

What could I tell this person instead?

What appreciation have I been withholding, and from who?

What is this costing me?

What could I tell this person instead?

What complaints have I been making lately?

What requests could I make instead?

Where am I avoiding asking directly for what I want?

In what ways am I trying to manipulate a situation rather than asking directly for what I want?

What requests could I make instead?

BONUS: PRACTICE IN ACTION

Do at least one thing today that either (1) asserts your true feelings to someone that you've been withholding from, (2) transforms a complaint into a request, or (3) has you let go of a manipulative attempt to get what you want by making a direct and specific request.

SUGGESTED STUDY GUIDE
FOR GROUP DISCUSSION

1. Who were you able to give up making wrong this week, and how might those people be right if you looked at things from their perspective?

2. What was it like for you to accept your life exactly as it is and, perhaps more important, as it is not? What attachments were you able to give up?

3. What fears have been running your life, and to what extent, if any, were you able to self-soothe and take fear out of the driver's seat?

4. What did you notice about your ability to be 100 percent responsible for the quality of your relationships at all times?

5. On a scale of 1 to 10 (one being the least and 10 the most), where are you when it comes to needing to know all the answers? How might you release some of this need to be in control?

6. What covert agendas do you bring to your conversations, and what has it been like to let go of them?

7. What requests were you able to make this week and how was your experience of doing so?

LIVING LOVE FULFILLED

The more we are, the richer everything we experience is.
And those who want to have a deep love in their lives
must collect and save for it, and gather honey.

—Rainer Maria Rilke

As we move into our final week together, we continue cultivating the characteristics of love, celebrating all that is beautiful and lovely in our lives today. This week:

✳ We explore the qualities of an enchanted life and examine how to increase the magical experiences we effortlessly draw toward us

✳ We allow the forces of love to move through us more and more in the ordinary activities of our daily lives

✳ We begin the transformation from a *me*-centered life to a *we*-centered life

✳ We focus on enhancing gratitude as the absolute best way to attract all that is good and wonderful

✳ We begin taking bold and brave risks to actively create more possibilities for love

✳ We center and anchor ourselves fully in the vision of love fulfilled in our lives

LESSON 43
The Enchanted Life

A bit of advice given to a young Native American at the time of his
initiation: "As you go the way of life, you will see a great chasm.

Jump.

It is not as wide as you think."

—Joseph Campbell

When we are looking at life from a loveless perspective, the chasm to
enchantment may seem daunting and vast. We watch others joyfully in
love with our noses pressed up against the glass, peering in at what
appears to be a rich, colorful experience of life—an experience that we
ourselves are deprived of. It's as though we were living in a world explod-
ing with music, while we ourselves remain hearing-impaired, acutely
aware of the rhythm to which others are swaying, as though we were
standing on the sidelines of a fabulous festival to which we ourselves have
not been invited.

Falling in love is an enchanted experience, a sudden eruption of color
in a previously black-and-white world. The alchemy of love transforms
the ordinary into the mystical and the mundane into the charmed.
Routine encounters suddenly occur as rich in nuance and possibility and
commonplace tasks take on new meaning and depth. Yet, just as easily as
we are caught up in this cyclone of delight, we can also be dropped from
the sky with nothing but the cold, hard earth to break our fall. Our love
affair with love affairs often forgets to take into account Plato's warning
in *Symposium* that love is both the child of fullness, as well as of emptiness. Love does *not* promise to heal all wounds and make straight all
crooked paths. Rather, love will often escort you straight into the most
wounded parts of yourself, leading you round and round in some strange
circuitous route right into the heart of disaster.

It is better, therefore, to separate the magic of enchantment from the experience of falling in love. We need to know that the mystical heights to which we aspire are not necessarily dependent upon any one person or any one kind of relationship. Love must be regarded as less the phenomenon of a particular connection, and more as a state of heart, body, mind, and soul that we are seeking to attain. For it is this intensely alive state of being, this thriving and optimistic perspective on life, that we enviously long for as we surreptitiously observe new lovers at play. We yearn to be so alive, so happy, so connected, and so inspired. It is the brass ring, the gold medal, the Academy Award, and the Pulitzer Prize rolled up into one. Its source is not necessarily to be found in a lover, however. Its source can be found within each and every one of us.

Synchronicity, a kind of happenstance in life that reveals a deep and pervasive connectedness, permeates the life that is in harmony with this inner wellspring of love. A lack of synchronicity is present when we insist upon finding enchantment outside of ourselves and occurs as a sort of frustrating fragmentation in life. The pieces of your life don't quite fit and all the dots don't quite connect. The various aspects of your life do not seem to operate well as a cohesive whole and the majority of one's time is spent trying to fix the many problems that are present. When life occurs without a sense of magic, all events are somewhat flat and all encounters somewhat unfulfilling. Yet when synchronicity and magic are present, all events seem somehow interwoven and related and all encounters are accompanied with a sense of purpose and meaning. Even those that are seemingly ordinary and mundane are often imbued with a feeling of connection and significance.

So many "how we met" stories are filled with this sense of synchronicity and magic. Is it that this experience is given to only a chosen few? Is it that some of us are "born lucky" while others are destined to be left out in the cold? Or is it that the "lucky" ones are those of us who have aligned ourselves with the mysteries of life—insisting that in *our* lives "all things work together for good," as the Good Book itself has promised, regardless of our current circumstances and challenges. For surely, this kind of faith must tempt the Universe to respond kindly. Such a childlike sense of trust and wonder must cast quite a spell on the forces of

Lovers think they're looking for each other. But there's only one search: Wandering this world.
—Rumi

I think it pisses God off if you walk by the color purple in a field somewhere and don't notice it.
—Alice Walker

> Strive to live the
> ordinary life in an
> extraordinary way.
> —Ralph Blum

fate, which would bring opportunity to some and a lack thereof to others.

The intensity of our emptiness and desperate longing for romantic union is directly related to our sense of separation from ourselves and from one another. We are all yearning to feel a deep sense of connection and belonging with others, and we believe that a romantic commitment is our fastest route home. For when we fall in love, we see in our beloved's face, the face of God. But isn't God everywhere? In every person we encounter? And every moment we experience? Must we wait indefinitely before partaking of the beauty of God?

What our craving for romantic love reveals to us is the need to return to a place in our consciousness where we are aware of and awake to our connection to our own heart, to one another, and, in fact, to all living things. Sufi poet Rumi once wrote

> *This is how a human being can change.*
> *There's a worm addicted to eating*
> *grape leaves.*
> *Suddenly, he wakes up,*
> *call it grace, whatever, something*
> *wakes him, and he's no longer*
> *a worm.*
> *He's the entire vineyard,*
> *and the orchard too,*
> *the fruit, the trunks,*
> *a growing wisdom and joy*
> *that doesn't need to devour.*

Please don't think that I am saying that a desire for romantic union is pathological. It's not at all, by any stretch of the imagination. But the extent to which we are waiting to begin our lives, or the boredom and the restlessness we feel in the absence of such a partnership is telling. We have to ask ourselves, if we are so numbed and asleep to the fullness of life, what then are we really offering another? Are we looking to share a love that we have cultivated and grown to the extent that we can no longer contain it within our own little lives, or are we simply looking to jump-start our own dead batteries? And how, then, do we plan on sustaining the magic of love after the initial excitement has cooled down, if we have no clue on how to create magic for ourselves right now?

Years ago, I met a middle-aged, divorced woman named Karen. She was rather plain looking, with straight, mousy brown hair and a wide, oval face. Her body was at least twenty-five to thirty pounds overweight and she wore loose clothing that hung rather poorly on her. Yet, talk to her for five minutes and your life was transformed. Her kindness spilled out in every gesture. She was filled with a sense of wonder and joy that was absolutely infectious and a delight to be around. Everywhere we went, some man asked Karen out on a date. She couldn't even keep track of them.

We cannot wait for someone to choose us before we begin experiencing enchantment and magic in life. That's like saying, I think I'll wait to breathe until I meet "The One." The deprivation could kill you, if not physically, then at least spiritually. We must fight the spiritual inertia that tempts us to rot away on the sidelines, letting the beauty of life go by unnoticed, and the sweetness of life go by untasted, until there is exactly the right person to see and taste it with.

We are all such perfection junkies. We have these very stringent guidelines about what we think we should have, by when and with whom. Yet, having rigid rules for your life is not the same thing as having a vision for your life. Being clear about what you want does not usurp being open and available to the boundless opportunities for enchantment and magic surrounding you today. There is tremendous freedom in being able to appreciate and relish the life you have right now, inclusive of all its quirky and peculiar imperfections. When we are busy making everything and everyone around us wrong (i.e., thinking we have the wrong bodies or the wrong jobs, we're the wrong weight or are meeting all the wrong people), we strangle the expression of enchantment in our lives. For magic only happens when one is fully present and available to what is so, and not preoccupied with what is not.

In order to live a blessed life, one must be a blessing. That means that we have to give up complaining about what we don't have and begin

Remember that the most beautiful things in the world are the most useless: peacocks and lilies for instance.
—John Ruskin

Waking up this morning, I smile. Twenty-four brand new hours are before me. I vow to live fully in each moment and to look at all beings with eyes of compassion.
—Thich Nhat Hanh

blessing all that we do. It means that we must consciously make an effort to see the extraordinary in the ordinary and the mystical in the mundane. We must make an effort to begin harnessing the forces of love in our most routine encounters. It is then that the hidden door will open to us, and we, too, will begin experiencing the magic and synchronicity that has, for so long, eluded us. And we will discover that we were *never* not invited to the party. The invitation was right there in our pocket all along.

PRACTICE

This morning, we are going to do a simple blessings meditation. Read the instructions once through and then do the meditation from memory to the best of your ability.

Sit up straight with your legs and arms uncrossed and resting easily. Close your eyes and relax your entire body. Starting at the bottom of your feet and working your way up through the body—your toes, your ankles, calves, knees, thighs, etc. until you reach the top of your head, release any tension you find. Breath in and out normally, without any effort, with your mouth slightly open and at rest. Feel yourself breathing but do not try to regulate your breath in any way.

Allow your mind to wander to the various aspects of your life—your physical environment, your job, your friends, your family, your exes, your finances, etc. Anything that comes to mind, pause and simply say silently to yourself,

"I bless (my) _____ exactly as it (s/he) is right now."

Do this meditation for several minutes.

BONUS: PRACTICE IN ACTION

Do at least one thing today that enhances the experience of enchantment and magic in your life (e.g., do something ordinary with extraordinary kindness and mindful attentiveness, allow yourself to become enraptured by a beautiful sunset, or spend some time lovingly tending to an animal).

LESSON 44
Let Love Live Your Life

The goal in life is to be a vehicle for something higher.

—Joseph Campbell

For years spiritual leader Marianne Williamson led a New Year's Eve service here in Los Angeles that I attended regularly. I was happy, then, to have her back in L.A. one recent New Year's Eve, this time hosting a call-in talk-radio program. The show was also aired on the Internet, allowing people from all over the world to call in. A woman named Grace from Sydney, Australia, got through.

Grace sounded like an intelligent, thoughtful woman who, like many of us, was devoted to her career. While she was quite successful in business, she often felt lonely and isolated from others during the hours she was not working. This, then, prompted her to devote more and more of her time to her work, and less time to tolerating the loneliness of her non-existent social life.

Marianne listened as Grace admitted that her idea of creating love in her life was to watch Hollywood movies and wait passively for her knight in shining armor to come along. When that didn't happen, she felt deeply disappointed and became resigned about ever finding love. Marianne challenged her by comparing the drastic, extreme measures she was willing to go to ensure her professional success to what little she did to create more love in her life. Grace acknowledged that she needed to become more proactive in cultivating love in her everyday life.

If we made a commitment to develop our ability to love and be loved with the same level of focus and devotion that many of us give to our careers, most of us would become enlightened beings in no time. We have a tendency to think that enlightened teachers such as Jesus, Buddha, and Muhammad were simply born that way. But each of these masters toiled for years to cultivate their ability to give and receive love before ascending to their positions as spiritual leaders. None of us finds a shortcut to fulfillment.

Love is a state of being that does not rest upon external circumstances. Regardless of what is, or is not, happening around us, love is something that we generate from within ourselves. Like Grace, many of us are waiting for a knight in shining armor to rescue us from our sorrow by bringing love to us, as though love were to be found only outside of ourselves. When it looks like our knight is not coming, we delve into depression, believing that our lives are void of love. The Universe is somehow withholding from us. We become frustrated and angry. How awful it is to be at the random mercy of fate that smiles upon some with the light of love yet frowns upon others by its absence. However, the truth is that the only thing missing in our lives is the thing that we ourselves are not giving.

The forces of love are always available for us to dance with and cultivate. It's just that we're so concerned with the form that love takes, that we miss the constant opportunities that come our way. We're trying to get love to look a certain way—the ring on the finger, the white picket fence or whatever version of that you have for you. When we do not get exactly what we want, we often withhold our love from the world in response. Like a two-year-old throwing a tantrum, we refuse to do it any other way, as if to say, "If I can't have love *this* way, then I won't have love at all." But love itself is not interested in form. It is interested only in you expanding beyond yourself and your expectations to include whoever and whatever is in your life *right now*. If that one special person has not yet appeared, the best one can do to prepare for his or her arrival is to keep the channels of love itself wide open. Since like attracts like, if one wants to attract in more love, then one needs to foster and nurture the opportunities for love that are present *now*.

Spiritual teacher Eckhart Tolle, tells us, "Love is not selective, just as the light of the sun is not selective. It does not make one person special. It is not exclusive." It's inauthentic to say that you want to be in a loving relationship if you have no interest in growing your capacity to love in general. Your ability to create a loving union is directly related to the amount of love you are able to surrender yourself to in any given

> The heart is like a garden. It can grow compassion or fear, resentment or love. What seeds will you plant there?
>
> —Jack Kornfield

Don't think of what's
being said but of
what's talking.
Malice? Ignorance?
Pride? Love?

—Joseph Campbell

There is no way
to peace.
Peace is the way.

—A. J. Muste

moment. Good relationships require a tremendous amount of generosity, kindness, compassion, and self-awareness. Too many romantic unions fall far below their potential due to the limitations of one or both partners to bring these qualities with them when they enter into the relationship.

We have to extend ourselves beyond our religious beliefs or our philosophy in order to cultivate these qualities. We can't afford to just be a Buddhist or a Christian. We actually have to have some capacity to *be* the Buddha. We must develop some ability to *become* the Christ.

Remember those bumper stickers "What would Jesus do?" In allowing ourselves to become a conduit for love, we ask ourselves throughout the day, "What would love do now?" When we are willing to surrender ourselves to the qualities of love—compassion, forgiveness, graciousness, and kindness—we discover that we are never left void. Rather, we find that vast amounts of wisdom and kindheartedness are available to us in any given moment, just for the asking. In her book *Enchanted Love,* Marianne Williamson quotes her minister friend Mary Manin Morrisey as saying, "God can only do for us what He can do through us." It's foolish to ask God for a great love without being willing to become a great lover. Just as it would be foolish to say that we wanted to become a great doctor without being willing to go to medical school.

The first response to the thought of yielding to love over remaining petty is usually resistance of some sort. Attacking thoughts that would justify an unloving response come to mind, and the mind attaches itself to them. However, if we are able to observe these thoughts and choose to move beyond them without acting them out, we allow for the possibility of love to move through us. Rather than clinging to being right, we surrender to the possibility that the other person might have a point. Rather than exposing someone's flaw, we yield ourselves to kind-hearted compassion, instead. Rather than punishing an offense, we find ourselves deferring to graciousness and understanding. In doing so, we enlarge our hearts. We feel inordinately better about ourselves—bigger somehow, more grounded and more mature.

The biblical story of Noah comes to mind. One night, long after the floods had receded, Noah drank the wine from his vineyard and became so drunk that he passed out naked in his tent. His son Ham saw his father and condemned him by gossiping and complaining to his brothers, Shem and Japheth, about his drunken state. But Shem and Japheth had compassion on their father. They picked up a blanket, placed it on their shoulders and, so as not to shame him, walked backwards into the tent. Without looking upon their father's naked drunkenness, they covered him lovingly with the blanket and left him to sleep it off. And while they did not do this deed of kindness for any reward, their father was deeply touched by their compassion and extended a blessing to them and their descendants.

Many of us make the mistake of trying to expand our ability to love at the expense of ourselves. But a heart that is inappropriately open will cause a great deal of suffering. I used to believe that being a spiritual person meant that I had to keep my heart available to others, even if they were being disrespectful or unkind toward me. It took me awhile to understand that, by doing this, I was displaying a lack of self-respect and self-worth. Love is never fulfilled at my expense and being a loving person is not to be confused with being a doormat. Buddha said, "You can look the whole world over and never find anyone more deserving of love than yourself."

> God loves the world through us.
> —Mother Teresa

PRACTICE

Take out your journal.

First, write a list of four or five qualities that you believe define love (e.g., patience, empathy, peace, etc.).

Second, write down three situations in your life that are irritating to you (e.g., I'm irritated that I'm being passed over for a promotion at work, etc.).

Next, write down the names of those directly involved in these situations. Next to their name, write down what your judgments of them are (e.g., Janice—for brown nosing the boss, being manipulative and greedy by taking what should have been mine).

Finally, write a response to the question:

**What would love (or any other quality you listed such as
compassion, kindness, etc.) do now?**

Write on this question for each of these three situations (i.e.,
Acknowledge that Janice has worked harder than I have these past few
weeks and that I took an extended vacation at a crucial time, even though
I knew it would cost me. Love would congratulate Janice for her accom-
plishment. Love would see my envy as evidence that I, too, wish to advance
in my career. Love would (1) begin to take actions consistent with that
desire, such as get to work on time each day, (2) go out of my way to go
above and beyond what is expected of me, and (3) let my superiors know
that I am committed to advancing as well and ask for their guidance and
support).

BONUS: PRACTICE IN ACTION

As you go through your day, each time you notice yourself irritated or
upset, ask yourself

**What would love
(or any other quality you listed such as compassion, kindness, etc.)
do now?**

Allow yourself to choose love over pettiness throughout the day. Stretch
yourself to become the most loving version of yourself possible by doing
that which you believe love would do in any given moment.

LESSON 45
From "Me" to "We"

Though modern marriage is a tremendous laboratory, its members
are often utterly without preparation for the partnership function.
How much agony and remorse and failure could have been
avoided if there had been at least some rudimentary
learning before they entered the partnership.

—Carl Rogers

In his book *Not Just Stories,* Rabbi Benjamin Twerski writes of a woman
who went to see the Miggid of Kozhnitz to ask his blessing, so that she
and her husband could conceive a child. They had been trying unsuc-
cessfully for several years and were quite discouraged. The Maggid said to
her, "My parents, too, were childless for many years. Then my mother
sewed a coat for the Ba'al Shem Tov, and after that I was born." The
woman excitedly replied, "I will gladly sew a coat for you, a beautiful
coat!" But the Maggid gave her a sad smile and replied, "No, my dear
woman. That will be of no avail. You see, my mother did not know this
story." The Maggid's story reminds us not to give something with the
expectation that we should receive something in return. His mother had
not sewed the coat in order to receive a blessing. Yet a blessing she did
receive.

What we give always comes back to us. But we cannot give for this reason. We have to give for the sake of giving. That is what makes giving an
act of enlargement and expansion. I am always amazed, however, at how
often couples come in to see me, keeping score. If I do something for you,
then you're obligated to do something for me. If I cook tonight, then it's
your turn tomorrow. It's such a stingy way to be in love. I almost want to
ask them why they bother. Wasn't it easier just to be alone?

Love is the extremely difficult realization that something other than oneself is real. Love, and so art and morals, is the discovery of reality.

—Iris Murdoch

Creating a "we" life as opposed to living parallel "me" lives requires a fluidity where giving to one another is as natural as breathing. In our excessively selfish society, this way of being is becoming rarer and rarer. The "me, me, me" mantra of modern day life is profoundly affecting our ability to be successful in our intimate relationships. We are coming to the table with little practice in being kind, thoughtful, and generous. We don't have an understanding of what it is to watch out for others in our community. We're too busy watching out for "number one." Our competitive indifference toward one another grows by leaps and bounds each decade. It's heartbreaking. Yes, there are moments, like right after a tragedy. Suddenly, life comes into perspective and the walls come down. For a split second, we understand our profound interrelatedness. However, within a relatively short period of time, we're back to business as usual.

American culture in particular places a profound emphasis upon the ideologies of autonomy and independence. These principles generally inspire us to be the best that we can be. Yet, taken to the extreme, they also can inspire us to be the worst. In this regard, we must stop defining our lives by what we got away with, who we pulled one over on, and how we made it to the top of the class. Long-term, committed love is an interdependent dance. As such, it requires us to think inside of the context of what it is to be deeply related, mutually dependent, and responsible to and for one another.

Culturally, we're more apt to call a generous gesture "codependent" than we are to call it "love." We're more apt to label kindness a weakness and sensitivity a flaw. We then expect our intimate relationships to provide all the love that's missing in our lives. But how can a relationship that so depends upon the unconditional generosity of both partners not be handicapped by the lack of generosity that is so common in our society? Because when you couple up with someone, you really do have to think "we" instead of "me" in order to have harmony and love in your home. You have to look out for one another.

I have been seeing a couple for close to a year now. Their marriage is a war zone. Yet for the sake of their children, they come back each week, in the hope that they can mature themselves faster than they can destroy what little love is left between them. It's a race against the clock. The main problem they have, we've discovered, is the way they conceptualize their marriage. Because they have no model of marriage as a "we" community, they see it more as "whoever dominates and screams the loudest, gets to have their way" type of arrangement. Either he wins or she wins, but always someone loses. It's all about a struggle for power and control so there's really only room for one of them in their relationship. It doesn't even occur to either one of them to explore the needs and wants of their partner, and then treat each other's needs as though they were their own. New concept entirely. Switch gears. Switch hats. Switch hearts. They're trying. But it is so much harder to do the work in hindsight. It is so much more difficult to change a dynamic once it's firmly in place, and has been reinforced over and over again. You, however, get to prepare yourself now. You get to practice living inside of a "we" paradigm so that when you meet "The One," you stand a good chance of creating a nurturing, loving dynamic from the very start. Whenever possible, preventive medicine is the way to go.

Marriage (and I include committed, same-sex unions in this category) is a community of two. It is about as "we" an experience as we can have in this life. Most likely, the movement from being a "me" to being a "we" will be one of the most profound adjustments you will ever have to make. Many of us fear entering into a "we" covenant because our sense of who we are is still fragile and delicate. We mistake the process of formulating a cohesive union as being one where we merge with the other, becoming "one" in the sense that we surrender our selfhood to the experience. We have misunderstood what it is to love. We fear it means that we will be overpowered by our awareness of the needs of the other before we have a good grasp on our own—the "how much of me do I have to lose to be loved by you?" dilemma. Yet, the best partnerships are formed between two people who have worked to develop a firm and resilient sense of identity within themselves. Put simply, you have to be a strong "me" in order to form a strong "we." Healthy "we-ness" always enhances and strengthens the individuality of who you are. It provides support that enables you to be more fully yourself in the world.

There is so much talk about the dysfunctional family. Sometimes I ask my clients if they know what a functional family looks like, so they have

> To live in love is life's greatest challenge.
> —Leo Buscaglia

something to emulate. Most do not. So, I think it's important to talk about what the goal is here. Functional families allow for the individuality of each member. People are free to express their needs, their wants, and their feelings. Those expressions are met with respect and with love. They are then taken into account in all subsequent decision making. True "we-ness" allows each person to be a fully formed "me," with likes, dislikes, beliefs, opinions, and attitudes. In true community, there is a spirit of inclusiveness and expansion. There is room for everyone. We don't have to agree; we can just agree to disagree, thereby making space for all of it, with an underlying foundation of respect and appreciation for differences. If we ever hope to have peace in the world, we will first need to be able to do this in our homes.

> What is love?
> It is that powerful
> attraction towards
> all that we ...
> hope beyond
> ourselves.
> —Percy Bysshe Shelley

PRACTICE

Take out your journal and answer the following questions.

What is my attitude toward marriage?

What is it about marriage that I want?

What is it about marriage that I fear?

Now, write a list of the important communities to which you belong (such as, family, spiritual community, professional community, etc.). One at a time, answer the following questions for each community on your list.

In what ways do I take care of others in this community?

In what ways do others from this community take care of me?

Do I give more, or less, than I take from this community?

What do I criticize and complain about regarding this community?

What actions, if any, have I taken to correct these perceived shortcomings? (i.e., rather than simply complain about the absence of something, consider what I could do to improve things.)

How committed am I to this community, and to what lengths do I or would I go to ensure its success?

> Let the property of
> thy fellow be dear to
> thee as thine own.
> —The Talmud

BONUS: PRACTICE IN ACTION

Take at least one action today to be generous to one or more of your communities. Do this not for approval or recognition, but simply to practice the art of being generous and in recognition of yourself as part of the whole. If possible, take your action(s) anonymously, without telling anyone.

LESSON 46
Seventy Times Seven:
The Challenge of Forgiveness

Jesus said we should forgive seventy times seven times, and I don't think He meant that we should find four hundred and ninety people to transgress against us. I think Jesus was trying to tell us that deep wounds require more than just one pass through forgiveness before they can be truly healed.

—Karla McLaren, *Emotional Genius*

We have it that forgiveness is good—that we *need* to forgive, that we *should* forgive, and the sooner the better. Anger, that gnarly, dark "shadow" emotion, should be released almost as soon as it happens, lest it cause our souls to become sick with the stain of resentment. Yet, when his disciple Peter, came to Jesus and asked, "Lord, how many times should I forgive my brother when he sins against me?" (Matthew 18:21), Jesus did not tell him to forgive only one time and implore him to do so immediately. Instead, he replied that we should forgive "not seven times, but seventy times seven" times, acknowledging that forgiveness is sometimes more of a process than an event and more of an ongoing practice than a particular occasion.

We get angry for a reason. We have been violated, our boundaries have been broken, our integrity attacked. And while absolute forgiveness is the sweetness of grace that we all long for, we often cannot push the river for its arrival. For some transgressions forgiveness must be coaxed, wooed naturally out of its slumber, and of its own accord. We can commit to doing the inner work that forgiveness requires, but we never want to confuse forgiveness with its counterfeits, repression and denial. True forgiveness is an emotional expansion of the heart that must be arrived at honestly and organically.

Forgiveness should only occur once one's boundaries have been firmly reestablished and personal safety restored. These two things happen in a climate of total acceptance and honoring of one's anger and indignation. I once had a woman come to a workshop that I was leading. She spoke with contrite agony about her difficulty with forgiving her ex-husband for all the horrible things he'd done to her. Upon exploration, we discovered that her ex-husband was still perpetrating abusive actions against her—in the present. He lied constantly about his activities with their children, didn't pay his child support on time, and bad-mouthed her to their daughters. I instructed the woman *not* to forgive this man until she was able to secure better boundaries with him, whether that be through the setting of rules directly with him, or doing so through the courts. At that time she needed her anger to help mobilize her into much-needed action.

It's when we do not rise to the occasion of anger that we end up festering with its impotent sidekick, resentment. Anger is like a blazing sword meant to cut through the perpetrations and violations imposed upon us. Normally we have only two choices when it comes to being angry—repression or expression. Because it feels too dangerous and scary to deal with, we'll often repress anger, concealing our feelings even from ourselves. Our other option is to lash out hurtfully, attacking back in the way we feel we've been attacked. Yet there is a third, more healthy way to deal with intense feelings of anger. Feel the anger. Be with it. Listen to its power and its fury. Underneath the resounding whirlwind of rage is a very important message that we obviously need to hear. When anger consumes us, there is information present that is much like gold that must be searched for and mined. That information is frequently about how we ourselves have failed to provide adequate protection for ourselves through the setting of appropriate and secure personal boundaries.

In her book *Emotional Genius,* Karla McLaren points out that anger always begs an action. Fortunately it need not be a reactive, destructive one. The action that anger calls for will usually have something to do with (1) reestablishing, or establishing for the first time, a necessary boundary, and (2) restoring personal safety and integrity. Once constructive action has been taken, then and only then is it really appropriate to forgive

And when ye stand praying, forgive if ye have aught against any: that your Father also which is in heaven may forgive you your trespasses.
—Mark 11:25

Forgiveness is not an emotion. It is a decision made by your whole self after your true emotional work has been done.
—Karla McLaren

someone. If you forgive someone prematurely, you rob yourself of vitally needed energy to take actions on your own behalf.

"I had often fantasized about running into my ex and his wife. In those fantasies, I was running into them with a truck," says Carrie, the protagonist in *Sex in the City.* If you have a disempowered relationship with anger, then the desire for revenge is normal. If you focus your anger outwardly, as though it is others that have to change without examining what you yourself need to alter, then you'll miss the opportunity that anger presents. The woman whose ex-husband was abusive to her admitted to us that she'd always been a doormat for someone—her father, her older brother, and then a series of boyfriends who treated her poorly. One bully after another seemed to somehow find his way into her bed. Was it that *they* had to change? No. She herself was the one who needed to change. She had to start standing up for herself in life and insist that people treat her better. At the very least, she had to stop giving out her phone number to abusive men.

Howard comes to me week after week complaining of profound feelings of rage toward his ex-girlfriend with whom he is trying to maintain a friendship. The terms of the friendship, though, seem to address her needs without addressing his. Since she rejected him, he has been the one who has done most of the work in trying to adjust to this new direction. She remains emotionally and financially dependent upon Howard, expecting him to continue caring for her, even though she is already dating another man. He is trying. She calls him to talk about her insecurities with the other man until he becomes furious and blows up at her. He then apologizes the next day and tries to be there for her again, out of some ideal that this is the "loving, spiritual" thing to do. She again begins talking about her problems with her new boyfriend, and he again becomes angry, although this time he manages to keep it to himself. However, after their phone conversation, Howard goes out and promptly has a car accident. This is a clear example of someone who is not using their anger to inform them of how to renegotiate their boundaries and need for personal safety. Anger is like the flame of a fire. I'll burn you if you don't make a move.

The person we are usually the most angry with is ourself—for letting

---

Thou hast permission at all times to say "NO," to change thy mind, and to express thy true feelings.
—Catherine Cardinal

it happen; for not listening to our intuition; for making choices out of the weakest parts of ourselves. But when you find yourself ruminating about how disappointed you are with yourself, you are not allowing the process of transformation to occur inside of you. We must learn to be fully present with our feelings of disappointment, and allow ourselves to sink deeply into the sorrow that arises when we display a disregard and a disrespect for ourselves. Forgiving yourself begins by becoming so present to the profoundness of your disappointment that you allow yourself to be transformed by that experience.

I had a client once who was furious with herself for letting her abusive ex-boyfriend back into her bed one night. She was horrified to think he might judge her as someone he could so easily use and then discard. She desperately wanted to call him (since he was not calling her) and tell him that she's not normally "that kind of woman." Given that he'd already displayed his lack of regard for her by predictably disappearing after "getting the goods," so to speak, I suggested that instead she focus on restoring her own regard for herself. She needed to be with the embarrassment and shame that she felt about giving herself so completely to someone who had consistently demonstrated that he has so little regard for her welfare. By doing so, she had an opportunity to channel the pain she was feeling into making a deeper commitment to herself—one that caused her to develop strong boundaries that honored her need for safety and connection before she opens up emotionally and sexually again.

Eckhart Tolle says that "forgiveness is to offer no resistance to life—to allow life to live through you." When it comes to forgiving ourselves, we must note that it is really only our ego, our false and fragile sense of self, that becomes indignant by the mistakes we've made. It is a distortion to think that we should be perfect or superhuman. Part of being human is to struggle with moral and ethical challenges. It is to struggle to grow ourselves beyond our own wounds and weaknesses. It is to allow ourselves to see that we are no better and no worse than anyone else. In truth, not forgiving yourself while being willing to forgive others is an act of arrogance. For it is a gesture that suggests that we think we should be above the human experience. But, truly, being "above" the human experience is to simply allow ourselves to sink deeply into it. In this way, we heal our sep-

> The most beautiful thing that man can do is to forgive a wrong.
> —Rabbi Eleazar of Worms

arateness from ourselves, which was the fundamental cause of our ability to violate ourselves in the first place.

In order to hold a space for love, we want to learn how to lighten up. We can't really be open and available to love when we are weighed down by the burden of chastising ourselves and others. Without learning the lessons that anger is trying to teach us—how to say no, how to set healthy limits with others—and allowing those lessons to transform us, we simply cannot trust ourselves to form an intimate partnership. We will always pull in the same kind of destructive, abusive person, and we will always wind up upset with ourselves, struggling with all too familiar feelings of rage and victimization. If this has been so for you, look to see what it is that you have not yet implemented by way of setting good, clear personal boundaries that you can trust, and that establish a sense of safety. For once you've managed to restore well-being and balance to your life, your ability to forgive the transgressions of others will follow that much more fluidly.

PRACTICE

Few of us have so mastered forgiveness that we are able to instantly clear ourselves of all angers and petty resentments. Most of us need a daily discipline to help us move toward this ideal. I invite you to try this practice on for size.

Take out your journal. Write a list of three to five people you feel angry or resentful toward and why. You may include yourself on this list.

Now, one by one, go through your list and identify the boundary violation and/or loss of personal safety you've suffered as a result of this transgression.

Write about the ways in which you've allowed and sometimes even colluded with others in the violation of your own boundaries and need for personal safety.

Now, make a list of actions that you are going to take and/or promises that you are going to make to yourself to restore wellness and balance to your life.

Finally, reread your list and see if there is anyone who you are now ready to release and absolve.

BONUS: PRACTICE IN ACTION

Take at least one action today that firmly establishes your boundaries and/or restores personal safety to your life.

As a result of taking this action, if forgiveness is now an option, then forgive someone you've been holding resentment toward.

> Anyone can become angry—that is easy. But to be angry with the right person, to the right degree, at the right time, for the right purpose, and in the right way— that is not easy.
>
> —Aristotle

LESSON 47
On Giving Thanks

Gratitude helps you to grow and expand; gratitude brings joy and laughter into your life and into the lives of all those around you.

—Eileen Caddy, *The Dawn of Change*

Several years ago I was captivated by a romantic relationship that alternated passionately between feelings of euphoria and deep despair. As the despair took over and began to dominate the relationship, I became more and more despondent. Unable to excavate myself from a destructive situation, I was terribly upset and confused. Not only had I lost respect for my then-boyfriend, but my inability to end the relationship was causing me to fast lose respect for myself as well. I began berating myself for what appeared to be a weakness of character on my part. Finally, not knowing what else to do, I surrendered. I must need to be here, I told myself, and I gave up resisting my predicament. I began to chant over and over in my mind, "Thank you, God, for this relationship. Thank you, God, for this pain that is sitting on my chest and causing my heart to break open. Thank you, God, for using this man to teach me to be a more loving and compassionate person." Miraculously, after just a few minutes of repeating this prayer to myself silently, my heart began to lighten. Although I still saw no way out of the impossible situation I was in, a sense of peace washed over me. Encouraged, I began this practice each time I'd get knotted up into an emotional pretzel (which was often). Each time I was able to alleviate the emotional agony I felt. Eventually the relationship worked its way out of the state we were in, and we were able to part ways in a kind and respectful fashion.

Sometimes the value of a relationship (even a miserable one) is that it provides an opportunity for you to grow and mature in ways that you might not have done otherwise. There were many lessons I learned from this challenging encounter and the extraordinary power to gratitude to transform us was one of them. In his book *The Power of Now,* Eckhart Tolle says, "Your task is not to search for love but to find a portal through which love can enter." Gratitude is such a portal.

When we think of gratitude we think of turkey and pumpkin pies, notes written in haste, sweet, superficial lists made up of life's little blessings, and childlike utterances of "God is great, God is good." That is *not* the gratitude that I am talking about. While all expressions of gratitude are valuable, I'm talking about gratitude as a kind of alchemy that transforms our very experience of life. I'm talking about gratitude that moves the heart from contraction to expansion, from broken to whole.

Out of my experience with my former boyfriend, I began to understand the power of giving thanks. I decided to do an experiment. Every day for thirty days, I set my alarm clock a half hour earlier than usual. I woke up, grabbed my morning cup of coffee, took out my pen and notebook, and wrote five full pages of things that I was grateful for. Not as a list, mind you, but as though I were writing a journal entry. "Dear God: Thank you for the beautiful hardwood floors throughout my apartment, thank you for how sweet and loving my cat, Clover, is to me each and every day, thank you for my health, thank you for this quiet time . . ." Pretty soon I'd run out of things to thank God for that I actually felt glad to have. I'd have to start stretching myself. "Thank you for this red pillow, since I love the color red. Thank you that the flowers in the kitchen are once again in bloom. Thank you that my neighbor downstairs has finally stopped drinking, so I don't have to worry about him burning the building down with his cigarettes." But pretty soon I'd run out of those things to say as well. That's when I *really* had to stretch. "OK, God, well, thank you for the fact that I'm broke again because I appreciate the opportunity to once more practice having faith. Thank you that I have no date on Saturday night, giving me the opportunity to push past my feelings of social inadequacy and go to the movies alone. Thank you that I gained five pounds with my period because I get to love my body even when I don't necessarily like its shape . . ." You get the gist. I had to dig pretty deep.

Now, this is the miracle. During that thirty-day period, I began to feel

And only when we are no longer afraid do we begin to live in every experience, painful or joyous; to live in gratitude for every moment, to live abundantly.
—Dorothy Thompson

Let the beauty you
love be what you do.
There are thousands
of ways we kneel
and kiss the earth.

—Rumi

a pervasive sense of joy. This sense of joy was completely unattached to whether or not my life was going the way I wanted it to. I simply began to feel blissful most of the time. I was truly happy just to be alive.

What I learned about gratitude is this. When we give thanks for *everything* in our lives, specifically and exactly for *the way they are,* regardless of our preference for them to be different, *our lives become lit up with joy.* And when we are lit up with joy, we become an absolute magnet for the blessings of life.

Our minds are generally overwhelmed with thoughts of what we *don't* have, and we're usually in an upset about that to one degree or another. "I don't have enough love." "I don't have enough money." "I don't have enough sex." "I don't have enough time." Now that's understandable. After all, when you have a toothache, you aren't thinking, "Well, gee, I'm awfully glad that my feet feel fine and that my hands don't hurt." No. You think about the agony your tooth is in. Yet the danger of our preoccupation with the lack in our lives is that we are creative beings, and whatever we give our attention to is what we create more of. Our constant attentiveness to our deficiencies does *not* create abundance—it actually creates more deficiencies.

Gratitude shifts our perception from what we *don't* have to what we *do* have. In shifting our focus this way, we increase our sense of abundance and appreciation. In turn, this attracts more abundance to be appreciative of. That is what Jesus meant when he said, "To him who has, more shall be given." Gratitude is an inner map that instructs the Universe how to respond to us. Just as depression is an inner map that says, "You will never have what you want no matter how hard you try. It's hopeless. You should just give up"; and anxiety says, "Life is terrifying and dangerous. Better be careful, hedge your bets and don't get your hopes up. Be attached to something specific, but don't dare believe that you'll actually get it," so does gratitude affirm, "Good things are always coming to me. Look, there's another one right now. Life is good to me even when it doesn't appear to be so at first glance. I know that love belongs to me because I have constant evidence of its beautiful presence in my life."

When Jesus fed the multitude, his first action was to give thanks. He then broke bread and turned five loaves of bread and two fish into enough food to feed thousands. Jesus understood the power of gratitude to create an abundant life, filled with all that is needed in any given moment. When he admonished us to "consider the lilies of the field, how they grow," he was beseeching us to give up worrying so much about what we don't have and to fill our minds instead with what we *do*. Our constant worrying and fretting about life must have seemed as foolish to Him as if the lilies of the field were all huddled around, whispering words of fear to one another; "What if there is no more rain? What if the sun doesn't shine tomorrow? What if there is an earthquake and we become uprooted from our soil? Oh, what will become of us then?"

As life is constantly redefining itself according to our consciousness, gratitude is the absolute best way to attract all that is good and lovely and wonderful into our lives. It begins with something both simple and profound—giving thanks for exactly the way things are and exactly the way that they are not in your life right now.

PRACTICE

Take out your journal. In journal style, write five full pages of things that you are grateful for. While five pages may be a lot to ask, the ability to shift your awareness from "lack" consciousness to "abundance" consciousness promises to completely alter your experience of your life. Because of this, I believe it's worth the time and effort.

BONUS: PRACTICE IN ACTION

Today, I invite you to take on the practice of being grateful for everything exactly as it is, and exactly as it is not. Throughout the day, regardless of whether or not you are pleased with what is occurring, say a prayer of thanks that things are just the way they are.

Giving up on the idea that we *simply have to* find a soulmate may be a necessary prerequisite to actually finding one. For one thing, it amounts to a decision to dissociate ourselves from our … insatiable neediness and entitlement, and to be grateful for what life has given us already.
—Carolyn G. Miller

The measure of mental health is the disposition to find good everywhere.
—Ralph Waldo Emerson

To be upset over
what you don't have
is to waste
what you do have.

—Ken Keyes Jr.

At least once today, express your gratitude to someone. Tell this person exactly why you are grateful for their presence in your life. Be very specific (e.g., "I always feel like I can I can talk to you without being judged," "You always try your best to take my complaints seriously," "You inspire me to be a better person.").

LESSON 48
On Being a "Yes" to Love

If one wishes to be a lover, he must start by saying "yes" to love....
A lover says yes to life, yes to joy, yes to knowledge, yes to people,
yes to differences. He realizes that all things and people have
something to offer him, that all things are in all things.

—Leo Buscaglia, *Love*

When I was seven years old I loved the TV show *Batman*. More accurately, I loved Batman himself. He seemed to me to be the ultimate strong, masculine hero. To a little girl who was estranged from her father, this was potent stuff. The producers of the show must have known that the bulk of their audience were swooning little girls, because one night they announced that they were holding a contest—and the grand prize was a date with Adam West, the actor who played Batman. I was excited beyond belief. For weeks, we were encouraged to send in postcards with our names and addresses written down. I wanted to send in my card so badly, but I was horrified with embarrassment at the idea of confessing to my mother that I wanted to win a date with Batman. I kept procrastinating asking her help in sending in my postcard. On the day of the drawing, I was mortified to realize that I'd not entered the contest. I couldn't bear the thought that I wouldn't be the one to win. So I began to fantasize that someone, although I didn't know who, must have sent a postcard in on my behalf. I waited patiently until the end of the episode, hoping against all odds that I would hear my name called when they announced the winner. Alas, I was devastated when they called out the name of another girl and not my own. My heart broken, I cried myself to sleep that night. That's how so many of us are. We pine with all our hearts for love to be ours, but we're too scared to take the risk of doing whatever it takes to be in the game. Still, we continue to hope and pray that some-

Progress always
involves risk;
you can't steal
second base and keep
your foot on first.
—Frederick Wilcox

one, somewhere, will know how desperately we want to be loved. Regardless of our refusal to put ourselves out there, we fantasize that someone, somehow will come along and rescue us from our longing.

Deanna, a lovely, bright woman in her thirties, complained for months that she wasn't meeting any men. She had this idealistic notion that she should meet someone "naturally" while going about her day-to-day life, not putting herself out in any special way. From her perspective, "trying" to meet someone felt "too contrived." She described herself as "picky" when it came to men, and she just didn't believe that the ones she'd be interested in would be "working that hard" to meet someone themselves. Refusing to go to singles events, join a dating service, or even ask her friends to set her up, left her alone, and lonely, on many Saturday nights. Finally, out of my constant and, I'm sure at times irritating cajoling, she attended one singles event, even though she felt shy and somewhat embarrassed by being there. But that night she met someone whom she actually liked, and began dating him. Although the relationship didn't go the way she'd hoped, she was inspired by her success and subsequently joined an Internet dating service. In the last few months she's met several promising men who are all seriously looking for their life-partners. One, in particular, is a man that she likes and is now dating exclusively.

Sometimes we use the excuse that we are being "selective," as a way to avoid risk. We long to surrender ourselves absolutely to the forces of love, yet we want to remain in full control of every aspect of the experience. In truth, Deanna was just afraid that if she actually let others know how much she wanted a relationship, she might be rejected and humiliated. She was afraid to validate her belief that "all the good ones are taken." On some level it was easier to stay in the fantasy that her prince would just magically appear one day—at the dry-cleaner's, in the market, at a traffic light. As long as she didn't "try" to meet him, she thought that she couldn't be that disappointed when he didn't show up.

We complain about how little love there is in our lives, all the while closed and defended to the world around us. It's easy for us to *say* we want love in our lives, but that will require us to let down our guard and risk being open and available on a whole new level. Many of us are so busy trying to impress people that we've forgotten to be vulnerable as well. Our need to look good blinds us to the many opportunities for authentic and meaningful connection that constantly surround us. If I say I'm looking to expand the experience of love in my life, then I've got to become present and available to everyone I meet, and not just the people whom I immediately assess as being the ones who may be able to give me what I want.

Love comes to us in many ways. We have no idea, really, how or when it will come. Nor do we know what it will look like when it does. There is always the thunderbolt, the "one glance across the room and I knew" experience that most of us are hoping for. This kind of encounter is the one most often reinforced in our collective psyche and is the one most often referred to as "true love." However, there is also this other love, the slow and steady kind, which is often not recognized immediately. It is the love that slips itself through the backdoor when you aren't looking or steals itself into your heart while you sleep. One of the most delightful couples I know worked together for years before they both happened to break up with their respective partners around the same time, and suddenly recognized one another while on a routine business trip. We don't always know the person we are looking for the moment we see him or her. That's why it's important to remain open and curious with everyone in our lives, anticipating the possibility of a meaningful connection in every encounter.

In seeking "The One," we look for a person who complements and balances us, as well as someone who shares values and concerns that are similar to our own. Remember, however, that we are not looking for a clone. At its best, marriage is an exercise in diversity. We never marry someone who is exactly like us. Rather than being irritated by this, we need to appreciate the gift of someone who is so completely different than we are. In order to do that, we have to get used to being open and available to ideas and experiences that are new and perhaps even foreign to us.

When getting to know new people, remain neutral, yet receptive until you have the information you need to see more clearly what they have to offer. Someone can be a great person and yet not be available to love. You want to learn how much someone has to give by watching how they show up in life. If they are consistent, do what they say they are going to do,

Ever tried.
Ever failed.
No matter.
Try again.
Fail again.
Fail better.
—Samuel Beckett

It is only those who do nothing that make no mistakes, I suppose.
—Joseph Conrad

Most of us die
with our music
unplayed....
We should try
to step out of our
comfort zones and
do the things
we're capable of.
—Mary Kay Ash

are sensitive and considerate toward you and others; then you can open up more. If they tell you things such as "I'm commitment-phobic," if they don't keep their word or behave in ways that convey a disregard for your feelings and the feelings of others, then don't open up. We can't allow our desire for love to blind us from seeing what it is that another person does, and does not, have to offer at this particular time in their lives.

There are reasons why we defend ourselves against the possibility of love, and they have their merit. Ask a widow or widower to share from their heart what it was like to lose their beloved, and you may begin to understand. Falling in love is one of the most vulnerable experiences that one can have in life. None of us know for sure what's coming next, and that can be terrifying. Before I met Mark, I was engaged in life and very much invested in being alive. On some level, though, I was always aware of my own mortality. As a deeply spiritual person, I felt somewhat prepared for the inevitability of my own death. But once I fell in love, you'd think I'd never done any spiritual work at all in my life! Suddenly, living to a hundred didn't seem long enough. I wanted more time. I wanted invincible time. I wanted forever. I understood, for the first time really, how fragile we are, and how tenuous life can be. Worst-case scenarios haunted me. What if I get sick? What if his plane crashes? What if, what if, what if. Our inescapable passing-away and the awareness of the temporality of both our lives made the experience of loving him like an ache inside of me. If you've ever been a parent, you probably understand. Loving absolutely and with complete abandon is a terrifying yet exhilarating experience. That is why it takes most of us so many tries before we are finally willing to open wide our hearts and run naked into the fire.

To love is to risk. There is no way around it. If you are one to shy away from failure in life, if you are someone who plays only the games you believe you can win, then you are probably living a life that is way too small and far too boring, even for you. Taking a risk means that there is no sure way to predict whether you will win—and get what you want, or lose—and not get what you want. A risk with an assured outcome is not a risk. That is simply you playing small in your life. Until you embrace failure, loss, and disappointment as part of a life well lived, then you will most likely have a life that doesn't really light you up or inspire you very much.

Taking risks means that you are willing to take actions that are outside of your comfort zone. It means living life in a way that allows you, even challenges you, to expand yourself beyond who you know yourself to be. A certain amount of resistance is normal, but you have to remind yourself that the way you have been living is what has produced the life you now have. There is simply no way to change your life without changing how many risks you are willing to take.

In order to create more love in your life, you may just have to say yes to things you might have said no to in the past. You may have to give up your defenses of judging and finding fault with everyone you go out with. You may have to tolerate the discomfort of not being in control. You may even have to give up the paralysis that comes from allowing your fear of making a mistake to stop you. Remember, if it weren't for mistakes, most people on the planet wouldn't even be alive right now. There is a big difference between playing full out in life by taking a risk that may or may not pan out, and plowing straight ahead even though you know, in your heart, that what you are doing is a mistake. The latter is motivated by neediness and displays a lack of belief in yourself and others. The former is where all things worth having in life begin. Don't let your fear of making a mistake dictate your chances for love. Remind yourself that at least one good thing came out of every mistake you've ever made.

There is surely evidence in our world of why we should remain closed and defended with one another. Yet there are beautiful openings for love every day, reminding us of the very real possibility of a world where love is more real than fear. Since we are creating this possibility in your personal lives, I invite you to be present to the possibility of this for our collective life as well—considering what it would be like to live in a world where people say yes to one another, yes to the risk of being more open and receptive, yes to the possibility of a more profound, thoughtful, and kindhearted way of relating to one another.

Marriages stop. Marriages change. People are always saying a marriage "failed." It's such a negative way of putting it.... Failure is terribly important.... The notion that failure is a negative thing is wrong.

—Emma Thompson

PRACTICE

Take out your journal. Make a list of all the risks you've not taken and actions you've been avoiding in your quest for love. For each response, do the following sentence completions, writing as many answers as are true for you.

I'm afraid if I do this, I'll . . .

By avoiding doing this, I'm protecting . . .

The action(s) I could take that would represent a risk are . . .

Those actions that I am willing to take are . . .

I will take these actions by . . .

BONUS: PRACTICE IN ACTION

Your job is to fail at least one time today. Take at least one action(s) today that puts you at risk for rejection. Make an unreasonable request, a bold assertion, or an attempt to go for something that is pretty much an assured disappointment.

Also, try to be more accessible and available than you normally are. Say "yes" to the invitations, requests, ideas, or suggestions of others that come your way today, unless it is clearly not in your best interests to do so. Consciously remind yourself throughout the day to remain as open and receptive as possible.

LESSON 49
Holding the High Watch

When love isn't in our lives, it's on the way. If you know
that a special guest is coming at five o'clock, do you spend
the day messing up the home? Of course not.
You prepare. And that is what we should do for love.

—Marianne Williamson, *Enchanted Love*

Sitting with my husband over dinner, I confessed why I don't encourage people to make lists of the things they want in a partner. It is not because I don't think they are useful. Rather, it's because I myself had not made one before I met him, and I wasn't actually sure it would have helped me much if I had. I admitted that, when I was single, I did not have the ability to visualize the relationship that we now have for two reasons: (1) because I'd never experienced anything so wonderful and did not even know that it was possible for people to have such good relationships, and (2) I did not have the self-esteem to imagine that I could have it, even if I knew that it existed for others.

"How did you do it, then?" he asked, genuinely confused. "How did you attract in this relationship?" I had to think about it for a long time before I knew how to answer him. The truth was, I didn't have a strong visual on what it would look like to have this kind of love in my life. I mean, even though I was "doing the course" (although it didn't yet exist as such), and believed strongly that *someone* was coming, I simply had no reference point for the kind of relationship I now have. If ever there was evidence·that you do not have to do this course perfectly in order to have it work for you, I'm it. What I did see upon reflection, however, was that, years before, I'd made a decision. I had decided to dedicate myself to cultivating an ability to give and receive love, not in order to get something but simply because I wanted to do something beautiful and good with my

By night on my bed
I sought him whom
my soul loveth.

—Song of Solomon 3:1

life. It was a goal that moved me for no reason other than I felt it a worthy and noble one. I didn't want my entire life to be used up by frustration and anger because life wasn't giving me what I was demanding that it give me. So I had made a choice to love myself, and everyone God put in my path, to the best of my ability; and I had been actively, passionately engaged in doing all that I could to fulfill this aim. Hindsight now tells me that this way of living had helped me to pretty much move beyond the issues I had with low self-esteem or any doubts I was holding about my ability to create what I wanted in life.

It is good to be clear and specific about what we are looking for. I don't think that my former inability to believe myself worthy and capable of having a great love is of any merit. But I do think that sometimes the lists we make of what we want in a mate really reflect the characteristics that we ourselves would be cultivating if we were being true to our highest aspirations. If I had made out a list of the things I wanted in a mate (happy, spiritual, kind, etc.), but was not doing everything I could to be those things myself, I would probably have felt too intimidated to date a person who had all these qualities. I would have had to tell him to come back in a year or two to give me a chance to catch up. That's why we always begin with the self. Because the lists we make are usually the vision we have of ourselves living our best life. I've never known anyone to write a list of attributes like unsuccessful, depressed, broke, humorless, and mean. Of course we want someone great. But you know who usually winds up with great people? Other great people. Contrary to popular opinion, all the good ones are *not* taken. They are, however, holding out for someone as fabulous as they are. So, I'd rather encourage you to spend your energy cultivating your own greatness. Instead of spending your time judging and assessing whether or not others are everything you think they should be, concern yourself with whether or not you yourself are everything you've ever dreamed of and hoped for. If you are fully engaged in being the absolute best that you can be, I guarantee you, you won't choose an amoral, negative, and abusive person as your partner in life.

"How long must one remain in the dark?" asks author Florence Scovel Shinn. "Until one can see in the dark," she cleverly answers. Holding the high watch is such a mystical sight. Holding the high watch is not so much about standing in what you are going to *have* in your life, as much as it is standing for who you will *be*. I had to make a commitment to be the best person I was capable of being before I was able to bring in a partner whose number one commitment to me is to support me in becoming all that I am capable of being. It is a spiritual axiom that whenever we truly commit ourselves to something that requires us to stretch ourselves, miracles begin to happen that support the fulfillment of that goal. I met Mark when I did because I had gone as far as I could go without him. He is the one who has given me the support that I have needed to birth my daughter and to write this book—both profound opportunities for me to expand even more into the possibilities that my life holds. He is essentially a launching pad for me to be all that I can be. But first, I had to be committed to being all that I could be.

We have it backwards. We want to *have* love so that we can *do* loving things so that we can *be* loving. But the opposite is true. We need to activate an experience of expanding our hearts to feel love (being), and then behave in loving ways (doing), so that we might draw toward us those things that create more love and fulfillment (having). Rather than have, do, be, which is how most of us are trying to create our lives; it's actually be, do, and then have. We've got it reversed.

In the Book of 2 Kings in the Old Testament, there is a story about three kings who were wandering in the desert without any hope of finding water for their thirsty men and horses. The prophet Elisha was called upon to help them. When Elisha prayed for water, God answered, "Thus saith the Lord, ye shall not see wind, neither shall ye see rain; yet make this valley full of ditches." Sometimes, we just have to dig ditches before the rains will come. We have to love and care about those right in front of us. We have to "act as if" we love ourselves and that love is abundantly fulfilled in our lives. And not long after, the story continues, ". . . it came to pass . . . [that] the country was filled with water."

We must surrender ourselves completely to our desire to learn the ways of love. We must allow our commitment to actualize a great love to dominate the choices we make right now, and the actions we do or don't take each and every day. Sometimes we confuse the idea of surrendering our quest for love with resignation or giving up. This is the difference.

> You will have wonderful surges forward. Then there must be a time of consolidating before the next forward surge. Accept this as part of the process and never become downhearted.
> —Eileen Caddy

At times the kind
of perseverance
required is patience.
—Ralph Blum

The temptation when
the path to success
gets too bumpy is to
leap back into the
comfort zone. Don't.
Keep pushing
forward, always
forward. The comfort
zone is the land of
dreams and wishes.
Success is
the land of results,
where all those
dreams come true.
—Mark Burnett

Surrendering is like floating on the water. You relax, allowing the water to fully carry your weight, knowing that you are completely supported and that you are safe to let go. Resignation, on the other hand, is like sinking. You have a feeling of dread, knowing that you are not safe and that things are not OK. When you feel this way, try reminding yourself of the buoyancy and strength of water to hold the entirety of your hopes and dreams and see if you can get yourself above it.

New York Times wedding columnist Lois Smith Brady writes, "Whenever anyone asks me about love . . . I always say wait for that feeling, wait, wait, wait. Wait with the patience of a Buddhist fly-fisherman." When we consider the Buddhist fly-fisherman, we intuitively know that he or she is a person who knows how to generate who they are from the inside out. They are, as we say, living from center. They are not in reaction to the externals of their experience—the weather, the force of the current, the temperature of the water, or the amount of time they've stood standing there waiting for a nibble. They are true to their intention to catch a fish. They stand unflinching and unwavering in their commitment to align themselves with that aim.

There will be days when you will feel quite discouraged. I know, because I was. Sometimes when you set this intention to call in "The One," you begin creating near-misses. I remember the agony of meeting Robert, before I found Mark again. I thought he was the greatest guy I'd ever dated—handsome, heartfelt, funny, and altruistic. When he decided not to go for a fourth date because he'd gotten involved with another woman, I was devastated. I could barely keep from crying as he drove me home. It will happen. Just don't make it mean that the work you've done is for naught. Think of it only as a need for refinement, and acknowledge yourself for getting closer. In those disheartening and frustrating moments, remember the sage advice of Woody Allen in his movie *Hannah and Her Sisters:* "The heart is a very, very resilient little muscle."

We've declared our intention and petitioned God boldly to send a great love into our lives. We have prepared ourselves wisely and thoroughly. We have cleaned the skeletons from the closets and thrown away all that no longer fits. We have visioned and stretched ourselves fully to learn and become practiced in the ways of love. All there is left to do is to affirm its pervasive presence in our lives and continue to expand our ability to give and receive its grace. As the farmer who has planted his crops does not go out to his garden and tug on his plants in an effort to force them to grow, we wait. It is an active waiting, not a passive one, knowing that 99 percent of all creation takes place beneath the soil. We stand ready and alert. We till the ground. We know that the miracle is coming and we receive that miracle now. And together we say yes, yes, yes, and yes.

> Remember.
> What is yours will
> come to you.
> —Ralph Blum

PRACTICE

OK, *now* it's time to make "The List." Take out your journal. Write down those qualities that you are looking for in a life partner. Do this now.

When you are finished, read through your list. Narrow it down to your top five qualities by circling those things that are the most important to you. Do this now.

Next, review these items and make a promise to yourself to date those who appear to have these qualities and to refrain from dating those who don't.

Now, go through your list once more. For each quality that you circled, I invite you to also make a promise to yourself that you are going to do your absolute best to develop and cultivate this very quality within yourself (e.g., "Spiritual" becomes "I promise to prioritize my spiritual path and to grow myself spiritually each and every day." "Funny" becomes "I promise to see the humor in every situation, to learn to poke fun at myself, and to have fun each and every day." "Smart" becomes "I promise to be an avid reader and learner of new things and to do all that I can to develop my mind each and every day").

BONUS: PRACTICE IN ACTION

Create a statement that serves as an affirmation of your ability to attract in your beloved. Read through the following list to see if any of these affirmations resonate for you as true. Feel free to create one of your own.

My heart has
burned with passion
and has searched
forever
for this wondrous
beauty
that I now behold.
—Rumi

Thank you, God, in advance, for bringing me
a great and lasting love.

I am open to love and I receive my beloved now.

Who I am is love and I am attracting in the love of my life
in this very moment.

I know that my beloved is coming to me right now.

I am already connected deeply to my life partner
and I receive that partner now.

I now receive the miracle of spiritual partnership,
knowing that ours is a blessed union.

Allow this affirmation to become your mantra, speaking it to yourself over and over again and writing it often in your journal. Allow yourself to feel the joy and gratitude for the anticipated arrival of your beloved each time you speak your mantra. Receive the miracle of love, reverting back to your mantra in moments of fear and doubt. Let this mantra be the sacred song of your heart and soul. Sing it often and sing it loud.

And I join with you now, holding the high watch with you and for you, knowing that as you have asked, so shall you be answered.

SUGGESTED STUDY GUIDE
FOR GROUP DISCUSSION

1. Share with the group the qualities that you believe define love and how you were or were not able to apply these qualities to a situation that was disturbing you.

2. Share your feelings about surrendering yourself to becoming a "we" instead of a "me." What, if anything, are you reluctant to give up in order to belong to something larger than yourself?

3. Who in your life has been difficult to forgive, and why? What boundaries do you see you could set in order to move you closer to completion with this person? What, if any, resistance are you having to setting them?

4. How was it for you to write out five full pages of things that you are grateful for?

5. What risks did you take this week, and what happened as a result? How is it for you to fail?

6. Share with the group the top five qualities you are looking for in a mate, and how you yourself are cultivating those very same qualities in your own life. Share your affirmation if you created one.

NOTE: On your final meeting together, I suggest you go around the room and acknowledge each member of the group as a way to create closure. One person at a time is invited to be on the "hot seat" while other members have an opportunity to express their appreciation and admiration for that person.

POSTSCRIPT

The end is where we start from.

—T. S. Eliot

If you have taken this course seriously, as I imagine you have, then you have probably hit a few bumps in the road. Transformation is never an easy path. As Shakespeare once said, "The course of true love never did run smooth." Quite likely, the most challenging of all has been the utter aloneness that one inevitably encounters along the way. For whenever we take a major step in our own personal growth, we cause upheaval in the lives of those around us. No longer can they count on us to silently pick up the slack, martyr ourselves to the role of doormat, and/or suffer the covert and not-so-covert misuses that we've tolerated in the past. By now, I imagine you've pissed off more than one of your friends or family members, and I just want you to know how OK that is.

When we grow, we force those in our lives to grow as well—and they don't always like it. As a matter of fact, they will often resent us for it and sometimes even choose to leave our lives. This has to be OK. Because the alternative—betraying ourselves by putting on the brakes and reverting back to old, toxic ways of being—is simply unacceptable. And in some way, not really even an option anymore. For once you've crossed the line into self-awareness, you can never really go back. Diminishing ourselves by hiding our greatness has never really helped anyone. In fact, it has only served to encourage them to stay small as well. While it is often sad to allow people to leave our lives when they choose to, it seems to be a part of life that we must simply accept. Allowing loss. Allowing death. Clearing out the old as a way to make room for new, more appropriate relationships to enter our lives. And while they may rant and rave that we have abandoned them or disappointed them or let them down in a big way, the truth is, the best we can possibly do for anyone is to continue the task of getting healthy and well ourselves.

No doubt many of you began this course in order to attain a particular goal—that of love realized in your life. Indeed, *all* of us are working in some way to realize love, those of us who are in committed partnerships, as well as those of us who are not. Love is not a goal as much as it is a journey. It isn't suddenly realized simply because you have your beloved in your life. Love is a *verb*, not a noun. It is not something tangible. You can't put it in your safe-deposit box. Love exists to the extent that you give it away. It is as old as the last encounter you had, even in the most ancient of your relationships. Love will always require of us more than we initially intended to give, for it will take no less than everything we've got. Love rarely behaves itself, complying with our preconceived notions, our lists of demands, and our constant desires that it show up a certain way. Rather it insists that we rise to the summit of what it is to be human, constantly stretching ourselves beyond what we had previously believed to be our limitations. Love is a 24/7 job. It will never be contained in a particular form of a particular relationship on a particular time schedule. The fulfillment of love is not to be found in the future. The fulfillment of love is always to be found right now.

In my work over the years I have come to see that people are divided into two categories. Those who want love in their lives and will faithfully do the work to actualize love; and those who want love in their lives but won't. Those who *will* do the work understand love as a creative action that they are free to choose in any given moment. Those who *won't* do the work tend to see love as a thing to get or as a place to hide out. I pray with all my heart that I have enticed you toward the former. For that is the fulfillment of my purpose in life—to ever expand my capacity to give and receive love with all those who cross my path, and to help others to do the same. You, dear reader, are the fulfillment of love for me. And now I beseech you to please pass it forward.

Bloom where planted.
—Mary Engelbreit

Two roads diverged in a wood, and I—
I took the one less traveled by.
And that has made all the difference.
—Robert Frost

References

Adrienne, Carol. *The Purpose of Your Life*. New York: William Morrow and Company, 1998.

Anand, Margo. *The Art of Sexual Magic*. New York: G. P. Putnam's Sons, 1995.

Capacchione, Lucia. *Living with Feeling*. New York: Jeremy P. Tarcher/Putnam, 2001.

Chödrön, Pema. *When Things Fall Apart*. Boston: Shambhala Publications, Inc., 1997.

Chopra, Deepak, ed. *The Love Poems of Rumi*. New York: Harmony Books, 1998.

Dalai Lama, His Holiness The. *Ethics for the New Millennium*. New York: Berkley Publishing Group, 1999.

Dalai Lama, His Holiness The, and Howard Cutler. *The Art of Happiness*. New York: Penguin Putnam, Inc., 1998.

Forward, Susan. *Emotional Blackmail*. New York: HarperCollins Publishers, Inc., 1998.

Frankl, Viktor. *Man's Search for Meaning*. New York: Pocket Books, 1959.

Gawain, Shakti. *Creative Visualization*. New York: Bantam Books, 1978.

Gibran, Kahlil. *The Prophet*. New York: Alfred A. Knopf, 1962.

Goleman, Daniel. *Emotional Intelligence*. New York: Bantam Books, 1995.

Gray, John. *Men Are from Mars, Women Are from Venus*. New York: HarperCollins Publishers, Inc., 1994.

Gurmukh. *The Eight Human Talents*. New York: HarperCollins Publishers, Inc., 2000.

Hafiz, translations by Daniel Ladinsky. *The Gift*. New York: Penguin Books, 1999.

Hollis, James. *The Middle Passage*. Toronto: Inner City Books, 1993.

James, William. *The Varieties of Religious Experience.* New York: Macmillan Publishing Co., Inc., 1961.

Krystal, Phyllis. *Cutting the Ties That Bind.* York Beach, Maine: Samuel Weiser, Inc., 1993.

Masterson, James F. *Search for the Real Self: Unmasking the Personality Disorders of Our Age.* New York: Simon & Schuster, 1990.

McLaren, Karla. *Emotional Genius.* Columbia, Calif.: Laughing Tree Press, 2001.

Miller, Carolyn Godschild. *Soulmates.* Tiburon, Calif.: H J Kramer, 2000.

Moore, Thomas. *Care of the Soul.* New York: HarperCollins Publishers, Inc., 1992.

———. *Soul Mates.* New York: HarperCollins Publishers, Inc., 1994.

Myss, Caroline. *Why People Don't Heal and How They Can.* New York: Three Rivers Press, 1997.

———. *Sacred Contracts.* New York: Harmony Books, 2001.

Peck, M. Scott. *A Different Drum.* New York: Simon & Schuster, 1987.

Rumi, translated by Coleman Barks. *The Illuminated Rumi.* New York: Broadway Books, 1997.

Schiffmann, Erich. *Yoga: The Spirit and Practice of Moving Into Stillness.* New York: Pocket Books, 1996.

Schucman, Helen. *A Course in Miracles.* Glen Ellen, Calif.: Foundation for Inner Peace, 1975.

Shafir, Rebecca Z. *The Zen of Listening.* Wheaton, Ill.: Quest Books, 2000.

Shinn, Florence Scovel. *The Game of Life and How to Play It.* Marina Del Rey: DeVorss & Company, 1925.

Tolle, Eckhart. *The Power of Now.* Novato, Calif.: New World Library, 1999.

Vanzant, Iyanla. *In the Meantime.* New York: Simon & Schuster, 1998.

Walsch, Neale Donald. *Conversations with God, Book I.* New York: G. P. Putnam's Sons, 1995.

Williamson, Marianne. *Enchanted Love.* New York: Simon & Schuster, 1999.

———. *A Return to Love.* New York: HarperCollins, 1992.

Zweig, Connie, and Jeremiah Abrams, eds. *Meeting the Shadow.* New York: Jeremy P. Tarcher/Putnam, 1991.